"Hunter Baker's volume is a much-welcomed addition to the debate on the role of religion and faith in the public square. To the confusion regarding matters of religion and politics, Baker brings illuminating clarity. To the ambiguity regarding the meaning and place of pluralism, he provides thoughtful analysis. To the directionless arguments for secularization, he offers an insightful and discerning response. This much-needed volume provides a readable, historically-informed, and carefully-reasoned case for the place of faith in our public deliberations. It is with great enthusiasm that I recommend it."
—DAVID S. DOCKERY, President, Union University

"Hunter Baker is a gifted writer who knows how to communicate the issue of secularism to an audience that desperately needs to hear a critical though winsome voice on this matter. In many ways, the book is a twenty-first-century sequel to the late Richard John Neuhaus's classic, *The Naked Public Square*. Baker understands the issues that percolate beneath the culture wars. They are not merely political but theological and philosophical, and they are rarely unpacked in an articulate way so that the ordinary citizen can gain clarity. Baker offers his readers that clarity."
—FRANCIS J. BECKWITH, Professor of Philosophy and
Church-State Studies, Baylor University; author,
*Defending Life: A Moral and Legal Case Against
Abortion Choice*

"Hunter Baker is one of the sharpest thinkers in contemporary American Christianity. This work will provoke the same kind of conversation ignited by Richard John Neuhaus's *The Naked Public Square*. Read this book slowly with a highlighter and a pen in hand as you think about questions ranging from whether the Ten Commandments ought to hang in your local courthouse to whether there's a future for public Christianity."
—RUSSELL D. MOORE, Dean, The Southern Baptist
Theol

"The task of discerning the alternative to practical atheism lived by many nominal Christians and the pretense of a neutral secularism has been made easier by this rich study. Once authentic Christians grasp the ramifications of the incarnation of Christ, then and only then will it be apparent that, as Baker argues, 'secularism only makes sense in relation to religion.'"
—ROBERT A. SIRICO, President, Acton Institute

"*The End of Secularism* debunks the widespread myth that secularism is the inevitable wave of the future, coming at us like an unstoppable force of nature. Baker shows instead that the secularization of society was the result of deliberate planning and concerted effort by a relatively few determined ideologues. Baker makes it clear that what they did can be undone. We shall be hearing more from this promising young man."
—JENNIFER ROBACK MORSE, Founder and President,
The Ruth Institute

"Hunter Baker has produced a powerful and carefully constructed argument against the secularists in our midst who are attempting to subvert the traditions that gave birth to our unique national enterprise."
—HERBERT LONDON, President, Hudson Institute; author,
America's Secular Challenge

"Secularism was supposed to have displaced religion before the end of the last century. It failed. Baker has done an immense favor for every Christian interested in a faithful life in the public square. As an important and emerging young evangelical scholar and public thinker, he doesn't cower at the seemingly imposing face of secularism but intelligently reads its vital signs and confidently declares its inherent weaknesses."
—GLENN T. STANTON, cultural researcher; author,
Marriage on Trial and *My Crazy Imperfect
Christian Family*

the end of secularism

hunter baker

:: CROSSWAY WHEATON, ILLINOIS

Trade paperback ISBN: 978-1-4335-0654-3

PDF ISBN: 978-1-4335-0655-0

Mobipocket ISBN: 978-1-4335-0656-7

ePub ISBN: 978-1-4335-2323-6

Library of Congress Cataloging-in-Publication Data
Baker, Hunter, 1970–
    The end of secularism / Hunter Baker.
      p. cm.
    Includes bibliographical references and index.
    ISBN 978-1-4335-0654-3 (tpb)
    1. Christianity and politics. 2. Christianity and politics—United States.
3. Church and state. 4. Church and state—United States. 5. Religion and
politics. 6. Secularism. I. Title.
BR115.P7B143   2009
211'.6—dc22   2009005813

VP		18	17	16	15	14	13	12	11	10	09
14	13	12	11	10	9	8	7	6	5	4	3	2	1

Contents

Preface

There was once a professor who had a fantastic dream night after night. In this dream, he would stand before the great philosophers of the ages as they made their cases and send them away defeated one by one with a single devastating sentence. The problem was that each time he woke, he could never recall his powerful refutation. His psychiatrist suggested he keep a pad and pencil on his nightstand as a means of willing himself to wake just long enough to record his rejoinder. The professor dutifully did as his doctor advised. Sure enough, the dream returned that very night. He managed to rouse himself and scribbled on the pad. When morning came and he returned to consciousness, the professor reached for his notebook with a sense of awe and expectation. With disappointment he read, "Well, that's what you say!"

I had a dream of my own while writing this book. In my nocturnal imaginings, the great clergyman and church-state scholar Father Richard John Neuhaus would have something complimentary to say about *The End of Secularism* in his monthly column, "The Public Square," in *First Things*, a distinguished journal of religion and culture. Regrettably, like the professor in my little story, I was destined to be disappointed. Before the book could be published, Father Neuhaus died after a return of the cancer that nearly killed him several years ago. The worldwide community of academics and autodidacts who quickened their step on the way back from the mailbox with copies of *First Things* in their hands mourned his passing. There would be no more chances to read his many thousands of words of erudite and witty commentary each month.

According to Joseph Pearce's biography of G. K. Chesterton, when Chesterton met his final reward T. H. White is said to have announced to his class, "G. K. Chesterton died yesterday. P. G. Wodehouse is now the greatest living master of the English language." Richard John

Neuhaus held that kind of importance for a great many of us who devote ourselves to understanding the nexus of church and state.

Though I won't have the chance to gain a favorable notice from the great RJN, I have an outstanding debt to pay. *The End of Secularism* would never have been written had not his seminal volume *The Naked Public Square* preceded it by more than twenty years. I suspect there will be more tributes like mine in books to come. The remarkable Neuhaus inspired many of us during his brilliant career.

I hope this book successfully follows *The Naked Public Square* and the mountain of commentary Neuhaus piled up behind that celebrated title by demonstrating that the segregation of religion to private ceremonies and weekend events marks a collective giving in rather than a social victory. Real-life human beings developed the institutional separation of church and state as a sensible and organic reaction to the lessons of the Reformation and the wars of religion that followed. The attempt by some elites to move a society with a healthy church and state interacting with each other, sometimes as friends and sometimes in tension, into the arrangement we call secularism, which privatizes religion, is a step too far. And it is a step we resent for good reason. That is the idea to which Richard John Neuhaus so eloquently gave voice. That is the work I have tried to build upon here.

Neuhaus was the wise tutor I never met. I dare not conclude this preface without a brief acknowledgment of the professors who trained me in person. Francis Beckwith and Barry Hankins, I remain thankful for your teaching and your sterling examples of intellectual honesty. A career spent chasing the two of you would be gratifying, indeed. Thanks also to Robert Sloan, president of Baylor University from 1995 to 2005, for making that institution the kind of place where I could pursue doctoral study with men like these.

A.M.D.G.,
Hunter Baker

Introduction:
My Story

I was once a secularist. I believed in God, but I didn't see what difference that made to anything outside my private world. Private religion is at the heart of secularism. My relationship with God was simple. If I felt fear, I asked him to protect me. If I wanted, I asked him to provide. His character was not particularly of interest to me. The God who existed in my mind during my life up until college was essentially a cosmic genie.

Beyond the realm of my personal desires and wishes, I saw no place for God other than in ceremonies like baptisms, weddings, and funerals. That god is an accessory to occasions. He is like a magical charm designed to do what we want him to do. There are times when we bring him out with ornaments, bows, and ribbons. Otherwise, we box him up in the attic and only occasionally remember or contemplate him. For me, the private god-in-a-lantern model was the appropriate way to think about God and/or religion.

To discuss such things at my public school or at the mall or walking to the basketball court informally with friends seemed gauche and embarrassing. I think I would rather have ripped my pants in public than talk about God in the middle of a "mainstream" gathering. I felt shame for other people who crossed that line. The reaction I had is pretty typical of a secularist's feelings about public religion. It is distasteful, out of place, and irrelevant. In retrospect, I now believe those feelings of discomfort drive secularists to encourage the privatization of religion. Expressions of public faith offend them in the way pornography offends certain other people. Something that should have been kept behind closed doors has been exposed for all to see. Better to make ideological zoning laws to force such things to the outskirts of town.

Those were my views despite the fact that my parents attempted to raise me as a Christian. There was nothing heavy-handed in how they went about it. They took me to church and Sunday school. I was so mentally disengaged that I went through those many years without ever understanding why the Romans crucified Jesus. Religious friction in my family led to personal secularism in my life. My mother was Catholic. My father came from the restorationist Church of Christ. While they did not fight with each other and worked in good faith to compromise, there was tension in other family relationships that left me with the opinion that my life would be simpler without thinking much about any particular religion. I was satisfied with my private God of no particularity. The famed sociologist Emile Durkheim thought that societies created their own gods as a way of worshiping their collective identity. Based on my experience, I think the charge is better directed at these private gods who make no demands and exist purely for the purpose of potentially fulfilling wishes. They are simply more powerful versions of the human submitting requests to them.

It was only when I left home to attend college at Florida State University that I began to think differently. On my own, away from family life, I met people who took their Christianity quite seriously. Whether this was the sovereignty of God or happenstance I leave to the reader. The only answer I will not accept is that I was seeking these Christians. I wasn't. The first time someone asked me if I had a personal relationship with Jesus Christ, I felt uncomfortable and put upon. I was annoyed in the same way one feels when approached by a stranger asking for money on a pretense. However, it happened that I made friends with a number of Christians. I observed their lives and listened to what they had to say. Importantly, I began to read the Bible and also to pay attention to Christian claims about the resurrection of Christ. Over time, I experienced a largely rational (somewhere Richard Dawkins is snorting) conversion to Christianity. By that, I simply mean I became convinced that what the New Testament says about Jesus Christ is true. There was no single moment when it happened. I can recall reading about a professor who described losing his faith by saying it was as if he had put his beliefs in a drawer and shut it only to find when he opened the drawer there was nothing there.

My conversion was the opposite. I started with a nearly empty drawer and closed it. When I returned it was nearly full.

Upon becoming a Christian, I became aware of the strangeness of my idea of religion as a private thing. Christians, at least the kind I had come to know, talked about their faith. They did Bible studies that were sometimes purely devotional but were at other times organized around themes like social justice, racism, the environment, or the sanctity of life. These were public matters. Before my conversion, I can remember listening disinterestedly to a high school debate over abortion. The only thing that stayed with me was a moment of hilarity when one debater mistook the meaning of the word "euthanasia" for "youth in Asia" and exclaimed with outrage, "I don't see what difference kids in China make to this discussion!" I was utterly hardened and felt nothing when one of the participants tried to explain the violence wrought upon a fetus. But after becoming a Christian, I listened with growing horror as a friend in the dormitory gave his reasons for why he thought God cared about abortion. My conscience was pricked in a way I hadn't experienced before. I wonder whether others from a generation or two previous had similar experiences with regard to their views on race and segregation. What if God cares? It can be a sobering thought and a motivating one.

This bit of personal history offers a report from a life spent on both sides of the secular/public religion divide. I comprehend the disgust and discomfort the secularist has when listening to Christians or other religionists bringing God into public affairs. I also understand the feeling many Christians have that they must participate in public affairs to help maintain justice and to restrain evil. Pay attention to those words, *justice* and *evil*. When we talk about politics, we don't engage in a debate that revolves around pure scientific and mathematical certainties. There is more discussion to be had. What is justice? What is love? What is equality? What kinds of things should we do for people? What kinds of laws shall we make? Right and wrong will enter into the picture and there is no compelling reason to rule secularism in and religion out. As both a Christian and a professional student of law and religion, I have come to believe secularists are profoundly wrong to suggest that leaving religion out of the public square is a good thing for all involved. Secularism is neither necessarily fair, nor clearly superior to other alternatives. Secularism is supposed to provide a new way forward for humankind. It is, in actuality, a dead end. This book seeks to prove that point.

The secular understanding of religion and politics tends to divide the two things entirely as we see in Diagram 1.

Diagram 1: Religion and Politics per the Secularist

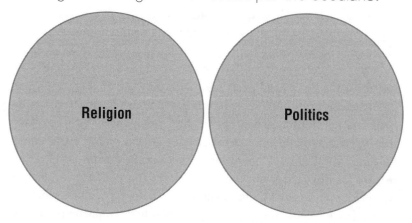

In reality, such thinking is too simple by far. More accurately, we could portray religion and politics as a Venn diagram (2), in which the two concepts overlap.

Diagram 2: Religion and Politics Rightly Understood

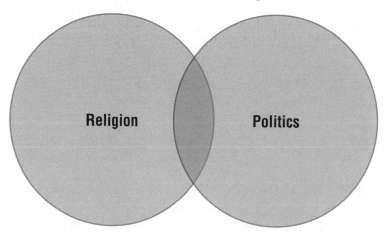

This representation of the relationship between the two concepts captures the situation much better than secularism, which would separate them entirely. Diagram 2 embodies an acknowledgment that there are many questions of value confronted by a political system in which secular understandings have no real advantage over religious counterparts. Indeed, there may be certain understandings basic to a political system, such as human equality, that might be incomprehensible outside of some metaphysical foundation. Religion and politics are not two totally distinct areas of human activity. It is also true, however, that they are not coextensive. As the renegade Puritan Roger Williams insisted, it is possible to govern well and justly without possessing a correct understanding of something such as the doctrine of the Trinity.

Another way to understand part of the difficulty with secularism is to consider it in terms of simple worldview analysis. Secularists think of secularism as a neutral space in the polity benevolently keeping religions from dangerous, disharmonious, and potentially oppressive activity. This view can be pictured in Diagram 3.

Diagram 3: Separating Religion and Politics Framework

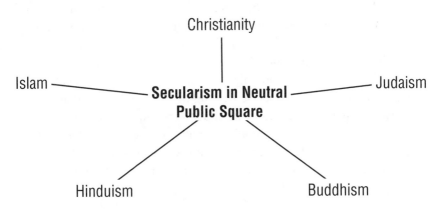

However, the reality is that secularism does not provide a neutral space. It is one of many conceptual players attempting to influence social and political activity. Consider Diagram 4.

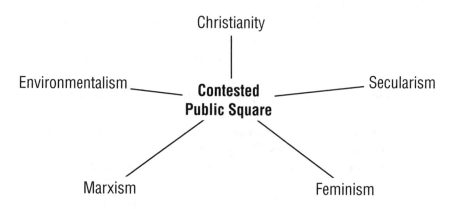

Diagram 4: Secularism as Part of the Competing Orthodoxies Framework

We could make Diagram 4 much more complex and attempt to create a detailed ideological and religious map of the world, but the basic point holds even with a simple depiction. Secularism represents a partisan position, not a neutral one. And secularists are partisans. They attempt to create a political community that suits their preferences. Remember my story about being uncomfortable with public religion. Secularists very often feel that way. Secularism is a way to suppress that which they find troubling and to bring about the existence of a political and legal regime more agreeable to their tastes.

In the above diagrams, I have made two key points. One is that religion and politics are not fully separable or, at least, that there is no strong rational warrant for separating them. The other is that secularism is a partisan position with supporters and thus cannot be seen as the neutral answer to pluralism. I will endeavor to illustrate these points in detail in the subsequent chapters. The primary method is to study Christianity and secularism together, for surely the fates of the two have been intertwined.

Secularism as an Academic Subject

There is an old joke that religion departments exist to make sure atheists have a home on campus. I've never surveyed religion professors to see if the joke is true, but there is little doubt that religion doesn't fare very well in religion departments. The historian C. John Sommerville has invited academics to treat secularism much as they have religion, which means he thinks it should be studied, written about, and taught critically.[1] What would it mean to accept Dr. Sommerville's provocative invitation? Imagine a university department full of scholars dedicated to studying the phenomenon of secularism. Where did secularism come from? What do its advocates and practitioners believe? Why do they believe it? Do their most cherished beliefs stand up to scrutiny? How do they approach politics? What are their prejudices? Just what kind of people are these secularists? Is secularism just another way for the people of wealth and fashion to maintain their prerogatives against religious appeals for righteousness?

If there were such a thing as a secularism department at large universities, these are the types of pointed questions that would surely be asked in series of debates, conferences, research papers, and books sent off to the nation's academic libraries. They are also mirror images of the questions that are currently asked about various faiths and believers in our university religion departments. Unlike academic departments centered on race and gender-based concerns, which are always staffed by sympathetic scholars, religion scholars tend to be critical of their subjects rather than identifying with them.

In introducing the subject, I have imagined a department of secularism studies as the opposite of a religion department. And to some extent secularism is the opposite of religion. Whereas religions typically seek to know God's will and to live in accordance with it, secularists see that quest as divisive and try to bring us together by focusing on what we have in common without God. In the sense that religion means "with God" and secularism means "without God," the two are opposites. But the relationship is more complicated than that. For example, many conservative Christians have argued that secularism is just another religion and should be treated as one for purposes of constitutional jurisprudence. The idea is intuitively appealing but not quite right. Secularism often implies a worldview, just as religions have worldview implications. However, secularism is an idea that seeks to privatize religion. It is not, itself, a religion even if there have occasionally been groups of people claiming to be part of quasi-religions such as secular humanism or ethical culture.

Because advocates of secularism present it as a solution to the "problem" of public religion, we become the audience for a caricature of the ways the two concepts are opposed to each other. Instead of "without reference to God" versus "with reference to God," the antonyms expand to look more like "reason and tolerance" versus "prejudice and superstition." This misunderstanding has not been accidental but is instead the thrust of the presentation pushed by advocates of a particular side. Thus, rational thinking processes, empirical verification, and social harmony are said to accompany a secular outlook. Religious associations, on the other hand, are tied to mysticism, violence, ignorance, and coercion. The secular take on religion is more Torquemada, Jim Jones, and Osama bin Laden than Augustine, Aquinas, Luther, Newton, and Pascal.

Garry Wills, writing for *The New York Times* after the reelection of George W. Bush, bemoaned the turn of Americans from "intelligence . . . and regard for secular sciences" to resembling America's fundamentalist Islamic enemies more than its cousins in Western Europe. One of his key evidences was that Americans believed in the virgin birth in greater numbers than they endorsed Darwin's theory.[2]

Former Clinton Secretary of Labor Robert Reich and a bumper crop of nouveau village atheists (e.g., Daniel Dennett, Richard Dawkins, and Sam Harris) perceive religious belief as a deliberate decision to ignore reason in favor of dangerous and arbitrary superstition. Prior to the 2004 presidential election Reich wrote:

> The underlying battle will be between modern civilization and antimodernist fanatics; between those who believe in the primacy of the individual and those who believe that human beings owe blind allegiance to a higher authority; between those who give priority to life in this world and those who believe that human life is no more than preparation for an existence beyond life; between those who believe that truth is revealed solely through scripture and religious dogma, and those who rely primarily on science, reason, and logic.[3]

On this view, religion is like white phosphorus. It should be submerged lest it ignite. This reading somehow forgets that a Christian culture gave birth to our Western emphasis on science and reason and that the church was an important patron of scientific work. But that can be forgiven. Dr. Reich has been brought up on ideological history of a particular sort as most of us have been. That is a matter to which I return in subsequent chapters.

Understanding Secularism

The provocative prose of Secretary Reich notwithstanding, the logic of secularism is persuasive on the surface when wielded a bit more delicately. The argument is simple:

1) We believe different things about God.
2) Throughout history, people have killed each other because of those different beliefs. They have sometimes done so on a large scale.
3) If we do not have indisputable empirical proof of God's existence and/or of what God wants, then the persecution of others who believe differently is unwarranted and gravely wrong.
4) In fact, given our lack of certainty regarding God, we should simply avoid the influence of religious ideas in our public space.
5) It is one thing for people of faith to gather together, in a place of worship, for example, and to talk about their religion, but it is another to bring beliefs into the diverse world in which we live together.
6) It would be better for all involved (the argument goes) if we would simply exclude religious considerations from commerce, politics, education, law, and any other public endeavor.

The virtuous person of faith, then, is a private person of faith. Religion, in the secularist's scenario, is sort of like a hobby. Enthusiasts should save their talk and activities for times and places they arrange together.[4]

Secularism is much more than a formal financial and legal separation of church institutions from state institutions. It is a way of living together in community that emphasizes clean conceptual boundaries over organic beliefs and traditions. Here we come to a critical point. Secularism is not and should not be synonymous with the separation of church and state. The separation of church and state, in the classical sense, simply means that the state does not collect fees to support the church; neither does it mandate membership in the church. Classical separation, as I have just defined it, is a wonderful arrangement Americans arrived at as a practical solution after many years of dealing with the difficulty of pluralism and the old European model of one church and one state.

When Christians rail against the separation of church and state and heatedly charge that those words do not appear in the Constitution, they are really reacting to secularism. The problem is that the language of the separation of church and state is often used to push for more secularistic understandings. Given a right understanding of secularism as the separation of religion from public life and the separation of church and state as nothing more than formal institutional independence of church and state, citizens should value church-state separation as the healthier and more justifiable state of affairs.

Secularism is a different concept. It is directly tied to secularization theory, which posits that advanced societies essentially outgrow religion and gain ever greater independence from it. Religion loses its relevance to the public world. Individuals and subcommunities may believe fervently, but that is not something to impact public business or our professional lives. The iconic sociologist Max Weber imagined a process in which virtually every human endeavor would freely discover its own excellence and its own boundaries without religion hovering above offering guidance or judgment.[5] This process may help explain why ideas such as medical ethics and business ethics often seem so useless in our time.

The development of secularization and secularism may seem attractive to many. Religious pluralism is a fact of the modern world in which people travel and migrate with a high degree of freedom. If it is possible to conduct most activities, particularly public ones, in such a way as to avoid religion and religious differences, then friction should diminish and social progress should increase. What person of goodwill would look askance at such a promising development? Secularism appeals to common-ground approaches to getting along with others. "Let's leave aside the things that divide us, like religion, and focus on those things we all have to deal with like jobs, transportation, food, and education." In a world divided into a growing number of religious factions, secularism has been supposed by many to be an answer to the fact of religious plurality. The logic of secularism is that by conducting our affairs without reference to God, we can avoid religious division and deal with each other in a peaceful way. Secularism, the argument goes, is a recipe for social harmony.

Advocates of secularism also advance the idea that secularism is rationally superior to religious alternatives in the sense that it hews more closely to the path of science and empirical rationality. The tie between secularism and science has two primary sources. The first is the story of warfare between science and religion, which first began to be told with frequency in the late nineteenth century[6] and was extended for a long run with the slowly deflating mythos of the Scopes trial.[7] The second is the sociological theory of secularization, which has (in its widest reaches) viewed secularization as the destiny of man as he shakes off the immaturity of religious faith and becomes an advanced creature of scientific rationality.[8]

Previewing the Path of the Argument against Secularism

Because secularism was born through a process of development rather than springing forth whole from the troubled brow of a Greek god, the next several chapters will necessarily deal with the story of the theo-political question in the West. The goal is to briefly replay the history of the West since the time of Christ in order to illustrate different stages in the relationship of politics and religion. Looking at the stages, the reader has an opportunity to appreciate the advantages and drawbacks of various approaches to integrating or segregating the church and the state. The reader is also able to see how secularism emerged after being essentially unthinkable for most of the history of mankind.

The next set of chapters takes a detailed look at the development of the American public order. Because there is a seemingly endless debate over whether the United States was founded as an explicitly Christian republic or, conversely, as a determinedly secular order, there is value in attempting to set the record straight. Analysis reveals that both parties, Christians and secularists, overstate their side of the argument. However, close analysis demonstrates that claims that the Constitution and its religion clauses somehow established a secular republic are simply incorrect. The reality is that Constitutional texts dealing with religion simply preserved the autonomy of the states in that regard, which helps explain the unsatisfactory result of Supreme

Court jurisprudence reading those phrases like tea leaves. This part of the book then documents how secularism ultimately did develop in the United States and how Christians reacted to the increased salience of a secularistic social philosophy.

Secularism presents as a guarantor of social peace in a religiously pluralistic environment. The argument of the middle chapters will be that a secular approach simply shifts the social burden from one group of citizens to another. That argument is developed in three key ways. First, I demonstrate the lack of neutrality inherent in secularism as an approach to regulating the social order by looking at the points made by postmodernists and Christian critics. Second, I use the work of Christian Smith and others to show that American secularism was not so much a natural development as it was something pushed by interested agents in sometimes very forceful ways. Third, I look to the existence of secularists as a demographic group whose preferences line up so directly with a secular social order that it may as well have been set up for their comfort. Studying secularism and its partisans, rather than merely employing the concept as a critical lens through which to view religion, yields a more realistic appraisal of its merits. If secularism is simply a device for advancing the agenda of a particular group at the cost of imposing a burden on other groups, then there are clear problems with maintaining that it is the best method of maintaining social harmony.

The penultimate set of chapters will address the assumption that secularism is rationally superior to theistic alternatives. This part of the argument begins by addressing the idea that science and secularism go together. The warfare model of science and religion presents religion as dangerous and backward and thus leaves secularism as the protector of all good things such as electricity, medicine, and air travel, not to mention the expansion of human knowledge that might lead to elimination of disease and even possibly to physical immortality. By examining that history and showing substantial problems with the warfare model, I seek to remove the impression that Christianity is naturally hostile to science, even in its orthodox forms, and to knock a leg out from under the idea that secularism is necessary to the productive social use of science.

I then move on to point out there is nothing necessarily scientific about a secular approach to formulating political ends. Rather, secular and religious approaches to formulating political ends such as justice, mercy, and fairness all fall into areas of knowledge that are simply not scientific; thus, neither can claim that mantle. Unless secularism reverts to a thoroughgoing positivism (the idea that nothing is real that we cannot confirm with our senses), then it cannot claim scientific authority for its proposals. Despite our penchant for easily accepting the contention that knowledge divides into the secular and the religious, the primary thrust of the critique will be that knowledge does not divide in that fashion. Rather, there is the knowledge that we can gain via scientific experimentation and verification and then there is everything else. The "everything else" happens to be where secularism and religion do their work along with a host of other attempts to make sense of the parts of life we really care about and that happen not to yield scientific answers. Secularism does not deserve to be seen as the representative of science in law and politics against the religious. Awareness of the reality erodes the appearance of a special affinity between science and secularism, which thus far has counted for much in public debate.

In the concluding chapters, I offer a striking case study from a few years ago when a Christian law professor and a state governor set out to reform the tax code in line with the philosophy of Jesus Christ. The events of that strange year down south demonstrate much about the political motivations and unprincipled selectivity of the guardians of secularism.

The idea that rests at the foundation of this entire investigation and critique of secularism is that though it is a way of addressing problems of religious pluralism, it is far from the only way. It is certainly more extreme than simple institutional separation of church and state because it entails religious privatization. Just as microsurgery proves more effective than the amputation of a limb, there are better ways to deal with religious pluralism than removing religion from public life. In short, there are good reasons to question whether secularism is the enlightened path to living together.

My studies have led me to conclude that the case for secularism is partisan, shallow, and under-examined. In these pages, I have assembled the bill of particulars against secularism that I have long wanted to read in one volume but have never found.

1

The Early Church and the Empire

As defined in the introduction, secularism means that religious considerations are excluded from civil affairs. We live in a time when public secularism is something of a taken-for-granted reality in the United States. Although the U.S. is one of the most religious of the developed nations, there is still an expectation among those who define public reality in the media, academy, and government that appeals to God should be saved for one's private life. When someone breaks the pattern by publicly invoking God as the reason to either embark upon or avoid a course of action, the reaction is typically one of distaste, surprise, or feeling threatened. The reason for the adverse reaction is that secularism is widely believed to be rationally more attractive than the alternatives and a superior strategy for attaining social peace in a pluralistic setting. To swim against the tide of secular modernity indicates one may be uncivil, unbalanced, and possibly even dangerous.

The question posed by this book is whether public secularism is desirable and, more specifically, whether it lives up to its billing. In order to answer that question, it is useful to look back at how we reached the current cultural and political moment, in the West generally and in the United States specifically. Just as atheism is by definition a reaction against something, which is belief in the existence of God, so too, is secularism a reaction against something. In the West, where the concept was born, secularism is a reaction against the notion of a religious state, particularly a Christian one. Thus, if one proposes to make a critical study of secularism, then one must obtain a degree of familiarity with the story of the Christian church and the state since the time of Christ.

The Rise of Christianity and the Challenge of Power

For most of human history, religious and political authority has been unified. Typically, both governmental and religious rule have been united in a single structure or the two have occupied distinct organizations but with a mutually reinforcing relationship.[1] Christians and non-Christians often attribute the eventual growth of church-state separation in the West to the enigmatic statement of Jesus who famously said, "Render to Caesar the things that are Caesar's, and to God the things that are God's."[2] The statement referred to a coin bearing Caesar's image and appears pregnant with possible meanings, but a common lesson drawn from the scriptural moment, employed repeatedly for two millennia now, is that God cares about sacred things, such as a pure heart and religious observance, and delegates more prosaic matters such as regular law, order, and commerce to earthly rulers. This single interpretation of what Jesus meant—the idea of separating the sacred from the pragmatic business of community governance—is the seedling of the modern secular arrangement of public affairs. In fact, secularism is sometimes referred to as the gift of Christianity to the West.[3]

Although the Christian thus instructed aimed to be a good citizen of the empire into which the early church was born, obedience carried one important caveat. God must be obeyed rather than men, so where God's law differed from the law of men, Christians were forced to follow the higher law.[4] The paradigmatic example of a clash between the two realms involved emperor worship. At first, Christians were able to employ the same exemption from the practice that Jews enjoyed, but ultimately the government sorted out the two camps and began to persecute stiff-necked Christians whose refusal to subordinate their unique religiosity to the civil cult of the emperor posed an apparent threat to the legal order.[5]

From Persecuted Minority to Rule by the Lord's Man

Faced with growth of Christian churches, the empire had the choices of secularization (which was unthinkable), extermination (which had not worked), or conversion of the ruler to Christianity.[6] What meaning would Christ's words about the image on the coin take on if Caesar himself were a Christian? After battling to win the rule of the whole empire, Constantine did convert. Because conversion was seen as a way of dealing with the growth of the Christian cult and because of his deathbed baptism, his status as a believer is often questioned. In answer one might note that the empire was not yet majority Christian, and the practice of baptism at the end of life was commonly considered a prudential way of cleansing all sin right before death.[7] Constantine held the traditional Christian belief that God was the God of history and had revealed himself through the resurrection of Christ. He referred to the faith as "the struggle for deathlessness."[8] Historian Henry Chadwick asserted that whether or not Constantine's grasp of the Christian faith was subtle, the ruler was quite certain that the Christian God was the author of his military victory over his rival Maxentius in Rome.[9]

Christians and non-Christians alike often speak disparagingly of Constantine's conversion, as though Constantine made Christianity the state religion and thus ruined the purity of the faith by corrupting it with power and wealth. Contrary to popular belief, however, Constantine did not impose the Christian religion on the empire.[10] His regime is more accurately described as having embraced "provisional religious pluralism." He believed and said that "the struggle for deathlessness must be free."[11] His legislation did favor the Christian church in some instances though. He gave residences to the bishops of Rome and gave large percentages of provincial revenues to be used in church charity. The law itself also took on a more Christian flavor. He generated greater protection for "children, slaves, peasants, and prisoners."[12] He ended the practice of branding criminals' faces because of the image of God in man. Courts closed on Sundays unless there was a slave to be freed.

Although Constantine's Christian humanitarianism continued to influence the law, his policy of religious toleration gradually fell by the wayside in the West. For a long time afterward the church was possessed by a different view, which was that of the loving constraint of heresy and apostasy.

The Religion of the State, but Not the State's Religion

Under Constantine, the church first escaped persecution and then gained the bounty of endorsement by the most powerful man in the empire. In the latter half of the fourth century, Theodosius did what Constantine had not, which was to set up a Christian state where heretics had their civil rights sharply curtailed and pagans were tolerated but controlled. Half a century later, Theodosius II made serious doctrinal divergences subject to the death penalty and no longer allowed pagans to serve in the army.[13]

Ambrose set a precedent for the independence of the church when he refused Communion to Theodosius for his massacre of townspeople in Thessalonika after an imperial officer was killed in a riot there. The emperor did penance.[14] He was the head of the state but not the head of the church and lacked the power to absolve himself or to declare his actions right. The action not only established the church's independence but also showed that it was not a slave to its private interests.[15]

Augustine's State: Necessary Evil or True Justice

Augustine was one of the first major Christian commentators to live in an empire that was to some degree a projection of Christianity rather than a threat to it. For that reason, perhaps, his assessment of the state was thoroughly mixed.

Augustine viewed the natural state as little more than the most successful power play in a world of theft and contest. In one justly famous passage, he remarked:

> Without justice, what are kingdoms but great robber bands? What are robber bands but small kingdoms? The band is itself made up of men, is ruled by the command of a leader, and is held together by a social pact. Plunder is divided in accordance with an agreed-upon law. If this evil increases by the inclusion of dissolute men to the extent that it takes over territory, establishes headquarters, occupies cities, and subdues peoples, it publicly assumes the title of kingdom! This title is manifestly conferred on it, not because greed has been removed, but because impunity has been added. A fitting and true response was once given to Alexander the Great by an apprehended pirate. When asked by the king what he thought he was doing by infesting the sea, he replied with noble insolence, "What do you think you are doing by infesting the whole world? Because I do it with one puny boat, I am called a pirate; because you do it with a great fleet, you are called an emperor."[16]

For a state to reach out and subdue peoples who have not endangered it is little more than grand larceny.[17] Great legends arise out of conquest, but Augustine viewed that path with contempt. In an unfallen world, no one would ever have servant status imposed upon him by another man.[18] Man was not created to serve a state. And man was not created to serve another man under coercion.

Augustine's account of the pre-Christian state is definitely that of the glass half empty. In addition to being a robber band with better publicity, the state is something to be endured. Temporal life is training for eternal life,[19] and one should not complain too much as long as he lives under a state that does not compel him to commit impieties during his short life.[20]

With the coming of Christ, however, the state could aspire to more. The government could, if led by servants of the Lord, seek true justice and thus form a real republic rather than continuing to exist as a noble veneer covering larceny. God placed the empire in Constantine's hands for the very purpose of proving that his people could rule rather than exist as a permanent protest movement. In fact, the event of continued Christian leadership would prove extraordinarily "felicitous" for the people of the republic.[21]

Socrates already had part of the puzzle. He realized good morals were required to purify the mind so that it might then grasp higher things.[22] Taking on the mind of Christ is necessary to apprehend real justice upon which to found the republic; consequently, the Christian emperor should rule justly and remember he is human. He will use power for the greatest possible extension of the worship of God and he will fear and love God, be slow to punish and ready to pardon, punish for ends of government and not for his own hatred, and grant pardon in hope of correction. There is an important distinction to be made here where Augustine spoke of serving God. The old way was to serve God in the hope that he would grant dominance and power. The way of the Christian is to serve God through charity and caring. Finally, the Christian ruler will restrain extravagance as much as it might have been unrestrained by his predecessors.[23] This is the picture of the city of God.

To the extent possible, the earthly city should seek to identify its destiny with that of the city of God. In this way it could rise above theft, coercion, and temporality to strive for an eternal destiny. The city of God recognizes that there can be no right to do anything unless it is done justly. There is no right that proceeds simply from strength. What Augustine declared was later echoed by Martin Luther King Jr. many centuries later, as he wrote from the Birmingham jail, that an unjust law is no law at all. He appealed implicitly to the city of God and explicitly to Augustine's claim that God's justice has little to do with martial superiority.[24]

Despite his desire for republics ruled by Christians seeking after true justice—Christ's justice—Augustine realized that members of the city of God sometimes live in the earthly city without political power (as had been the pattern for the faith for the majority of its existence) and that cities where they do reign are surrounded by cities with different allegiances. Christians can live obediently in cities that seek mere earthly peace as long as those cities do not impede worship.[25] When in power, they are not to seek war with an adversary unless visited by iniquity.[26] The differences between the city of God and the city of man get sorted out in the last judgment. God holds the responsibility for sorting wheat from tares.[27]

Though Augustine's work seemed to point in the direction of something like religious toleration, he, like so many other great theorists, found himself compelled to make hard choices based on events. His community in Africa was one of the most contentious spots for Catholic-Donatist strife. While all involved were Christians, there was little forgiveness and occasional violence.[28]

Ironically, the subject of the long-running dispute was the persecution the church had been through in the past. Those Christians who appeared to have lapsed under coercive pressure wished to rejoin the church or regain their clerical positions. In the main, the Catholic Church was willing to forgive with appropriate penance, but there were others (the Donatists) who held the stricter position that apostasy could not be forgiven, and they clashed with the rest of the church. They cherished the memory of martyrs for the faith and argued that forgiving the offense of the lapsed demeaned the martyrs' sacrifice.[29]

Dissatisfied with the existence of a nearly century-long dispute within the church, Augustine moved to conclude the issue with a council. Though he was in principle opposed to coercion as a method of resolving the controversy and tended to think it would merely result in fake conversions to his side, Augustine eventually came to embrace the opposite point of view. The government began putting pressure upon the Donatists and met with some success in changing hearts and minds. Augustine began to believe that a mind changed by coercion might eventually find itself in true agreement and thus be really reconciled. Slowly, he embraced a policy of moderate coercion and thus put his own imprimatur on "paternal correction" of dissidents.[30]

The council in Carthage (411), which addressed the situation, finally settled on fines, exile of Donatist clergy, and confiscation of Donatist property. Even with official policy against them, the Donatists continued on in Africa for nearly three more centuries. Perhaps the only reason we are not talking about them today is that they were eventually wiped off the map by expansionist Islam in the seventh century.[31]

The decision to suppress through the vehicle of law was one the church (in various manifestations) and Christian states would make at several points in history. Examples include the Medieval Inquisition directed against heretics such as the Cathars, who were clearly non-Christian, and the Waldensians, whose heresy looked a lot like mere Protestantism before its time; witch trials; and the suppression of both Catholics and Protestants by each other in Reformation and post-Reformation Europe. The idea behind the suppression was that of loving constraint. Love toward the community and toward the heretic himself required coercion and hopefully persuasion toward repentance so that the offender might save his soul. The "struggle for deathlessness" was no longer free. Rather, it was guided by church and state for better or worse.

2

By What Right? By What Power?

Throughout the period of the Christian church's greatest political power (approximately from the time of its establishment as the faith of the Roman Empire until the Reformation), the notion of secular and sacred spheres of authority recurred often as the church and kings of Europe wrestled over their relative powers. Pope Gelasius analyzed the state and the church as "the two swords" but left uncertainty over whether the church claimed to be superior to the state and that the state merely derived its power from the church.[1] Thus, we have the series of iconic moments described in Brian Tierney's *The Crisis of Church and State*, such as the crowning of Charlemagne (800) by the pope, possibly unintended by Charlemagne;[2] the Investiture Contest (1075–1122) in which kings battled with the church over who had the power to appoint bishops (which the church ultimately won);[3] King Henry IV standing barefoot in the snow to ask the forgiveness of Pope Gregory VII (1077) who claimed the right to depose wayward rulers;[4] and the Peace of Venice in 1177.[5] In these events we see the church seeking to supervise kings, and kings seeking control over the church. It is very much the situation that still obtained later at the time of the Reformation, when Martin Luther complained in *On Secular Authority* that no one does their duty and we are left with the ridiculous circumstance of souls "ruled by steel" and "bodies by letters."[6]

At all points in the history of church and state in the West between establishment of the Christian church by the Roman Empire and the period prior to the Reformation, the primary question was not which church was the true church or what religion kings would embrace. Kings became Christian. Their realms followed. The church was the Catholic Church. The social order was a Christian one, and the battle between church and state was over which institution had the mandate from God to exercise various powers. Did emperors hold their power from popes and could popes depose them? Who had the right to appoint clergy with responsibility for religious services and religious fee-taking in certain geographical areas? These were the sorts of questions that created the most controversy, not the kinds we have been dealing with during the past few centuries in which the questions have been which religion will give form to the social order, if any, and to what degree will religion be permitted to impact the public square.

As for secularism as we know it today, meaning the ordering of the community without reference to God, it did not exist. In its place, there was the idea of the secular, which carried the simple meaning "in the world." The best example is the distinction made between clergy of the Catholic Church who served in segregation from the world, such as those praying and working in the monastery, and those who had responsibility for a parish. The priests with parish duties were known as secular clergy. The modern definition of *secular* is "without reference to God," but the older meaning of the word was quite different, as the above demonstrates. The idea of "secular" clergy going about their work administering the sacraments, giving aid to the poor, and, yes, even collecting tithes, burial fees, and other church revenues without reference to God is ludicrous. In the world we are discussing, *secular* simply referred to activities conducted in the world as opposed to those directed toward a purely supernatural plane.[7] State and ecclesiastical authorities wrestled, but they wrestled within the context of Christian right and wrong.

To give the proponents of secularism their due, one can point to a church practice that favors their point of view. The pre-Reformation Catholic Church proposed different standards for how people differently situated should live. Christians were separated into two classes. The first group, composed of monks, nuns, and others who had given their lives to the church, operated like a team of spiritual athletes that embraced poverty, celibacy, and pacifism in order to better plead for the world before God. This group lived by the counsels of perfection as set out (though without any such distinction) by Jesus in the Sermon on the Mount. The second group, which included just about everyone else in Christendom, lived in the sinful world on terms more amenable to ordinary human behavior and dirtied their hands with commerce, marriage, and just war.[8]

It would be a stretch to say that the second group was expected to establish a public order that operated without consideration of God, but it certainly operated with a different set of expectations and definitely contributed to the idea of true religion as something that is private and mystical rather than publicly relevant. Abraham Kuyper (1837–1920), former Dutch prime minister and Calvinist exemplar, would later imply that the Roman church created secularism by wrongly dividing life into consecrated and profane sectors.[9]

The Surprising Return of the Classical World

Although the pre-Reformation West was based on a union between the church and the crown, there were intellectual movements stirring in the twelfth and thirteenth centuries that began to open the door to the idea of a society without "the one true church" as its bedrock. Such stirrings could be seen even within the church. For example, Pope Innocent IV wrote about government as a necessary human activity and suggested that infidels could have legitimate human governments. He was possibly influenced by his study of Roman natural law arguments and implied that Christians had neither the right to dethrone pagan rulers nor the authority to pillage their goods.[10]

The impact of classical sources on Innocent's thinking was not an isolated instance. By the end of the twelfth century, the Crusades were beginning to yield an unexpected cultural influence upon the West. The Eastern world had successfully preserved and engaged the work of Aristotle and other classical scholars who were nearly lost to Europe. These rediscovered works presented a different way of thinking about society. The major consequence of the reemergence of Aristotle into a Christianized society was to make it possible to think about the state without necessary resort to theology.[11]

Thomas Aquinas is a key figure in any study of secularism and the church. Though he is to this day the Catholic Church's prime interpreter of faith and reason, Aquinas is also a key figure in setting up the premises for a secular state.

When put to a specific question involving the church and its prerogatives, Aquinas seemed to favor something like theocracy, which of course fit the world in which he lived where the Catholic Church was at the height of its power. For example, Aquinas thought that those who had always been unbelievers, including Jews, should never be coerced to embrace the faith. However, appropriate force could be used in preventing them from interfering with the Christian faith via blasphemy, "evil inducements," or persecution. This appropriate force was Aquinas's justification for the Crusades. Once a person had accepted the Christian faith, he was fairly subject to physical compulsion to render his fealty to the church and to God.[12] The same logic dictates that a Christian ruler could protect the fealty of his subjects by dealing with a religiously motivated invader like the Moors.

Aquinas also entertained the question of whether it was acceptable to have unbelievers governing believers. While it was tolerable for unbelievers to govern for reasons we will explore further below, he insisted that the church had the option to use its God-given authority to direct the end of that dominion by unbelievers. The rationale for this power invested in the church was that unbelievers deserve the loss of their control over those "who are being transformed into sons of God." Per Aquinas, the church exercised or refrained from exercising this power as it felt was necessary.[13]

Despite the answers Aquinas gave on the specific questions of the church and its authority over unbelievers, heretics, and blasphemers, it was his broader reasoning on the nature of the state that has contributed to the Western tradition of thought about the nature of the state as it regards religion. Aquinas did not have the same grim assessment of the world without Christ that Augustine did. Instead of a world so desperately alienated from God that it did not even know what justice was and could only hope to find a lesser earthly peace, Aquinas saw a world incompletely understood without God but still capable of realizing much good, including justice. The state arose from the social nature of man and existed entirely within the realm of reason.[14] Aquinas's state was actually prior to the family or even the individual because it represented the body of mankind, while subsidiaries like families and persons were merely parts like fingers and arms. People are naturally dependent on the state and cannot live without it. If they do, they are not human but are, rather, "a beast or a god." Natural men have a social instinct.[15]

What Aquinas failed to address was the tension created between his two perspectives. If he was right that the logic of the state proceeds directly from man's social nature and that we can know that without knowledge of God, then the state could theoretically operate independently of the church. Aquinas did not spell that out, but it was a natural deduction from his work, despite the fact that Aquinas declared earthly rulers subject to the pontiff.[16] Then again, the conflict was perhaps more apparent than real, because Aquinas insisted upon the truth of biblical revelation and the need for the church to provide full understanding of God's world as faith extends the powers of reason by giving it information beyond what the senses can assemble on their own.

Regardless of Aquinas's own ultimate settlement of the church's authority over a state that existed even in unilluminated nature, he poured water on seeds of secularization. In a world where popes and kings regularly disputed their bounds, it was a near certainty that new voices would pick up on the Aristotelian/Thomistic notion of the state's natural existence established by pure reason and develop that into a brief for the superiority of the state over the church for ordering society.

In the early fourteenth century, Marsilius of Padua did just that. Invoking Aristotle as his authority, Marsilius declared that all governmental power arose from the will of the citizenry who together hold a "primal law-making power."[17] This group would produce good laws after debate and discussion because "no one consciously injures himself." In essence, good laws would follow from the exercise of self-interest by the governing group.

On the spiritual side, Marsilius used Scripture to deny the primacy of Peter or any other centralization of the authority of the church. He also asserted that it is God who can punish or remit sins rather than any representative of the church who claims to be able to do so at his own discretion. Not only were the claims of the papacy erroneous, but also the papacy had failed to realize that Christ set a model of humble subservience before it. The church and its agents should be thoroughly obedient to the state, just as Christ had been even to the point of death on the cross. For a pope to claim to rule anything was in direct contravention of the gospel.[18]

Marsilius's theoretical church was completely subject to the power he called "the legislator," which represented the will of the citizens. This church had not even the power to deny sacraments or to excommunicate. Only the "legislator" would wield those powers. In short, the church was owned by the state, lock, stock, and barrel. One might pause to note that Marsilius's use of Scripture was extraordinarily selective, as was his selection of quotations from church fathers such as Ambrose.[19] Although his arguments against the papacy and some of its claimed potencies may have held water, his view of the church as a spiritual subsidiary of the state and "the legislator" could not survive a trip through the New Testament. Why exactly were the apostles in trouble if they were not obeying God rather than the state? At best he could argue that the church should conduct its activities and take its punishment if deemed illegal, but he could hardly argue that Christ or any of the apostles simply offered meek obedience to the state. In some ways Marsilius anticipated the Reformers, as with his attacks on the presumed power of the papacy, but in others, such as his notion of the utter subservience of the church, he anticipated totalitarian states of the future.

In their reliance on Aristotle, both Aquinas and Marsilius prefigured the Renaissance period that would emerge nearly contemporaneously with the Reformation in the fifteenth and sixteenth centuries. Renaissance humanism gloried in the information about the Greco-Roman classical world that became more readily available and emphasized careful study of original sources both with regard to classic texts and Christian ones. The interest in classic texts damaged the claims of Rome directly—as did the exposure of the forgery of the Donation of Constantine, which purportedly deeded a large chunk of Italian real estate to the church—and indirectly by focusing attention on Scripture rather than on the tradition of the church. As deconstructionists of Catholic claims, humanists were in consonance with the spirit of the Reformation, but as enthusiasts of the classical world who found inspiration in a civilization built on a basis quite different from Christendom, they were a different sort of men.

3

New Winds Blowing:
Two Reformers and a Schemer

Although the Reformation is often noted as the period that
made religious pluralism a hard reality in Europe, pluralism was
not the goal of the Reformers. Martin Luther, John Calvin, Ulrich
Zwingli, and a host of others entered into intense confrontation with
the reigning Catholic Church. They were not fighting for the right to
be tolerated or to tolerate. Rather, they sought to reorganize society
along Christian lines more suited to their beliefs than those of the
Catholic Church. In addition to taking issue with various doctrines
of the church regarding matters such as indulgences, the proper
number of sacraments, the status of the pope, and marriage of clergy,
Reformers had their own ideas about the correct way to resolve the
contest between church and state with regard to social authority.
Luther and Calvin, Reformers *par excellence*, contributed directly to
the further drawing of lines between religious authority and secular
authority in their writings.

Calvin

Calvin's idea of secular authority very clearly resolved the boundaries between church and state. Rather than having the church answer
to the state or the state answer to the church, Calvin proposed that
each entity answer directly to God for the responsibilities entrusted
to their care. The church was to provide for teaching of the Word of
God and worship. The state would have sole authority over governing, subject to the church's non-binding guidance.[1] Such a state as
Calvin envisioned, however, could not really be thought of as secular

in the modern sense because a Calvinist government would take great care to suppress heresy and blasphemy. To Calvin, the king held his power only through the hand of God, and it would be ridiculous for God not to care whether his chosen servant protected right worship and doctrine.[2] If the king failed to do his duty by God, the people could expect punishment from God directed against the nation. In the face of Catholic persecution of Calvinists, the Reformer suggested lesser magistrates could represent the people and bring correction to a wayward ruler.[3]

Though Calvin's solution to the theo-political problem had little in common with secularism as understood by the modern reader, it clearly contributed to the idea of separation of church and state by decisively making the state independent of the church. Calvin's scheme ironically rises out of an explosion of pluralism but does not do much to account for it in terms of toleration. His state still wields the sword in enforcement of orthodoxy.[4] Of course, in Calvin's view the great difference was that a state such as the one he envisioned would enforce a substantially more correct orthodoxy than what went before. The end result of Calvin's formulation came down squarely on the side of kings and emperors who contended through the ages that they did not have to account to the church for their leadership; rather, they were accountable directly to God and had personal responsibility to protect right religion.

Luther

Luther's solution to the church-state issue was decidedly more radical. Rather than take a side in the debate that had raged through the centuries, Luther redrew the map.

Luther wrote *On Secular Authority* to answer a pressing question: how can the sword of the state be reconciled with Christ's Sermon on the Mount, wherein meekness and nonresistance are commended to the believer? Because of his dissatisfaction with the traditional Catholic answer—that the Sermon represented a "counsel of perfection" (itself a secularizing idea)—Luther developed his own doctrine of the two kingdoms and God's use for each. His approach maintained the authority of the Sermon on the Mount for every believer, while explaining the continued existence of the state and God's purpose for it.

Thus, he argued that all mankind must be divided into two parts: "the first belong to the kingdom of God, the second to the kingdom of the world."[5] This first group, living in the reality that Christ came to establish his kingdom in the world, has no need of the sword. The entire secular apparatus would disappear for lack of need if all the world were truly Christian.[6] After all, Paul told Timothy that laws are for the unjust, not the just.[7] However, the second group is not living according to Christ's gentle counsel and neither are most who would take the name "Christian." As a result, it is God's will that the secular sword and laws are to be rigorously employed "to punish the wicked and protect the just."[8] The law also helps us recognize our sin. Without our subjection to the secular sword, the world would become a "desert." But because God has ordained government, enough peace exists to allow men to support their families and serve God.[9]

So, we have two governments: a spiritual one to fashion "true Christians and just persons through the Holy Spirit under Christ" and a secular one to maintain outward peace. No land will tolerate a truly Christian government without disaster. The wicked are too numerous.[10]

Bear in mind that Luther's tough-minded view of the need for a secular sword does not devalue the necessity of the spiritual government. The secular arm alone will be marked by hypocrisy and a lack of justice. It needs the spiritual government as much or more than the spiritual government needs the secular.[11] In fact, the spiritual government plays a key role in making fit citizens and rulers.

Despite their lack of need for the restrictions of secular government, the Christians are not called to separate themselves from the state or object to their participation in it. They should willingly hold themselves in subjection to the state in order to "attend to what others need." Participating in government is no different from any other service rendered unselfishly to another. The Christian visits the sick, though he is well himself; so should he support the work of government, though he does not need its restraining hand. The Christian is helping his weaker brother to "enjoy peace" and have "his enemies kept in check."[12]

> And therefore, if you see that there is a lack of hangmen, court officials,
> judges, lords or princes, and you find that you have the necessary skills,

then you should offer your services and seek office, so that authority, which is so greatly needed, will never come to be held in contempt, be powerless, or perish. The world cannot get by without it.[13]

Far from being a passive spectator or holding himself pure behind the monastery wall, the Christian is to be active in government. Although it is not stated directly here, one might make an inference that the importance of preventing authority from being held in contempt would include keeping the government just.

Because service in the secular government is a service to God's mission of restraining villainy and maintaining order in the world, it would be wholly unchristian to say that there is anything that serves God that a Christian should not do, for there is no one more suited to serving God than a Christian.

In the same way it is right and necessary that all princes should be good Christians. The Sword and power, as a special service rendered to God, are more suited to Christians than to anyone else in the world, and so you should value the Sword and power as much as the married state, or cultivating the soil, or any other trade instituted by God.[14]

Nevertheless, the Christian must bear one thing in mind. His business with the state is always done as a community service. He is never to use the state to vindicate his own claims. On the personal level, the teaching of Christ remains "a strict injunction to every Christian. And rest assured that those who avenge themselves and litigate and quarrel in the courts for their goods and honour are mere pagans bearing the name of Christians, and will never be anything else."[15]

The two kingdoms have their own kind of law. "Where the soul is concerned, God neither can nor will allow anyone but himself to rule." Authorities must "see the folly of trying to compel belief . . . by means of laws and commands." In the area of faith, the church is supreme and should not encourage the state to create Christians by compulsion. Even the church should take care only to command "what is certain in God's Word," particularly with regard to salvation.[16]

Force cannot bring about belief. The individual has a responsibility before God. Each must decide at his own peril what he is to believe, and must see to it that he believes rightly. Other people cannot go to heaven or hell on my behalf, or open or close [the gates to either] for me. And just as little can they believe or not believe on my behalf, or force my faith or unbelief. How he believes is a matter for each individual's conscience, and this does not diminish [the authority of] secular governments. They ought therefore to content themselves with attending to their own business, and allow people to believe what they can, and what they want, and they must use no coercion in this matter against anyone.[17]

At this point, Luther offered a revolutionary idea. By placing the individual's belief or nonbelief in the government of the church (which is controlled by the Sermon on the Mount), he created room for a substantially new liberty and for the flowering of more genuine religious commitments. The church will now be responsible for seeing that no master other than God will be permitted there, and it shall not employ the sword in the process.

Secular rulers should forget trying to rule souls, while bishops should cease ruling towns. Secular rulers and bishops who do not understand this proper relationship are experiencing the punishment of God.

God has made them to be of perverse minds and has deprived them of their senses, so that they want to rule spiritually over souls, just as the spiritual authorities want to rule in a worldly manner. And [God's purpose in all this is] that they should thoughtlessly pile up on themselves the sins of others, earn his hatred and that of mankind, until they are ruined along with bishops, parsons, and monks, all knaves together.[18]

Paul clearly teaches that while we are to be subject to civil authorities, their power has a limit. They have mastery over evil-doing but not faith. Christ distinguished what belongs to Caesar and to God to make exactly that point.[19] A prince is not even empowered to deal with heresy. Bishops must fight false doctrine, because God's Word is needed more than the sword. Heresy is spiritual and cannot be put down with secular power "even if it were to fill the whole world with blood."[20]

But no one does his duty, and we are left with the ridiculous circumstance of souls "ruled by steel" and "bodies by letters." As a result, lawless princes earn the contempt of God and the people. The established order may not be able to hold in the face of such a vast loss of confidence.[21]

It should be clear from the foregoing that Luther was not anxious for the church to abandon the secular kingdom but, rather, that it would stop jealously reaching for the power of the state while neglecting its own duties. At the same time, the state must focus on restraining injustice and chaos instead of attempting to set church doctrine or punish heretics. The bottom line is that Luther called for the church to *be the church* and the state to *be the state*. The point is not that they should ignore each other and exist in isolation, but rather that they should fulfill the purposes God sets before them.

In summary, Luther's state was God-ordained, just as Calvin's was, but its competence was much more limited. Theology was for the church. Law and order were for the state. Lest we go too far and consider Luther's state completely secular in the modern sense, we should recognize that Luther thought blasphemy was a punishable offense and assumed a Christian moral context within which the state would operate.

The entire reason for the existence of the state in Luther's mind was that God cared for people living in a fallen world and wanted to give them protection. In addition, despite Luther's clear views on the proper distinction between the church and the state, he, like most, saw the church as an official entity established by law and accepted the notion of the nobility as emergency bishops during the tumultuous times of the early Lutheran church's emergence. Wolfhart Pannenberg described well this idea of the secular when he wrote, "The disassociation of the secular state power and its laws from the context of the dual power within Christendom led to the modern secular state, which is a completely different matter than the secular power of kings and emperors where the social order is based on Christianity."[22] Luther's groundbreaking work was rooted firmly in the latter historical context.

Machiavelli

Machiavelli was roughly contemporaneous with Luther and Calvin, but the Florentine political philosopher was not concerned with the correct theology of church and state. Nevertheless, his work made it very clear that neither love of the church nor some natural law of right should determine the way of the prince. In his thin classic *The Prince*, Machiavelli spoke to the matter of how a noble should rule. His prescriptions were not particularly concerned with pleasing God or honoring man. Instead, he focused on effectiveness. Perhaps a better word is *winning*.

In the Christian view of the world, defeat is no shame. After all, Jesus experienced a massive worldly defeat when he suffered crucifixion. What is right in the Christian sense is to succeed by God's standard rather than by the world's measure and to bear persecution rather than to do wrong. Even a king should wield the sword only in the cause of justice. Machiavelli's advice to the prince was based on a decidedly different scale of values. For example, he advised the prince to make certain any harm done to an opponent is severe enough to forestall any possible future revenge.[23] He also insisted that the entire line of a displaced ruler must be extinguished so as to remove all hope of its return.[24]

Machiavelli even undercut the noble concept of honor. He was unambiguous in advising the prince to break a promise whenever it was advantageous. He need not worry about ruining his reputation or the value of his word because there would always be others willing to be deceived. Appearances remained important, though. The prince should strive to be seen as faithful, religious, humane, merciful, and trustworthy. At the same time, he should be ready at any moment to break free from any of the above.[25]

Machiavelli treated the church and the pope as nothing more than additional players on the geopolitical scene, which was understandable given some of the church's activity in his day.[26] The strategist came closer in tone and content than any of his contemporaries to the secularism of the modern world in dealing with how a prince should conduct himself to achieve his goals. The prince was not to worry about higher concerns such as justice, holiness, and virtue. Weberian social science is largely predicated on this same basis. Effectiveness rather than what is right should govern. With *The Prince*, Machiavelli may have created political science as we came to know it in the twentieth century. He may also have created modern secularism.

None of these estimates mean to suggest that no one before

Machiavelli acted on the basis of raw interest rather than on a higher sense of the good, but he was certainly one of the first to say so with candor and to be widely noticed. In truth, much of Martin Luther's critique of the Catholic Church had to do with his perception that the church was conducting itself as though guided by Machiavelli's counsel of interest rather than by the Scriptures. He wanted the church to stop acting in a Machiavellian manner and to concern itself more with holiness.

4

Reformation's Wake: Uneasy Pluralism and Social Contracts

What may ultimately have been of more importance than the influential writings of figures like Calvin, Luther, and Machiavelli was the brute fact of plurality created by the upheaval of the Reformation. Although disputes predating the Reformation resulted in compromise and reunification or in dissenters being put to death, the popular movement behind the Reformers and the cast of nobility who supported them presented too large an obstacle for the Catholic Church to overcome. The result was that Christendom split and Europe developed an uneasy coexistence between Catholics, Lutherans, Calvinists, Anglicans, and others. The solution that emerged at Augsburg in 1558 after much loss of blood and treasure was to have each country follow the religion of its ruler, while providing for some degree of toleration.

We may not yet know the long-term consequences of the Reformation, but the aftermath brought the wars of religion and great suffering to Europe. Many were disappointed with the legacy of reform and wanted to get away from the divisiveness of religion and focus more productively on problems that might be more agreeably solved. This is the point in the story where we reach the nugget of most modern political thought regarding religion. It is a short step from disgust with the wars of religion to secularism in which religious concerns are carefully segregated from public discourse.

Besides war and a disdain among intellectuals for religious controversy, another key consequence of the Reformation was that kings grasped the opportunity created by the Catholic Church's new vulnerability to seize resources for their project of centralizing governmental control over their nations. The process of converting church resources to public use was referred to as secularization of church holdings, and it was widely supported by Protestant church leaders who felt the Catholic Church had enriched itself at the expense of local communities.

The Social Contract

Following the time period in which religious conflicts raged, Thomas Hobbes, John Locke, and Jean-Jacques Rousseau offered solutions to the problem of pluralism based on the concept of the social contract. These writers lived in a time of proximity to serious theo-political strife and persecution. Inspired to some degree by the example of wild America, looking like a new Eden for a world-weary mankind trapped in religious struggle in post-Reformation Europe, these three imagined how society would form itself if starting over from a state of nature. What bargain would men strike if the world were young again?

Hobbes

Hobbes's response was elegantly simple and presaged some of the totalitarian experiments of the twentieth century. He viewed men in a state of nature as being engaged in a war of all against all. Unregulated life would be "nasty, brutish, and short." Without government to manage the situation, all would be in nearly constant fear of violent death. In order to escape this fear, men would trade their shabby freedom to the immense governmental authority of Leviathan in exchange for safety from violent death. They would render their obedience. Rather than accommodate pluralism, Leviathan would simply take complete responsibility for social cohesiveness and would maintain total control over faith and doctrine.[1] There are echoes of Augustine and Martin Luther in Hobbes's estimation of the plight of natural man. At the same time, one cannot help but think also of ideologies employed by Hitler, Stalin, and Mao in this account of freedom and government.

Locke

John Locke had a different view of human nature. Even without government, people might be reasonable and tolerant, but they might also realize that their core freedoms, such as the right to enjoy private property, would be relatively more secure with a government formed by social contract. He dealt with the notion of religious pluralism in his *Letter Concerning Toleration* and recommended strongly against coercion and persecution. As a Christian writer living in a divided Christendom, Locke addressed his coreligionists theologically. In Locke's view, the New Testament presented a God who has no interest in being worshiped by people with swords at their backs and hands pressing down on their shoulders forcing them to kneel. If God wanted something like that, he would never have endowed human beings with free will. He would have simply created believers with correct doctrine.[2]

Locke also invoked his conception of the social contract in making the case for toleration. His people living in the state of nature were not desperate Hobbesian folk constantly in fear for their lives. Rather, they perceived a relative benefit in ceding some of their freedom in order to gain greater security of their temporal goods and their person. Thus, upon entering the social contract they did not give up their right to freedom of religious belief and confession. The social contract does not deal with religion, because it offers no benefit to the contracting person with regard to that part of his life. Toleration is part of the deal because the only part of religious belief that is relevant is that which enables a person to fulfill his or her part of the deal by not stealing, murdering, breaking promises, etc.

This last part is why Locke denied toleration to atheists. They had no religious foundation upon which to build and thus nothing to back up their commitment. They could promise, but why would they not break their promise without any concern for justice that one can never truly escape? The suspicion toward atheists serves to emphasize a discontinuity between Locke and modern secularists.[3]

Locke also argued for toleration against the overwhelming historical preference for one king, one religion, and one law because he thought there were concrete benefits to its practice. He argued that toleration of other religious opinions was not a costly activity. Rather, it actually could make the government more secure. People who are oppressed plot against the existing order. Those who enjoy their freedom support the regimes under which they live.[4]

Locke's vision of the church as a persuasive entity rather than as a partner in coercion and of the state as an instrumental entity focused carefully on its core competencies of the public good and safety carried echoes (so often uncredited and unnoticed) of Luther's view. His ideas about toleration came to dominate the Western liberal democracies of the future, particularly the United States.

Rousseau

Rousseau, who became one of the key inspirations for the French Revolution, did not buy into Locke's notion of the state focused on temporal goods. He saw the state as dealing with a larger part of the person than merely the protection of property and personal safety. Rousseau's state addressed hearts and minds as well as bodies and wallets.[5]

Rousseau knew that prior to the coming of Christ, political and religious authority had been united, and that while Jesus spoke of a kingdom of another world, the reality was that Christians tended to seek to unify political and religious authority just as others had before them. Rousseau identified the Christian states that overtook the pagan ones as "the most violent of earthly despotisms," but he might have changed his mind had he seen the French Revolution in action a few decades later.

On the one hand, Rousseau complained about the Christian states in which a kingdom of this world undercut the promise of a kingdom of another world; on the other, he complained that in Christian states one could never know which master to support—the king or the priest. He did not appear to consider the possibility that a degree of tension between the two authorities might be healthy.[6]

He thought Hobbes was correct in recommending a forcible reunion of political and religious authority under the Leviathan but wrong to suppose that Christianity could be part of a successful system. To explain his antipathy to Christianity as part of the public order, he divided religion into three types: the religion of man, the religion of the citizen, and the Roman Catholic type, which resulted (per Rousseau) in two systems of governance always in conflict. This third type he immediately discarded as unworkable. The second type, the religion of the citizen, is the old divine cult united with civil laws. Dying for country was martyrdom. Disobedience of the law was impiety. This civil faith was problematic because it was false and credulous. It also left the rest of the world outside of its relationship with God, thus creating "a natural state of war with all others." The first type, the religion of man, was a purified gospel Christianity. Rousseau saw Christianity as essentially antisocial because all true Christians would be otherworldly directed, and any tyrant could seize rule of the nation while Christians counted it nothing relative to the promise of heaven. He also thought a nation of such people would have the opposite problem of the civil cult group. While the civil cultists would be too aggressive with their tribal god behind them, the Christians would be too passive both domestically and with regard to invaders.[7]

Something new was needed, a system of belief that would unify leadership and the people under one simple rule that was neither superstitious nor antisocial, so Rousseau proposed a civil religion. Each citizen must have one so that he will love the duties that he owes to his fellows as part of community life. The apparent meaning was that civil religion should keep a merchant from lying but not instruct him on something like the nature of prayer. Existing above a civil religion that made a man love his country and deal honestly with fellow citizens, there was a theoretically acceptable cloud of opinions about the other world where the sovereign has no authority. Individuals could think what they liked about the "life to come" as long as they were "good citizens in this life."[8]

This religion of the state was to be direct and simple. It featured the god of the deists who rewarded the good and punished the evil in the next life. The social contract and the laws that resulted from it would be viewed as holy. The only "negative dogma" as Rousseau put it, was intolerance writ broadly. Rousseau refused to distinguish between civil and theological intolerance because he thought one could not "live at peace with those we regard as damned." To admit theological intolerance would have meant the sovereign was not truly sovereign and that some higher authority had other requirements. Anyone who dared to say there was no salvation outside the church would be driven from the state.[9]

Rousseau's argument is susceptible to significant criticism. For example, his portrait of true Christianity was clearly a caricature. He need have looked no further than Luther and Calvin (major intellectual presences by then) to see both arguing persuasively for the Christian soul to be completely engaged in society as a service to his or her brothers and sisters. His immediate dismissal of the two-authorities system of kings and popes embodied by Catholicism was also too quick. He was right about the potential ills of double authority, but he failed to consider the potential benefits. For example, a person with no remedy at law (even in a case of gross unfairness) could go to the ecclesiastical courts to seek justice via equity. It is also possible that having multiple authorities could be freedom-enhancing, as they have the potential to check the ambitions of the other.

In addition, Rousseau manipulated history for his own purposes. According to his version of events, when Rome fell to barbarians it was the fault of Christianity for having sapped the old pagan valor. But when Arabs were conquered by barbarians, Rousseau found causation in the Arabs' having become "prosperous, lettered, civilized, slack, and cowardly."[10] The bias against Christianity was evident in the comparison. Surely one could argue that the Romans, too, were civilized into vulnerability well before the Christian faith became powerful in the empire.

5

American Story:
Religious Expatriates, a New World,
and Awakening

The Puritans struggled first for simple survival as a covenant community of American émigrés. Having gained some measure of safety and security, they later battled to retain the spiritual nature of their union as subsequent generations eased away from the covenant existence they had valued so highly in the seventeenth century. The Puritan culture was based on Calvinistic theology, particularly that of calling and the close relation of church and state. Calling meant each person inhabited his or her particular place in society by the sovereign hand of God. The baker was called to be a baker, the farmer a farmer, the preacher a preacher, the governor a governor. Each station had clear duties and one should perform them rather than agitate for a different station. To do other than to perform one's duty would be a kind of rebellion against God. The result was a sort of frozen hierarchy in which deference was expected. To present the matter so starkly, however, is not completely fair because there was an underlying tenderness toward family and brotherhood toward the community that coexisted with the rigidity of calling.[1]

The Puritans saw the state as a covenant entity with a sacred relationship to God. Unlike Luther or Locke, who saw the state as mostly instrumental, Calvin viewed the state as a matter of priority to God. Because God invested rulers with authority over other men, Calvin concluded that God would be concerned that rulers acknowledge that their authority proceeds only from him and that ensuring correct doctrine and worship were primary duties of the governing authority.[2] To some extent, this arrangement is similar to that sometimes endorsed by the Catholic Church in the past. The key difference, however, was that Calvin's state did not answer to the church at all. It had its own direct calling from God and made decisions independent from the church. One sees this understanding played out in the events of John Winthrop's life, in which he as the governor had to deal with the religious variances of Roger Williams and Anne Hutchinson. He encouraged Williams to leave[3] and excommunicated Hutchinson outright for her refusal to be corrected in matters of the faith.[4]

Roger Williams

Roger Williams matched his Puritan forebears in religious zeal and perhaps exceeded them in his desire for a pure and righteous church. Where he differed so greatly as to require that he take his leave from the community (despite an apparent affection for him on the part of Winthrop) was on the matter of the connection between the church and community governance. Unlike the Calvinist Puritans, Williams thought the government should not be at all involved in ensuring proper religious doctrine. He did not think God cared much for the holiness government could bring about.[5]

Although Williams was full of concern for religious purity, he also reasoned like Locke about the nature of human society. He saw government as something inherent in human society that seemed to work reasonably well, whether run on the principles of Christians, Indians, or Turks. In fact, it sometimes worked better with those who were not Christians. He had his experience living with Indians from which to compare and draw conclusions. This phenomenon suggested to him that governing was a practice with something like an independent excellence. Either one knew how to do it well, like captaining a ship, commanding an army, or doing the work of a doctor, or one did not. The competence to govern did not depend on one's opinions about God. This competence focused itself on bodies and property, but not on beliefs, at least not on beliefs about religious particularities.[6]

Although he is often embraced by secularists because of his courageous stand against loving constraint of heretics and for religious liberty, it is not clear whether Williams would pass muster with the secularisms of the modern day. Government for everyone (Christian or not) worked in part, Williams was sure, because of the six things written on the heart of every person: "1st. That there is a Deity; 2d. That some actions are nought; 3d. That the Deity will punish; 4th. That there is another life; 5th. That marriage is honorable; 6th. That mankind cannot keep together without some government."[7] These beliefs were the basis of common government. Correct Christian doctrine may not have been needed for earthly community in Williams's view, but God clearly was.

Just as Williams thought the nature of governing precluded making faith the center of it, he believed the nature of faith precluded government working as the guarantor of orthodoxy. An iconoclast like Luther, he knew coercion could not make a man believe something he did not accept in his own mind and heart. Instead of turning him around, religious coercion would only have the negative effects of either turning its object into a hypocrite or tarring its employer with the evil of violence. Williams was ahead of his time but not by too much. He eventually set up his own successful colony in Rhode Island on the principles he espoused.

Jonathan Edwards, New Lights, Old Lights

The descendants of Puritans in the era of Jonathan Edwards were noticeably different from their forebears in Winthrop's (and Williams's) time. One key difference was the presence of the Awakening. Individuals had direct experiences of God that threatened to upset allegiance to a standing order of spiritual supervision. Distinctions developed between the Old Lights and the New Lights. The New Lights wondered whether the Old could even understand them or have the same kind of relationship to God they did.[8] Should one who had been so close to God give deference to one who had obviously not been awakened or was even actively opposing the Awakening as some kind of dangerous spiritual fraud?

Edwards was a partisan of the Awakening. His community was significantly less settled than Winthrop's as they dealt with the problem of finding the right answer to the question of a voluntary, regenerate church versus a comprehensive Christendom model, which attempts to bring everyone into some relationship (even if only formalistic) with the church. Edwards encountered a Christendom model and tried to move it in the direction of a regenerate church membership. In consequence, he lost his pastorate.[9] Edwards's course had implications for secularism in both directions. A move toward a regenerate church was inherently secularizing because large portions of the community would have little to do with the church and would surely become less and less attuned to Christian expectations about society. On the other hand, continuing the comprehensive Christendom model kept lots of lukewarm individuals in the church and led, historically speaking, to stagnant churches that declined through the centuries. The strong covenant model of the Puritan community did not ultimately survive the tensions it created. Although the first generation was composed of those who desperately wanted to worship according to their beliefs and wanted to maintain those beliefs, they ultimately could not maintain their cohesion with a model of church intended to be synonymous with geographic communities.

American Awakening

The Great Awakening revivals had a powerful impact on colonial America. They were the most significant public events of any kind during the period from about 1740 to 1840.[10] As was mentioned earlier, the Awakening divided Christians into groups such as New Lights, which saw authenticity in spontaneous religious experience, and Old Lights, which was skeptical of experience and preferred to see established clergy lead parishioners along. The division reinforced the sense already kindled by the openness and freedom of the New World that the individual was more important than anyone previously believed. The absolute individual was replacing the absolute ruler and the absolute church.[11]

The great historian of American Christianity Mark Noll notes that what began happening in the Awakening was greatly facilitated by the conditions of frontier existence. The established churches could not compete with those who adapted to the situation at hand and who preached from commitment rather than from credentials and training.[12] Patricia Bonomi saw the Great Awakening as having been critical to the development of the urge to stage a revolution against the mother country. For the first time, many Americans developed the willingness to challenge settled authority, particularly if it failed to comprehend the awakened self.[13]

How the new willingness to challenge authority if one felt he had God on his side played into the Revolution is not the business of this book, but the impact of the Awakening on the divide between church and state is. By giving rise to a group of persons who were more intensely seeking God and had had an experience they felt was authentic and needed to be explored, the Awakening gave force to the notion of the regenerate church fellowship independent of ties to the state. Awakened Christians did not want to continue to support the old order. They wanted to voluntarily support their new one.[14]

The colonial United States leaned toward established churches, but the reality of increasing pluralism, a lack of clergy, and the simple fact of tremendous availability of land and freedom eventually overcame the logic of establishment completely. More because of social realities than by design, the United States became a nation of disestablished churches, which also happened to become some of the most vigorous churches in the world, particularly in comparison to their European counterparts. Thus, although the new nation's Constitution explicitly ruled out the idea of a nationally established church, the U.S. was a nation in which the churches were increasingly influential rather than less so.

The United States is a particular focus of this book and will thus be revisited in detail in subsequent chapters. For the purpose of this survey, however, it is sufficient to say that the American Revolution differed from European counterparts in that it took on the throne of England without need of an anticlerical campaign designed to cripple a centrally established altar operating as a buttress for the state.[15] The result is that the American approach to politics, law, and religion has been marvelously productive of freedom but has also been a frequent source of controversy.

6

France:
A Different Kind of Revolution

In America a new thing was happening both for the church and for the state. Though it was not planned, the combination of vast spaces and lack of church enforcement mechanisms scattered the carefully ordered pieces of church-state union and eventually resulted in a free-wheeling pluralism that energized churches for the challenge rather than enervate them, which conventional wisdom expected. The Catholic Church was a player looking for toleration rather than to be a dominant force, and Protestants vied with one another for the hearts of the people. Although there were state establishments, they were far from secure in the dynamic religious environment of the new lands.

To Topple Throne and Altar

Europe, on the other hand, was still Europe. Throne and altar were still intertwined and royalty occupied the top ranks of the church just as it did the state. To want to change society meant to reform both the state and the church together. France became host to the Revolution that upended the old arrangements entirely, at least for a time. Although the Revolution failed and ended with Napoleon and a new concordat with the Roman Catholic Church, the intellectual influence of those few years has been felt through the last two centuries. It was, as Alec Vidler memorably wrote, "a sort of atomic bomb of which the fallout is still at work" that initiated the fall of the *ancien regime*.[1]

The Revolution occurred at a time when the Catholic Church still possessed a great deal of political power. It was said of the bishops that "they administered more provinces than sacraments!"[2] Although it was incongruous with Christian theology, most of them were nobles of some sort.[3] The lower clergy were more humble men who often knew more about farming than theology. The difference in station between the two groups led to different attitudes toward radical reform. Unsurprisingly, the lower group favored change.[4]

Although Voltaire may have been careful to keep his servants from hearing his ridicule of the church for fear they would steal the silver in a fit of liberation, he was not shy about spreading his views to the literate class. Skepticism and unorthodox views were in fashion in Paris, where men like Voltaire and Rousseau were celebrities.[5] Between the growth of skepticism, the failure of the church to act with spiritual vigor equal to its political zeal, and a humble lower clergy looking up at bishops living in opulence, the church was not well situated to handle a revolution. Its vulnerability rapidly became evident when the pace of events accelerated to the point of radical change that would be deemed so even to this day.

Dividing Loyalties

The Revolution began in 1789 when Louis XVI convened the States-General to help deal with a financial crisis. The solution grew much larger than the problem to which the assembly had been directed when it developed into a full-fledged transferal of political power controlled by members of the bourgeoisie. The part of the Revolution that interests us in our current investigation is the shape of church-state relations that resulted. In the swirl of early revolutionary activity, it came to pass that the national church was completely remade. Unlike radicals of the later Russian Revolution which would aim at destroying the church and putting no new one in its place, the French revolutionaries, influenced by their hero Rousseau, thought a religion of the state indispensable. Thus, the new government constructed the Civil Constitution of the Clergy in 1790, which equated dioceses with civil department boundaries without the pope's permission, left the pope without authority (maintaining primacy of honor) over the national church, and made appointment of bishops a matter of civil election.

This first move already represented a potent intrusion on the church's usual prerogatives despite the fact that the French had typically enjoyed a fair amount of independence from Rome. The Civil Constitution of the Clergy also made clergy employees of the secular government, which paid them a salary. The encroachment upon the church brought about heavy opposition from within the church and has been blamed for making the Catholic Church a long-term enemy of political liberalism. Battling against the opposition, the government required an oath of clergy to support the new measures. About half refused and were forced out of their clerical functions. The refusers attempted to continue their work. The pope condemned the new governing documents, and the French people suffered divided loyalties.[6]

Goddess Reason and the Supreme Being

Later came the Reign of Terror, when the revolutionary government embarked upon a course of dechristianization. In 1793 the Republic unveiled a new calendar starting with the opening of the Revolution. Each tenth day rather than the seventh was a day off. Shortly thereafter the government declared the Cathedral of Notre Dame as the Temple of Reason. Members of the legislature traveled to local communities and enforced the new policy by closing churches, forcing priests to marry, and generally engaging in persecution of the faithful. Interestingly enough, the most infamous of the revolutionaries, Robespierre, opposed the dechristianization for its likely negative political consequences.[7]

Robespierre became dissatisfied with the abstract worship of reason and initiated a new civil cult more in line with Rousseau's earlier proposal. The Republic established the worship of the Supreme Being, which declared in part:

1) The French people recognize the existence of the Supreme Being and the immortality of the soul.
2) They recognize that the worship worthy of the Supreme Being is the observance of the duties of man.
3) They place in the forefront of such duties detestations of bad faith and tyranny, punishment of tyrants and traitors, succoring of unfortunates, respect of weak persons, defence of the oppressed, doing to others all the good that one can, and being just towards everyone.[8]

The legislation went on to institute festivals reminding man of the divinity of God and of human dignity and with names based on revolutionary events, benefits of nature, and human virtues. All who had talents sufficient to contribute to the greater beauty of the festivals received a general call to embellish the events.[9]

Reconciliation and Surging Nationalism

Robespierre did not last and neither did the Cult for the Worship of the Supreme Being. The Thermidorian reaction that ended the Reign of Terror saw the practice of Catholicism once again permitted, and a revival of genuine Catholic piety followed. Napoleon took advantage of the instability that followed the Revolution and came to power as a military ruler. He reestablished relations with the Roman Catholic Church whereby the two parties negotiated a concordat declaring Catholicism the religion of a great majority of the French people. The state paid salaries for bishops and parish priests in exchange for the church's relinquishment of claims for the return of its confiscated property. The Organic Articles of 1802 established the supremacy of the state over the church. Bishops gave oaths of loyalty to the nation.[10]

Although the French Revolution featured powerful fireworks between church and state, the most impressive religious consequences of the Revolution and of Napoleon's leadership may have been indirect. One of the primary reasons Napoleon had so much military success was that the Revolution had given common men and women a much greater sense of participation in the nation. Thus, when Napoleon went to war, he could put massive numbers of fighters in the field and could conscript more from the populace as needed thanks to their loyalty to the nation and their charismatic leader. Modern nationalism was becoming a great force in the world and was beginning to show that it (often paired with ideology) could provide a potent substitute for religion in the hearts of men and women.[11]

7

Analyzing the Evolution of Church, State, and Secularism

The foregoing survey and comment on church and state in the West covers about eighteen centuries. It is impressive to note the incredible importance Western culture has placed on working through the question of church and state in terms of both concrete events and answers proposed and considered. Rome solved the problem by permitting pluralism under a sacred canopy of common emperor worship. Constantine led as a Christian and supported the church with public funds, but willingly tolerated members of pagan faiths as full citizens or something close to it. In very short order the pattern for government in the West became enforced religious conformity. Given the patterns of history, it is not surprising that the newly Christian empire so quickly succumbed to the logic of one king, one law, and one faith. On the other hand, given the radical nature of the Christian faith and its emphasis on mercy, weakness, and values distinct from those of the world, perhaps disappointment is warranted.

In working through the history of church and state in the West, we discover a set of questions that guide the course of development. At the risk of oversimplification those questions are: (1) What is the state? (2) What is the church? (3) What is the proper relationship of the two?

What Is the State?

What is the state? The question is susceptible to many answers. In our experience and in that of our forebears, the state is and has been the institution responsible for the leadership of the community. It makes and enforces laws to regulate our interactions. It levies taxes to fund its activities. It protects the community from other states. In the course of doing these things, the state has a tendency to generate a moral identity. Just as a person can be judged by his or her attitude toward certain things and by actions, so too can a collective institution. It can be compassionate or harsh, generous or tightfisted, wise or foolish, democratic or totalitarian.

Through most of the course of Western history, it is fair to say that the state has been Aristotelian and/or Christian in the sense that it has striven toward some kind of community excellence.[1] The state (and the church with it) has been seen as something to guide persons toward a good life (and sometimes the afterlife). The obvious drawback to that view of the community is that it requires a pretty high degree of conformity from citizens whether they agree with the program or not. Thus, those who were not true believers or were true believers in something else, ended up as either hypocrites or martyrs. The result was a loss of human life and the sapping of the vitality of institutions such as churches, which ended up watered down with everyone (the comprehension model) instead of thriving independently with those who participated voluntarily (the regeneracy model).[2]

The idea of the state as a collective venture into the good life fits the thinking of Augustine's Christian republic exercising loving constraint, as well as the thinking of Aquinas, Marsilius, Calvin, Rousseau, the Puritans, and the French Revolution. Although all of these are placed together here, they are quite far apart in many respects, yet they are the same in the sense that each endorsed a state leading its citizens toward some ideal that includes religion as part of the required program with at least partial control of religious affairs by the state. The diversity of the group underscores how strongly people have historically believed that religion and state must travel together under unified control.

Over against that group we might collect another gathering of persons with a much more limited idea of the state. This second set sees the state as a much more focused venture with a role that is primarily negative, in the sense that it prevents things from happening rather than positively leading people toward a good life. To be more specific, one might characterize this group as seeing religion as very important to a community but on a voluntary basis and thus not subject to regulation by an earthly sovereign. Such a state is instrumental rather than ideal or ultimate. It is a state designed to restrain evil and to exercise tolerance about the things that are not primary in its competence. In this stream, one might place Constantine, Augustine's non-Christian state, Luther, John Locke, Roger Williams, and probably the American founding generation.

For this second group, however, religion remains critical to making citizens and is the glue of society in the sense that it underscores commitments and makes everyone accountable to a heavenly judge who witnesses all things. Some might question the inclusion of Williams in this list, but his belief that religion was unnecessary for a properly functioning society was undercut by his certainty that everyone believed in a deity who would punish in the next life.

What Is the Church?

The other major question is that of the church. What is the church? Is it a mass movement destined to cast a perpetually challenging vision toward the prevailing social ethos? Is it a retreat from the world where saints gather to live the Christian life away from the irredeemable rest of the world, which has no eternity in its future? Is it the basis of Christ's kingdom with a charge to grow and eventually bring all of life into harmony with God? Is it a partner to the state in building the kingdom of Christ, or shall it overwhelm the state's worldliness? We can find in our survey Christians who thought very differently about the role of the church. Their views were surely influenced somewhat by the position in which they and other believers found themselves relative to history. For example, the early church was essentially born as an embattled minority. When an emperor became a Christian, surely it seemed like a long-awaited deliverance from persecution and a potential boon to the world, because the message could spread unhindered.

Imagine the situation of the medieval church. For centuries after the fall of the empire, the church had been the center of civilization every bit as much as or more than various kingdoms. Its claims were universal rather than centered on the territorial rights of a bloodline or conquest. The cultural situation helped the church to see itself as the true source of government over all peoples. It is not surprising that in the age of Gutenberg the Reformation occurred and that pluralism took hold as the interpretation of the Bible became the activity of many rather than few. Pluralism eventually overwhelmed the Reformation's confessional states just as surely as it had overcome the Catholic Church's leadership of Christendom.

Even today the many different models of the church exist simultaneously. The one difference is the loss of adherents to the view that the church should hold a position of primacy over the state and that the state actually derives its power from the church. The advocates of real theocracy among Christians are very few. The live debate between Christians in the present has more to do with the degree to which the Christian faith should inform politics and how explicitly Christians should appeal to their faith in political debate and policy formation. It seems to be the consensus of Christians in this millennium that the church is a voice calling the state to righteousness and justice rather than a state or a supervisor of the state itself.

Whence Comes the Power?

The question of where the state gets its power has also been contentious. Certainly, kings and popes sparred over whether the state had an independent authorization from God and whether the church somehow conferred legitimacy upon the state. The Reformation effectively settled that controversy in favor of the state's having an independent license from God to do its work. Exactly what that work entailed was not agreed upon, but that the state's legitimacy came from God rather than from the church was the consensus of the Protestants and eventually became the position of the Catholic Church as well. Deciding that the state was authorized to do its work by God did not end the matter though. There was still the question of how God empowered a state. Was it simply that whoever managed to mount a throne had God's blessing or that power somehow flowed from the people and that they, as the purported beneficiaries and servants of government, were also its earthly source rather than mere succession of blood?

Western liberalism eventually triumphed, bringing democracy and the will of the people as the determiners of who would wield power and how. Some parts of the church agreed with that course and others did not. In Europe, the established churches mostly sided with the crown and with the traditional structure of society. America was a different story. The American churches, particularly those that were growing and vital, were a key part of the movement toward democratization. The American story is the subject of the next chapters. The Christian faith could be seen as giving support to either the European or the American proposition.[3] The New Testament is clear in its claims that God places rulers on the throne for our good and at his pleasure. When bad rulers come, their power may be interpreted as a judgment on a given community. At the same time, the growing emphasis on the Bible text, increasing access to it, and the Protestant project of inculcating literacy in order to make Bible reading possible led very logically to democracy. A person standing on Scripture could very effectively oppose a public leader who was, in the Christian point of view, simply another fallen human being in need of a savior.

Secularism Emerging through Deism

The brief review and analysis of the history of church and state in the West prior to the modern period demonstrates a recurring intellectual, emotional, and spiritual need to reconcile the claims of faith, government, and pluralistic communities. That ongoing process of reconciliation has always been difficult and has at times been productive of extraordinary conflict.

Politically speaking, the spring of secularism was the wars of religion. As was mentioned earlier, the aftermath of the Reformation was disappointment, at least among certain classes. Instead of a newer, better church, there emerged several churches, different brands of confessional states, and decades of wars both internal and external. The crisis of religious war sparked a search for solutions. Hobbes advocated dictatorial control by a sovereign to whom the people would willingly submit for safety. Locke proposed toleration based on government sticking to its more pragmatic functions. Rousseau pushed for a new deistic civil religion that would act as a kind of common denominator for citizens. Hugo Grotius sought a basis for law outside of confessional religion, in natural law that all men could observe, laws that would exist even if God did not! All these efforts centered on finding a new common ground for people that extended more broadly than confessional religious bases for society.

In this vein of common ground the deism of the eighteenth century became popular as the "rational" alternative to Christian "superstition." Deists held to the traditional idea that a society had to have a religion as the foundation of good citizenship and moral accountability. Although there were varieties of deism, the typical beliefs encompassed a God who guarantees justice via the application of punishments and rewards in the afterlife. It is a distilled version of the Christian faith that avoids questions of miracles, complicated doctrines such as the Trinity, and ritual disputes such as whether a person should be baptized via immersion or sprinkling and at what age. Although we do not discuss deism very often outside of historical surveys, the propositions are highly recognizable as representing the worldview of a great many people today.

Proponents of deism such as Tom Paine, Thomas Jefferson, Benjamin Franklin, and Voltaire viewed the philosophy as a more scientific outlook on religion and as a more peaceful one. It was deemed more rational because it opted to accept the witness of "nature" over that of Scripture. Instead of embracing the revelation of the Bible, deists looked at the creation and deduced there must be a creator. They studied their hearts and found a desire for justice and reasoned the creator must be more scrupulously just than they were. Deists imagined their creed more peaceful because of its avoidance of disputes over Christian doctrines that caused potent divisions within the church. Of course, polemical deists such as Tom Paine attacked Christian revelation and/or the churches directly in order to make their case for natural religion and thus engendered hostility and tumult in religious affairs in the same manner that the deism of the French Revolution did.[4]

Deism represents a very important step in the process toward divorcing public affairs from any consideration of God for three reasons. First, the deistic God is more removed from human affairs. He has created the world and expects us to make our way in it. This is a significant difference from the God of the Bible, who dramatically enters history as with the Incarnation. Second, deism was at its height during the period surrounding the founding of the American republic, which was the first to be conceived in the Western world without a nationally established church. Third, deism depended heavily upon the design argument for God's existence. It is no mere coincidence that the enthusiasm for deism as rational religion virtually disappeared in the post-Darwin nineteenth century when the design argument was reeling. The death of deism corresponded with the rise of true secularism, which is its heir. The movement toward deism in the United States was parallel to secularism in its aims. It proposed to be a more peaceful approach to the theo-political problem endemic to the Western world and a more rational one.

Just as deism sought to drop specificity of religious beliefs in favor of a simpler and purportedly more natural conception of God and his interaction with the world, true secularism sought and seeks to drop God, in theory making the public order accessible to all persons, believer and unbeliever. Everything else, including general morality, yields to something better founded upon scientific understandings or our progressive enlightenment. The success, or lack thereof, of that project is the subject of the rest of this book. But first, we need to sharpen our focus on the United States of America. Because the United States formed its new republic during the period of deism's ascendancy and at the height of the Enlightenment, the claim is often made that the United States is founded upon a legal secularism and that public secularism is, in essence, America being true to its own best nature.

8

The American Model,
the American Controversy

Because the United States Constitution is a document
written mostly in broad generalities rather than in the specificity of an
annotated code, the original intent of the founders is a frequent focus
of argument. In the period since the United States Supreme Court
incorporated the religion clauses of the First Amendment against the
states and subsequently began making significant changes to earlier
practice, there has been constant battle over the question of what
state of affairs the founders were attempting to achieve and what they
believed personally about the Christian faith.

The contours of the debate at the popular level are fairly simple.
One group, which tends to favor strict separation of church and
state out of a belief that religion is dangerous, extraordinarily cor-
ruptible, or simply irrelevant, emphasizes the deistic secularism of
the founding: the contemporaneous Enlightenment critique of religion, a Constitution that did not mention God, a Tom Paine who
criticized the God of Israel,[1] a Jefferson who edited the supernatural
out of the Bible, and purportedly ultra-low church membership.[2]
Another group, which seeks to accommodate religion for the purpose of honoring God and/or maintaining the place of Christianity
in American public affairs, emphasizes the primacy of the faith in the
founding: a Declaration of Independence that made much reference
to God, a Washington who encouraged his men to keep up their religious practice, the public prominence of the minister/professor John
Witherspoon, and the Bible everywhere.[3] It was a Christian republic
or a godless one. We are encouraged to choose which.

The battle is so contentious in part because the United States was the first nation in the world to eschew a national religious establishment. Those who champion public secularism note the lack of establishment, First Amendment religious liberty, and the no religious test clause and take them to mean that the nation with the most successful constitutional regime is also the first truly secular nation. Unsurprisingly, those who resist secularization of the public order and who might even want to roll back the dechristianization they perceive as having already occurred argue that the intent of the American founders has been misunderstood. Not only were they not attempting to found a secular nation, but they were actually thoroughgoing Christians who wanted to found a Christian America. The reality is that both sides have overplayed their hand. What is more, the Constitution as originally adopted is far less relevant to the dispute over public secularism than is widely believed.

What Do You Mean by *Enlightenment*?

Henry May's *The Enlightenment in America* is a useful guide for navigating these choppy waters of faith, faithlessness, and ideology. May informs the debate by taking apart the idea of a monolithic Enlightenment and dividing it into different streams:

- *The Revolutionary Enlightenment,* which insisted throne and altar must be overcome to initiate a new golden age for mankind.
- *The Skeptical Enlightenment,* which concluded religion should give way to simple materialism.
- *The Moderate Enlightenment,* which emphasized reasonable compromise between Christian confessions.
- *The Scottish Enlightenment,* which viewed faith and reason as completely compatible and depended on a universe which is moral and intelligible.[4]

Considering the various streams of Enlightenment (May invokes others at different points in the book, but they roughly correspond with the four above), May examines the relevant American history and concludes that neither the Revolutionary Enlightenment nor the Skeptical Enlightenment ever exhibited a very great influence in the young country. Around 1800 the conflict between the different strains of Enlightenment began to crystallize, and the majority of Americans chose Protestant Christianity.[5] Surely, it is fair to say the Enlightenment helped America on toward revolution. It is when one asks what brand of Enlightenment that the answer becomes more interesting. The Moderate and Scottish strains have tended to be more consonant with American culture.

May's influential work is damaging to the claim that the America of the founding era tilted in the direction of secularism. Instead of an antireligious Enlightenment contending against a benighted Christianity, we see an alliance between members of both camps with neither as extreme or rigid as we often imagine. In America, Christianity and Enlightenment were wedded.

Mark Noll adds useful insight to the project of understanding the close alliance between Enlightenment and Protestant Christianity by looking to the special politico-religious situation in the United States. Because the English never achieved real Anglican national establishment and the Puritans were never able to control the spread of pluralism in a country with lots of space and not enough clergy to maintain control, America did not really play host to the kind of throne and altar arrangements that forcefully resisted Enlightenment liberalization in Europe.[6] Thus, for practical reasons it was the case that by the time of the Revolution there was only a foreign government that needed to be overthrown, not a church.

In addition, it is not at all clear that American Enlightenment enthusiasts would have been able to mount a frontal attack on religion in the same way the French revolutionaries did, because the Christian faith was so vital in America at the time. In the work of revolution the American *philosophes* wrote books, but the Protestants organized and provided lots of foot soldiers.[7] The American founding was a joint enterprise between Protestants and enthusiasts of a moderate Enlightenment. John Witte has aptly divided the contributors into four camps: Puritan, Evangelical, Enlightenment, and Republican. Two are religious (specifically Christian). Two are secular.[8] All were important. Neither avowed secularist nor Christian America exponent can claim victory.

When It Was Harder to Get on the Church Rolls . . .

Patricia Bonomi's *Under the Cope of Heaven* exhibits essential agreement with virtually everything stated above and makes an interesting additional contribution. Both before and after publication of Bonomi's book, advocates of the secular America thesis have regularly pointed to church membership statistics that seem to indicate only about 10 percent of Americans were involved in their local church. Bonomi thought the numbers seemed questionable when one considered the religiosity of the seventeenth century (high tide for the Puritans) and the potent American Christianity of the nineteenth century.[9] Her work adds confirmation to Gaustad, who said the problem in the eighteenth century was getting on the church membership rolls, not getting off them as is the case today.[10]

Bonomi ferreted out a number of factors that kept membership numbers down. For example, many churches counted only communicant members. On the Congregational side, communicant membership was low because it required a strong, public faith confession and examination by one's peers. It was a step many adults were not prepared to take. Among Anglicans, the lack of an American bishop meant that only members who had been confirmed in England were eligible for Communion. In addition, most Christians took very seriously the Scripture's warning against taking Communion unworthily.[11] Yet another factor was that many Americans lacked official clergy and met with unordained ministers or simply appointed one of their own.[12] All the above kept membership numbers far lower than the actual participation rate. Based on her research, Bonomi estimated that 60 percent of white adults were probably regular attenders of churches.[13]

Awakening to Independence

Bonomi also rejected the idea that the Great Awakening was not really related to the movement toward revolution. H. Richard Niebuhr noted that the Awakening aided the process of absolute kings and absolute churches giving way to absolute individuals.[14] It was a sentiment Bonomi echoed. While the Awakening would not have directly urged revolution against England, Bonomi noted that being "awakened" involved challenging settled religious authority of the clergy and seeing oneself as directly answerable primarily to God. The result of that change of orientation was that liberty seemed to become almost a requirement. Each awakened person was answerable to

God, not to some custom of giving way to old patterns of authority. The implications were democracy and freedom from an old empire and its spiritually dead state religion.[15]

Politics and Religion

Philip Hamburger's treatment of the presidential election of 1800 between Thomas Jefferson and John Adams also offers evidence against the secular founding argument. The election between two of the biggest names of the American founding involved significant religious controversy. Jefferson was widely suspected of being insufficiently Christian and too enthusiastic about the anti-Christian French Revolution. The Federalist Clergy of New England thundered at Jefferson directly from its pulpits. The key point for Hamburger is not just that the election carried such significant religious overtones, but rather that Jefferson's allies felt compelled to answer the attacks with strong denials. Were it the case that the America at the time of the founding had little regard for the Christian faith both culturally and in public affairs, then how to explain the raging controversy and the impassioned defense of Jefferson from the charges that he was an infidel? The answer is obvious. Religion mattered at the time of the founding and mattered greatly.[16]

Another key point Hamburger develops is that while the institutional separation of church and state had many champions, those who proclaimed the separation of religion and politics were deeply in the minority.[17] The contention makes a great deal of sense, particularly given the prominence of Calvinism in colonial America and in the new republic. Calvin offered nothing but fierce reproach for those who suggested religion and politics had nothing to do with each other or, even worse, that politics was an unworthy activity for the Christian. In his mind, paying attention to politics was a major duty. His view of the state as an object of intense interest for both God and the church was surely still prominent in the Congregational and Presbyterian churches of the early American era. For that matter, that view is prominent among Calvinists today.

In addition to the Calvinistic theological roadblock to separating religion and politics, there is the additional problem of the nearly universal agreement among all the founders of whatever spiritual stripe that religion was a necessary foundational element of the good republic. The men involved in setting up a new nation knew that no freedom would last long that was not self-limited by virtue. Religion was the single most likely source of virtue. The enormously influential Locke believed atheists to be beyond the pale of civil society because there was no metaphysical foundation to undergird their oaths.[18] A transcendent point of reference backed both human rights (as one can see in the Declaration) and the discipline of virtue, as was readily admitted by Washington, Jefferson, Adams, etc.[19] Though it was certainly the case that some founders took a more instrumental view of religion as something very useful to regulating the appetites and activities of a free people, the fact remains that tying religion and politics together was considered wise and appropriate.

Against the Christian Nation Hypothesis

While Bonomi and Hamburger seem almost to have been rebuking the champions of a founding secularism in their books, George Marsden, Mark Noll, and Nathan Hatch (all evangelical Christian scholars) turned their critical eye toward the pamphleteers of Christian America.[20] With the resurgence of conservative Christians in politics during the late 1970s and early 1980s came the forceful renewal of the myth of the American founding as a great Christian event performed by heroic Christian people orthodox and true. The implication was that the Christian right simply stood in the shoes of the founders when it called a wayward nation home. Marsden, Noll, and Hatch offered a forceful rebuke to those who held to the idea of a Christian founding myth. While Bonomi and Hamburger spoke to an elite class in academia and public affairs who needed to be corrected into accepting the importance of the Christian contribution to the American cause, the three Christian authors warned their intended audience of the dangers of making modern-day decisions on the basis of bad history.[21]

If one began with the premise that the founders were Christians out to begin a Christian republic and then searched through history looking for bits and pieces of data to confirm the hypothesis, then it would be possible to construct a collage to fulfill the desired purpose. But the result is not history and it is not truth, which is something about which Christians are supposed to be passionate.[22] Though the authors were speaking to Francis Schaeffer, Jerry Falwell, and others similarly situated, they could just as easily be speaking to David Barton's Wallbuilders today, who have turned collage construction of Christian America into high art and take the show on the road.

The balance of the story is that the Christian faith has had a major impact on American history, particularly the founding, and that various misperceptions that exist (due either to an overinflated myth of Christian America or to an equally unpleasant preening secularism, which has become increasingly prominent of late) require correction. When it comes to the story of the American founding as Christian- or Enlightenment-driven, it seems no one will be satisfied but partisans of the truth. Christianity (particularly the Protestant kind) cannot be unraveled from its intertwined position with the American experience. Some of the founders were Christian. Some were not (or at least, not as we typically define Christians). Christianity was not the driving force behind revolution, but neither was it inconsequential. As Gaustad writes, Christianity and Enlightenment were the twin founts of the new republic.[23] An account that suggests otherwise appears to be basically false.

A Better Understanding

Although it is useful to examine the personal beliefs and philosophies of the founding generation, the information gained only edifies the debate over the legal aspect of public secularism in the United States if those beliefs were somehow transmitted to the founding document. During the past sixty years, the Supreme Court has treated the religion clauses of the First Amendment as though they had established a form of church-state separation for the national government that was later extended to the states via the Fourteenth Amendment. The Court's treatment of the clauses has sparked a cottage industry of scholars and interest groups working to interpret the founding generation's intent to their various advantages. All that work (and a sizeable chunk of the Court's current jurisprudence) would go for naught if one were to determine the religion clauses did not stand for what we believe they did, which might be why relatively little attention has been paid to persuasive authors who have presented a compelling alternate view on the purpose of the First Amendment to the United States Constitution.

Robert Palmer's Contribution

American Robert Palmer is one of the best-known English legal historians in the world. From time to time he has torn himself away from that consequential island and its history to focus on the American legal tradition. Perhaps because he does not typically circulate among scholars of American legal history, he has been able to offer a striking and original critique of the mainstream view of the American Constitution as having been a source of positive liberties from the time of its initial promulgation. His critique, plus that of Steven D. Smith, which will be explored later, makes the case that the secular/Christian debate over the founders of the American government and their intent is essentially unhelpful even if the substance of the debate were to be better pinned down than it has been.

Perhaps the best place to begin is with a broad view of the Constitution. We have a tendency to treat the Constitution as though it were a governing treatise on the good, the true, and the beautiful. Some even go so far as to embrace it or portions of it as some kind of secular holy writ. Palmer repudiates that kind of thinking entirely. "Not much concerned with values, principles, and morality, the Constitution sought only to erect a genuinely federal system."[24] Our appreciation for the document can sometimes obscure its real origin and purpose, thus making interpretation more difficult than it need be.

The first thing to remember is that the federal government was different in kind, rather than merely in degree, from the state governments that ratified its existence.[25] State governments were governments of inherent authority whereas the new federal government was one only of delegated authority.[26] It was not intended to deal with the broad sweep of human activity that governments normally had to engage. Rather, it was a cooperative entity carefully limited by states that did not wish to see it grow to usurp their roles.[27] For that reason, the federal government lacked the broad police power usually natural to supervising authorities. It could only exert itself with a mandate from the relatively few words of the document that established its existence.[28] Matters of "safety, health, well-being, and morality" were "part and parcel of a vital policy-making unit of government" and were "too important for the states to surrender."[29]

The notion of reserved powers in the states has a poor pedigree thanks to the Southern use of the concept to resist attacks on slavery and segregation, so one might well expect that only southern states sought to maintain their relative independence during the constitution-making process. Palmer undercut that notion by pointing out that Pennsylvanians (one of the most anti-slavery parties to the process) were also determined to specify that the federal government was not only a government of delegated powers, but also of expressly delegated powers. New York State demonstrated similar concerns in its ratification debates.[30] Southerners were not alone in making the "continued vitality of state governments" a prime goal.[31]

Reasoning from the nature of the government established, one realizes that the liberties set out by the Constitution were not individual guarantees in the same way similar liberties were when announced by state constitutions. Instead, they were exceptions to power. Contrary to popular perception, the U.S. Constitution had "little to do explicitly with the protection of individuals." Rather, the provisions we take as placing a high value on individual rights "were actually federalism provisions." Though it is true that the Constitution was more powerful than many expected and derived power from the people rather than from the states, it is clear "from the structure of the document itself" that federalism concerns were "pervasive" and that the Constitutional Convention had done its work from a federal rather than national orientation.[32] Therefore, it is fundamentally misguided to determine the meaning of the First Amendment religion clauses by looking to Virginia's contemporaneous legislation providing for religious liberty. The character of the federal government was fundamentally different from that of the state governments. The *Everson* Court's failure to acknowledge that crucial difference was a failure to observe what Palmer highlighted as differences in context.[33]

Palmer did not specifically address the religion clauses in his work. Rather, he focused on the freedoms of speech and the press. What he wrote of those provisions remains true for the religion clauses. In short, if one wishes to know the meaning of the First Amendment, then one must make "direct reference to the structure of the document itself and the function of the provision within that document." Doing so can resolve questions of meaning because the approved document must logically be "the primary evidence of the intent behind it."[34]

Religion Clause Deconstruction and Reorientation

What Palmer called for is exactly what Steven D. Smith did. Smith considered the confusing state of affairs evident in religion clause jurisprudence and asked the obvious question: what does the First Amendment really say about the separation of church and state and religious liberty? For the sake of convenience, here is the text of the religion clauses in the First Amendment: "Congress shall make no law respecting an establishment of religion, or prohibiting the free exercise thereof . . . "

The first part of the statement is referred to as the establishment clause. The Supreme Court's prime exposition of the meaning of the clause was offered, presumably as dicta, in the majority opinion of the 1947 *Everson* decision:

> The "establishment of religion" clause of the First Amendment means at least this: Neither a state nor the Federal Government can set up a church. Neither can pass laws which aid one religion, aid all religions, or prefer one religion over another. Neither can force nor influence a person to go to or to remain away from church against his will or force him to profess a belief or disbelief in any religion. No person can be punished for entertaining or professing religious beliefs or disbeliefs, for church attendance or non-attendance. No tax in any amount, large or small, can be levied to support any religious activities or institutions, whatever they may be called, or whatever form they may adopt to teach or practice religion. Neither a state nor the Federal Government can, openly or secretly, participate in the affairs of any religious organizations or groups and vice versa. In the words of Jefferson, the clause against establishment of religion by law was intended to erect "a wall of separation between Church and State."[35]

This is a great deal of meaning to draw from ten words that do not clearly seem to mean what Justice Black indicated they do. An opponent would immediately say, "Well, it meant that for the federal government, and then the Fourteenth Amendment extended that meaning to the states." But is even that construction obvious from the text?

So much is built on a thin and confusing layer of words. A judicially enforced public secularism is the result. Is it correct? Are the contours of the debate over its meaning accurately drawn? Were the American founders attempting to frame a constitution for a secular public order, or were they doing something else entirely? Steven D. Smith's answer is that the framers of the Constitution dealt with the religious question far less profoundly than they are presumed to have done. His case is compelling.

Smith's initial point is that the courts and scholars have approached the religion clauses from the wrong angle. More specifically, they have asked the wrong question, which is something like, "What is the meaning and scope of the principle of religious freedom embodied in the Constitution?"[36] When we ask that question, we go off paging through the many different varieties of religious freedom that have been manifested in the development of the West. Certainly, at the time of the founding of the republic no single view of church-state relations was clearly dominant. And that is the first problem. If we were to answer the misconceived question, we would have to ask ourselves, "How do we know which among the various versions of religious freedom is 'the Constitution's version'?"[37] The answer to this knotty problem is not to ask what is the substance of the religious freedom or church-state schema announced in the religion clauses. Instead, the answer is to ask what was the "probable original meaning" of the religion clauses. When we do, we will discover "that the religion clauses have nothing of substance to say on questions of religious freedom."[38]

If the religion clauses do not address the substance of religious freedom, then what do they address? The answer is obvious in the first five words of the amendment. "Congress shall make no law . . . " The religion clauses were merely jurisdictional.[39] They kept control of religious matters in the hands of the states, which would maintain their own governments in a coordinated partnership with the new federal government. When one first hears or reads this claim, it sounds incredible. During the decade prior to encountering Smith's work, I professionally promoted an understanding of the

First Amendment that interpreted it as a statement on the substance of religious liberty and church-state affairs. I lobbied members of the Congress and their staffs utilizing that understanding. As a law student, virtually everything I read assumed that understanding of the religion clauses. Nevertheless, it takes relatively little examination to discover that Smith is almost surely correct.

The American colonies-turned-states viewed religious freedom differently. They offered different answers to questions of establishment of religion, non-preferential support of religions, punishment of blasphemy, Sabbath observance, and other religious matters.[40] Boiling the issue down to its essentials, one might distill two primary positions. The first, which Smith calls the traditional position, held that government support of religion was necessary to the preservation of social order. The second, labeled the voluntarist position, disputed the presumption of the traditional position.[41] At least part of the voluntarist group was certain that religious institutions would be far better off without government support. Both traditionalists and voluntarists agreed that a religious foundation was critical to the health of the social order. It is an open question whether there were many in America in the voluntarist camp who embraced what Smith calls the "heretical" view that Christianity needed to be overthrown entirely.[42]

What is important about these positions is that they show a definite difference of opinion about the question of religion and the public order. The idea that these differences would have been ironed out with relatively little debate and dealt with in substance by the very thin religion clauses is risible. What happened instead was that the framers of the Constitution avoided choosing one of the available substantive positions on the matter and clearly left the responsibility for religion and the social order with the states, each of which had developed its own solutions. The elegance of the solution is obvious. "Traditionalists" could support the religion clauses because they protected the ongoing ability of Massachusetts and Connecticut to give support to established religion. "Voluntarists" could likewise agree on the wording because it guaranteed that the federal government would not interfere with the new nonestablishment approach that had been adopted, with a far more fully orbed debate, in Virginia. So, if the question is what theory of religious liberty animates the U.S. Constitution's religion clauses, "the answer is none."[43]

Federalism was the only correct answer with regard to religion and the new republic. Both camps, traditionalists and voluntarists, had prominent advocates and important states behind them. The Constitution did not make a substantive choice between the two, because agreement was not possible, not in the late eighteenth century at any rate. In fact, the record indicates the framers of the document did not even attempt to address the substantive question of religious freedom. Compared with the incredible interest evinced by the issue in Virginia "half a decade earlier," the "almost palpable apathy in Congress" and in the ratifying states over the religion clauses appears "inexplicable." The reasonable corollary is that neither the framers nor the ratifying states thought an epochal decision was being made either in favor of long tradition or for a bold new consensus.[44]

The value of a theory can sometimes be measured by the number of problems it solves. If that is the case, then Smith's view of the religion clauses is valuable indeed. A view of the religion clauses as jurisdictional explains the extremely rare invocation of their guarantees as a basis for legal challenge prior to the mid-twentieth century. It also explains why we find the text so unilluminating for the proper litigation of the kinds of cases raised under their auspices. Dissatisfaction with religious clause jurisprudence is the rule rather than the exception, and the interpretation of them is felt to depend greatly upon the predilections of the justices, which in turn engenders a great deal of resentment from whichever side loses a case. Clauses intended to accomplish the purpose to which we put the religion clauses could surely have been constructed more clearly.

What about the "No Religious Test" Clause?

Although Smith does not reach the point, one might imagine certain proponents of the founding secularism model, such as Isaac Kramnick and R. Laurence Moore, moving the focus from the religion clauses in the First Amendment to the "no religious test" clause in the body of the Constitution. They argue that the prohibition of a religious test clause for holding federal office is an evidence in favor of a conceptually secular government.[45] In response, it is not difficult to extend

Smith's point (and Palmer's) to cover the no religious test require-ment. If there were a religious test written into the Constitution, then it could exclude prominent citizens from states with different require-ments from serving in the national government, thus effectively mar-ginalizing the influence of that particular state. If a vital federalism was a primary goal of the Constitution, as Palmer indicates it was, then a religious test would be out of the question.

More Important, What about the Fourteenth Amendment?

The Fourteenth Amendment to the Constitution has been held by the Supreme Court to incorporate Bill of Rights freedoms against the states and/or to prevent the states from violating certain fundamental freedoms. In reality, fundamental freedoms have not been developed jurisprudentially except in the areas of sex, parenting, and reproduc-tion, so in the religious context the First Amendment is the key. The Court incorporated the religion clauses against the states in the mid-twentieth century, which leads us back to the current day where we act as if the religion clauses carry a substantive principle of religious freedom or public secularism.

The first problem with that line of jurisprudence is that if the religion clauses were purely jurisdictional, then there is nothing to enforce against the states. To incorporate the clauses against the states would be like saying, "The regulation of religion is a matter for the states. And that goes for the states, too." It is nonsensical.

But there is a potential way out for the current jurisprudence. What if the Fourteenth Amendment was written with the intent to establish public secularism and the voluntarist position on religious liberty as part of its broad sweep rather than with a narrower goal such as protecting the rights of freed slaves as a follow-up to the Thirteenth Amendment's ban on involuntary servitude? The possible way out is another dead end though. However broad the sweep of the Fourteenth Amendment was intended to be, it seems fair to conclude that it simply did not establish anything like the content of rights claimed by modern interpreters of the religion clauses. The historical record simply does not support such a construction.

Smith and Hamburger both offer strong evidence on this point involving nearly contemporaneous events. Hamburger, for example, notes that in 1870 (and years following), a mere two years after the ratification of the Fourteenth Amendment, it is possible to find activists who wanted to place establishment and free exercise limitations upon the states and who argued persistently for a new amendment to accomplish that purpose. Elisha Hurlbut, formerly a New York judge, advocated on behalf of the new amendment. He explicitly assumed "that there is nothing in the Constitution as it stands, which prevents a state" from either "establishing a religion, or preventing its free exercise." Hurlbut admitted the desired prohibition might be achieved via "tortured" legal construction, but thought it more likely and more proper that the clauses would be deemed inapplicable to the states.[46]

In addition to the amendments offered by Hurlbut and members of the National Liberal League, there was also the better-known Blaine Amendment. The Blaine Amendment set out to employ the exact wording of the First Amendment against the states rather than against Congress. If the argument about the Fourteenth Amendment incorporating the First Amendment were correct, then the Blaine Amendment would have been entirely superfluous. According to Daniel Conkle, neither proponents nor opponents of the Blaine Amendment believed the Amendment was non-effectual on the grounds that the Fourteenth Amendment had achieved the goal.[47]

If it is true that the religion clauses of the First Amendment were merely jurisdictional and that the Fourteenth Amendment did not incorporate something from the religion clauses that was not originally there, then the sometimes celebrated, but more often hated, religion clause jurisprudence of the last century has been deeply mistaken. The United States Constitution does not place its imprimatur of approval upon either the Jeffersonian model or the slender establishment favored by John Adams. Consequently, the U.S. Constitution does not embrace a particular theory of church-state relations and thus does not ingeniously or otherwise create a secular public order for the United States and/or its constituent parts. In turn, these revelations indicate that the wrangling over the religious intentions of the founding fathers is a fruitless affair. The document they approved skipped past that minefield in favor of the status quo in which some states appealed to the voluntarist position while others were traditionalist.

Secularism was not somehow endemic to the founding of the American republic and the writing of the Constitution, but it has become a powerful ideal contending for primacy of place in the American polity. The religious history of the United States as it extends beyond the founding helps explain the development of secularism as a significant force in American law and politics.

9

American Christianity: Triumph and Trial

It was not until after the presidency of George Washington that the pro-Revolution camp began to divide along religious lines and a man like Thomas Jefferson, despite being a hero of the founding, could come under heavy fire for his heterodox religious beliefs. The antagonism toward Jefferson probably also had something to do with his close identification with the French Revolution, which had become clearly not only anticlerical, but anti-Christian.

Powerful Protestantism

Though originally tolerant of the antireligious antics of the French Revolution, probably because they construed it as merely anti-Catholic, the American clergy developed real antipathy and alarm toward events in France. Steven Bullock's volume on the history of Freemasonry in the United States detailed how the fraternity went from being well respected to being viewed as part of a larger anti-Christian conspiracy. Despite the fact that Masons could claim Americans as prominent as George Washington, who remained a saint of the founding, Christians turned on Masonry and eventually nearly destroyed it in the U.S.[1] After the Revolution in France and the tumult of the election of 1800, Christians became more protective of the place of their religion in American society. American Protestants began to draw a clear line in the sand and let it be known that the American Revolution had gone quite far enough in overthrowing the throne and that the altar would not be next. The point is worth remembering when we discuss whether the new republic had some kind of mission to endorse secularism.

In the early to mid-nineteenth century, Christianity experienced explosive growth, particularly among the evangelical ranks. Eschewing the comforts and museum-like preservative of state establishment, Baptists and Methodists made huge strides in converting the frontier.[2] America experienced a Second Great Awakening that furthered the democratization of the religious economy (as related by Nathan Hatch in his landmark book *The Democratization of American Christianity*) and firmly thrust the Christian faith into preeminence on the national scene. Edwin Gaustad writes that the Bible replaced George Washington as the central cultural symbol.[3]

What seems to have occurred is that Christianity, after centuries of institutional political sponsorship, returned to the voluntarism more typical of its early identity, which coincided with explosive growth of the church. Instead of being little more than the spiritual backing behind Caesar's authority, it once again became decisive in individual hearts no longer bound by extreme deference to learned clergy or the old hierarchies. In a free and democratic nation, the entrepreneurial possibilities for evangelism, education, and social enterprises of many varieties were massive.

And the Fall . . .

During this time American Protestants, flush with success, firmly grasped hold of the Scottish Enlightenment and declared that science and the revelation of the Bible stood hand-in-hand. Instead of the Bible's being a document that interacts with the reader and reveals spiritual truth, it became a ready storehouse of facts. The Bible was scientifically accurate and could be relied on as bulletproof evidence in all that it said. The theologian gathered specimens from Scripture in the same spirit in which the scientist probed the natural world. As Mark Noll related in *The Scandal of the Evangelical Mind*, the cultural, intellectual, and spiritual influence of Protestant Christianity had crested and was primed for a spectacular fall that came in the second half of the century.[4]

Three developments worked together to facilitate that fall from informal cultural hegemony. The first two were the increased awareness of German higher criticism, especially as it traveled back overseas with American students ready to take faculty positions, and the combined power of the deliverances of modern geology and the publication of Charles Darwin's *The Origin of Species*. German higher criticism raised substantial questions about the reliability and historicity of the biblical text, and Darwin's book offered a natural and potentially godless mechanism, or at least a seemingly nonbiblical one, to explain the development of life on the earth. The two together inflicted major damage on the intellectual prestige of Christianity.[5] Regardless of whether the strikes against the authority of the Bible scored with the public, they did make substantial inroads among elites.

To transform the Bible into a "storehouse of facts" in order to justify its cultural hegemony was to demean the profundity of the document and the challenging nature of its claims, and worst of all to turn it into a dry strawman at which critics could endlessly toss matches. The strawman was composed of a combination of biblical literalism and extreme reliance on Paley's design argument as the bedrock of the faith. The move toward literalism was consistent with a desire to make the Bible mesh with common sense and to "insist on the rationality of divine revelation."[6] American Christians began to read the Bible as though "any apparent fact" was taken as a "fact stamped with divine authority."[7] By insisting on this Bible-as-divine-encyclopedia approach, the advocates of Christianity-as-common-sense set themselves up for a stunning blow. The literalness of the creation account in Genesis, for example, would first take a massive hit from the findings of modern geology indicating the earth was probably millions of years old instead of being created in six literal days and existing (due to the calculations wrung from genealogies) only some several thousand years.[8]

The damage incurred was compounded by the fact that much of it was unnecessary, particularly from the scientific side. The appeal of Christianity has always rested on two pillars. First, the church has always agreed with the New Testament that Jesus really did rise from the dead and was actually seen by many people after the event of his death. The idea is that if he actually returned from the dead, which is something we believe humans are incapable of doing, then his claims and his message bear the imprimatur of God himself and are utterly trustworthy. Darwin's findings and those of geological science produced nothing that would raise doubts about the resurrection account.

The second strong appeal of the Christian faith has traditionally been its amazing insight into the human heart. Whether one believes the Bible or not, it is hard to deny that there is an incompleteness or longing within the human personality and that one is never really able to achieve the level of moral perfection one feels one should reach. Christians believe that breach in the innermost heart and mind is the result of a primal falling away from God, a separation occasioned by sin.

These pillars point to a mysterious element in our day-to-day life, a sense that God can dramatically break in and has, in fact, done so, and the sensation that we walk around with a strange irresolvability in our personalities that comes from being touched with the divine spark. So, while the New Testament insists that Christ's resurrection really happened and does so rationalistically, the Bible as a whole also deals with narrative, poetry, metaphor, and parables that are not always aimed at establishing historical or scientific truths so much as they make a more piercing point about the human condition relative to our need for God and our distance from him.

The Spiritual Price of Slavery

What was arguably more important than the intellectual events detailed above and certainly more difficult to avoid was the third development of the nineteenth century. The Bible's great moment in America was nearly capsized by a debilitating argument over slavery and the division of American Christianity into northern and southern camps. Both claimed biblical authority with a degree of reasonableness for their positions in support of and against slavery. Just as Christianity seemed to have been on the edge of bringing in a new millennium as the unifier of religion, science, morality, and culture, it all fell apart in an unwanted war with science, angry regionalism, and a civil war. The postwar South succumbed to an unbecoming mix of sorrow and sentimentality for a lost cause, and religion aimed primarily at consoling the losers. Aside from paying attention to things such as drinking, dancing, and gambling, Southern Christians withdrew from the kind of public religion that is deeply interested in justice and proclaimed the uncomeliness of associating religion with politics. The reaction of the Southern church to the civil rights movement, which would come later, repeated this same reality-avoiding tune in a way that seemed both self-serving and uncompassionate.[9]

The Apparent Denouement: The Fundamentalist-Modernist Controversy and the Public Embarrassment of the Monkey Trial

As the twentieth century dawned, Protestant Christianity was beginning to break into different camps based on orthodoxy. Northern Baptists and Presbyterians went to war with each other over how to react to the intellectual challenges to Christianity. Men such as Harry Emerson Fosdick and others pushed for the church to accommodate to modernism, while J. Gresham Machen, in *Christianity and Liberalism*, and the traditionalists maintained that a church that made its peace with modernism as Fosdick saw it would no longer be a Christian church.[10] In the short and intermediate term, Fosdick's camp would win by an appeal to tolerance.[11] Machen was not a comfortable member of the fundamentalist camp that developed and was eventually rejected by some of his new allies.[12]

The development of fundamentalism as a reaction to modernism had an interesting effect on conservative Protestants. As George Marsden demonstrated in *Fundamentalism and American Culture*, conservative believers went from being intensely interested in matters of social justice to being almost oblivious to those concerns in favor of intense evangelism and defense of the faith.[13]

Fundamentalism met its apparent Waterloo in the Tennessee Scopes Trial when Clarence Darrow (at least in public perception as interpreted by Edward Larson) overpowered William Jennings Bryan in a direct battle between science and the Bible. Fundamentalists undertook a retreat of sorts that gave the impression they had ceased to be a significant influence. As Joel Carpenter has documented, what actually happened was that fundamentalists began their own parallel set of institutions and achieved substantial growth throughout the period of their apparent exile,[14] which would publicly end in the late 1970s with the presidency of Jimmy Carter, who at least seemed to be one of their number, and with the rise of Christian conservatives.[15]

Comeback/Reengagement

While the fundamentalists were disengaging from the larger society during the middle years of the twentieth century, a group of former fundamentalists were intent on reengagement. Carl F. H. Henry's book *The Uneasy Conscience of Modern Fundamentalism* (1947) set forth a powerful critique of the insularity of fundamentalism and insisted that Christianity must engage the culture in every way, including by offering Christian solutions to social problems and evidencing a real interest in social justice.[16] At the same time, Billy Graham was bringing revivalism back to the front pages and Fuller Seminary opened its doors with the idea of keeping Protestant Christianity intellectually vital.

Over time, the Graham-Henry group succeeded in establishing evangelical Christianity as an important public religious force in the American culture and polity. It is not going too far to suggest that the neo-evangelicals pushed American Christians toward a confrontation with secularism. Henry's book indicted fundamentalism for restricting the application of the gospel to the private sphere and adopting a view that might be bluntly indicted as "allowing the unregenerate world to go to hell." He argued that Christian supernaturalism provided the "key element of social advance" and that the two must not be divorced. By focusing on drinking, smoking, card playing, and movies (all of which, to be fair, impact larger issues) to the exclusion of race, management-labor disputes, poverty, and a variety of other social ills, fundamentalists avoided their full stewardship duties to the larger society.[17]

Avoiding the bigger social picture ran counter to what Henry believed should be the natural purview of Christians because the gospel impacts the whole world and Christians have an organic connection to the community through marriage and family. The failure to connect the dots between the family (which is the building block of the society) and the community writ large created the appearance of uncaring pessimism.[18] Henry knew that the social gospel and premillennialism had hardened fundamentalists against social appeals and further saw that secular social reformers had an absolute difference of opinion with regard to diagnosis and cure.[19] Thus, he urged Christians in the evangelical tradition to cease self-defeating absorption with their competitors and to concentrate on transformation.[20] To do otherwise would indicate satisfaction with being the gadfly to the prevailing consensus.[21] Instead, fundamentalists should emulate the early church, which attacked a variety of social ills such as gladiatorial contests, infanticide, sexual promiscuity, and unfair commercial dealing.[22]

In pursuing this line of argument, Henry played upon the consistent concern of fundamentalists and evangelicals with the connection of Christianity to culture. Fundamentalists, premillennial or not, have always believed and to this day continue to teach that America has a special cultural mission that must be preserved.[23] Henry spoke to fundamentalists in the book, but his point of view was shared by other significant thinkers such as Reinhold Niebuhr and T. S. Eliot, who could have easily joined Henry in proclaiming that the genius of Western civilization was grounded in its Christian heritage.[24]

In his mind and theirs, the positive attributes of modern society such as care for the poor, freedom, and democracy could not have come about as they did without the persistent influence of Christ's example and various implications of the biblical text. Accordingly, he scolded fundamentalists for ceding the "Christian social imperative" to "those who understand it in sub-Christian terms."[25] A more appropriate course would be to remind the secularists of the essential connection between Christian ethics and Christian metaphysics.[26] In Henry's analysis, the value of human personality is only guaranteed in a redemptive context.[27] To allow that bedrock connection to loosen would be a recipe for the kind of secular-scientific disaster developing in the totalitarian systems threatening Europe and Asia. The concerns of Henry and others were not limited to secularistic threats, however. At the time, he and many others feared that an inward fundamentalism would self-destruct or become marginalized so that "Romanism" would be left as the only voice of Christianity in the voice against modernism.[28]

Over time, the example of the neo-evangelicals was almost surely key in motivating the subsequent activism of Jerry Falwell and the "New Christian Right." Although Falwell had previously been a Virginia segregationist and a devotee of keeping the church out of politics, whether that meant civil rights or the cold war, he completed an about-face and exerted influence on the 1980 presidential election of Ronald Reagan. How much influence is uncertain, but the fact that Falwell helped change fundamentalist attitudes about politics is unquestionable. It is rare today to hear any conservative Christian insist that politics is too dirty or irrelevant to the church's mission. After out-politicking the evangelicals, Falwell drew massive fire against the fundamentalist label he once embraced proudly. That label is not worn proudly very often in politics anymore. In the years prior to his death, Falwell referred to himself as an evangelical Christian.

The Old Establishment: Mainline Fade-out

At the same time fundamentalists built a counterculture in isolation and evangelicals brought conservative Christianity back into the public square, mainline Protestants went on a journey of their own. They had successfully won the battle with fundamentalists, and without their continued presence they managed to move their denominations doctrinally to the left. In *The Kingdom of God in America*, H. Richard Niebuhr, no fundamentalist, had many harsh words for this group. He designated them the preachers of "a God without wrath" who "brought men without sin into a kingdom without judgment through the ministrations of a Christ without a cross."[29] He further accused liberals of being joyous over any scrap of respectability thrown their way by the intellectually or scientifically prominent and of uncritically supporting the establishment.[30] As has been detailed in a variety of studies, the mainline churches suffered major losses in membership to the more conservative denominations.[31] Institutionally, at least, accommodating the Christian message to fit secular modernity has proven a losing proposition. Today, the question of secularism is contested by its own advocates, conservative Christians, other conservative religionists, and postmodernists. The mainline Protestant church is largely irrelevant to the proceedings.

Conclusion

A seemingly ascendant American Christianity peaked in the nineteenth century only to fall prey to the twin assaults of the Civil War and a scientific revolution that turned heads and provided opportunity to critics and opponents of the faith. Public Christianity of the type that would maintain a strong presence in law and politics receded in the public eye only to reemerge powerfully in the last quarter of the twentieth century. The reemergence of the faith's openly questioning the reign of secular modernity has prompted intense concentration on what the founders intended with regard to the religion clauses of the Constitution.

This chapter established that the question will have to be dealt with anew because the text of the founding document simply fails to resolve it. Secularism and public religion clash openly in the public square. There is no master text in the U.S. Constitution to end the debate. And so we go to the merits. In the next chapter, we ask whether secularism is a superior guarantor of the social peace among diverse claimants.

10

Secularism:
A Failed Strategy for Social Peace

In the introduction to this book, I asserted that the modern understanding of secularism identifies it as the public philosophy tied to the sociological theory of secularization. In order to advance the idea that this modern secularism is not a superior strategy for achieving social peace and/or honoring the rights of all citizens, it will be helpful to understand something of the history, development, and critique of secularization theory. Speaking broadly, the theory envisioned a future in which mankind would leave its religious childhood and would someday live in an age of pure reason uncorrupted by superstition of any kind.

The Rise and Fall of Secularization Theory

The theory of secularization has its genesis in the historical period often referred to as the Enlightenment. To be more specific, secularization theory arises from a particular stream of the Enlightenment, sometimes referred to as the skeptical Enlightenment or the French Enlightenment. It was in this more radical stream, which concentrated on obliterating evils it perceived as having their origin in religious belief and religious institutions, that secularization theory seems to have had its most enthusiastic early proponents. Thus, critics of the theory point to the historical context in which it was birthed and raise questions about whether objectivity is possible with regard to a framework conceived in the immediate aftermath of wars of religion and violent revolutions against a nexus of throne-altar alliances rooted firmly in the old status quo.

Poster children for the early beginnings of secularization theory might include Diderot, who rejoiced at the thought of "strangling the last priest with the guts of the last king," the French revolutionaries who enthroned a young woman (actually a prostitute) as the goddess Reason in the Cathedral of Notre Dame, and Comte, who envisioned the death of traditional religion to be replaced by a new order based on reverence toward the powers of human rationality.[1] To point to these early exemplars is not to cast the typical advocate of the theory as some kind of angry materialist with an unsavory agenda. Many thoughtful people have worked in the secularization paradigm and have done so in good faith. The point of reviewing theoretical predecessors is to show that a powerful metanarrative arose during the period of Enlightenment around the idea of the decline of religion as a natural, necessary, and *good* thing. Thus, the theory of secularization may well be loaded, as Rodney Stark and others charge, with much ideological freight and possibly much more than some of its advocates would admit.[2]

The work of Emile Durkheim and Max Weber, two of the most prominent early practitioners of the field, embodies (in much more reasonable form) some of the built-in presuppositions of the skeptical Enlightenment.[3] For example, Durkheim conceives religion as social glue essentially put in place by a society that personifies its agreement on values and turns it into a god.[4] The clear assumption made by such an analysis is that the God of Israel, or any other god, such as the one portrayed in the Koran, does not exist and is merely a useful illusion. Max Weber ties religion to ancient roots in charismatic leaders and the practice of magic that offers explanations for things that remain unexplained in the real sense. Religion routinizes the charisma of the early leader and preserves it for later generations.[5] Over time, a disenchantment of the world occurs as real explanations are found to displace the mysterious ones and the various spheres of life gain their autonomy from the control once exercised by magical religion.

Eventually, each sphere of life develops its own internal logic based on the scientific method and the routinization of expertise.[6] As with Durkheim, the implication of Weber's work seems to be that religion is purely a social phenomenon that is in the process of disappearing as its usefulness is dissipated. Again, neither of these outstanding scholars represents some kind of revolutionary atheism, but simple presuppositions against the possibility of religious truth seem to be in place.

By the middle of the twentieth century, secularization theory was comfortably accepted as the dominant paradigm and was clearly the working theory for the discipline of sociology of religion. Moving into a more contemporary and future-oriented mode, the theory of secularization was said to refer to "the process by which sectors of society and culture are removed from the domination of religious institutions and symbols."[7] Further, secularization meant more than just the "separation of church and state," "the expropriation of church lands," or "the emancipation of education from ecclesiastical authority."[8] Rather, it was said to affect "the totality of cultural life and ideation, and may be observed in the decline of religious contents" in a variety of areas such as the arts, philosophy, and literature.[9] Further still, secularization was said to indicate "the rise of science as an autonomous, thoroughly secular perspective on the world."[10] Consciousness, itself, was destined to be secularized.[11] During the heart of the twentieth to late twentieth century, sociologists such as Talcott Parsons, Thomas Luckmann, and Peter Berger offered influential works in the mainstream of the theory.

Parsons wrote influentially on secularization as functional differentiation, the process by which religious institutions, supposedly once firmly in control of a vast array of social functions, give way to new social actors, such as businesses and bureaucracies, more rationally fitted to execute tasks. In Parsons's view, differentiation could be a good thing for religious actors because they would be able to focus on their core mission.[12] Differentiation would prove more durable than other parts of the theory. On the other hand, Parsons engaged in some arguably shoddy inferential historical work by trying to reconstruct religious development/evolution by putting together a series of contemporary examples from around the globe to show the various stages through which man has progressed.[13] While such a methodology has immediate intuitive appeal, it is also one that yields questionable results. Contemporary primitives are not necessarily a reliable analog for primitives from other cultures at other points in history.[14]

Luckmann wrote on the idea of secularization as privatization of religion. During the time he was writing, the idea of privatization must have appeared nearly unquestionable. As faith became increasingly irrelevant, he supposed, society would be run by a rational bureaucracy, and no consensus over values would be needed.[15]

There were theologians who accepted the news from scholars such as Luckmann with enthusiasm and quickly harmonized the sense of onrushing secularization with their own ideas about religion. Perhaps the most memorable example was Harvey Cox's *The Secular City*. He tried to extend Bonhoeffer's never thoroughly explained "religionless Christianity" into a paean to the secular city that has moved into a postreligious era.[16]

Peter Berger is one of the most interesting figures in the debate and evolution of secularization theory because he was one of the most well-known advocates and is also the best-known convert to the other side, having repudiated the theory some years ago as inconsistent with the empirical evidence. Berger wrote about the existence of a sacred canopy composed of plausibility structures that reinforced social belief about religion.[17] In Berger's conception, the effect of pluralism would be to undermine plausibility structures, thus resulting in the decline of religious belief.[18] In a particularly memorable quote, Berger imagined tiny remnants of religious believers huddled together in the final stage of decline by the late twentieth century![19]

Secularization Theory and Politics

The broad logic of secularization theory was that religion in the modern world would inevitably yield to functional differentiation, privatization, and, ultimately, decline. As a relevant social phenomenon, and perhaps even as a part of culture at all, religion would cease to exist. If correct, secularization theory would have clear implications for political communities.

In the wrong hands, secularization theory can give the comfort of scientific logic to dictators who wish to gather all power unto themselves or to a particular state ideology. Anthony Gill has described religious actors as expert providers of ideology, which is the lowest-cost way to govern people. Sometimes, state actors will seek to co-opt religion to that task. If religious forces refuse to cooperate, then the state has a rational incentive to offer its own ideology (as with Revolutionary France). The goal would then be to have the state ideology reign supreme and to use the instrument of state coercion to help along the "inevitable" process of religious decline so as to eliminate competitors for the loyalty of the people and to prevent any challenge to their authority.[20]

In a more benign scenario, one can imagine a situation like the one that has characterized the United States for the last several decades, particularly after the Scopes Trial. In that case, secularization has been implicitly assumed by elites in government, academia, and the mass media though it is not characteristic of the populace at large. The result is that to outsiders the society appears much more secular than it really is. Religious believers themselves have a strong sense of decline because the reality-defining institutions of the broad community exhibit secularist presumptions about most things, including religion. Thus, faith is often seen even by many believers as something that is private and does not matter much in the discussion of serious issues, unless of course the story is that religious fanatics have committed crimes in the name of their faith. The faith of a favored figure such as Martin Luther King Jr. tends to be deemphasized. Resurgence of religion occurs publicly when discomfort mounts with the perception that taken-for-granted certainties are being undermined by an elite culture that is somewhat aggressive, particularly in education.[21]

In the United States, a loose Christian consensus prevailed until the latter part of the twentieth century. As it has unraveled, American Catholics and conservative Protestants have turned away from battling each other to join in common cause against the threat of secularism. The balance of power is still in favor of Enlightenment-based secularization in forming public perception among elites, but the democratization of mass media with cable and Internet technology has leveled the playing field considerably.

If secularization theory is correct, secular social elites in the U.S. could successfully wait out a dying contestant and impose a new vision on the social canvas without much opposition. It is perhaps no accident that most of the critical U.S. Supreme Court rulings underscoring the separation of church and state occurred during a time when the theory of secularization was at its zenith. With such an assumption in place, benign toleration combined with unacknowledged (or perhaps under-acknowledged) exclusion would appear to be a sound policy for achieving a secular society, seemingly without tears.

But what would it mean for would-be social architects if secularization was less than a fait accompli and was, in fact, unlikely ever to occur? The last few decades have diminished the feasibility of a strong secularization theory. In the 1960s, which was still part of the heyday of secularization theory, a few sociologists of religion began to challenge the theory as inconsistent with empirical evidence and not nearly complex enough to take cognizance of the great variety of historical exigencies that had produced various modes of community around the globe. David Martin[22] and Andrew Greeley[23] fit into this category. Rodney Stark, now enormously influential in the field, admits that he, like Berger, was a member of the other camp until he began to sense dissonance within the secularization paradigm.[24]

Over time, the group challenging secularization theory has succeeded in forcing advocates of the once-dominant paradigm to sharply circumscribe their claims. Berger, for instance, has performed nearly a complete about-face in his own appraisal of secularization theory. He now forthrightly states that the idea that modernization leads to the decline of religion as a social force and in the minds of individuals has turned out to be wrong. In his view, secularization theory has been falsified by religious revolution, rejection, and the comparatively great power of groups that chose not to adapt versus the diminished credibility of those that have adapted.[25] He observes that internationally it is conservative/orthodox/traditional movements that are on the rise. Counter-secularization is as prominent a feature of the modern world as secularization. As a result, Berger concludes that modernization and secularization are not synonymous.[26]

José Casanova has written influentially on the spectacular deprivatization of religion that became obvious in the 1970s, when America was suddenly bursting with celebrities in both entertainment and politics talking everywhere about being "born-again," not the least of whom was President Jimmy Carter. Casanova points specifically to four social developments from the late 1970s and early 1980s that were decisively damaging to the notion of privatization: the Islamic Revolution in Iran, the emergence of the Catholic Solidarity

Union as a focus of public protest against the Soviets in Poland, the reemergence of Protestant fundamentalism in the United States, and the rebirth of Catholicism in Latin America.[27]

While Casanova maintained a place for secularization theory in the slimmed-down form of functional differentiation, Rodney Stark flatly declared the death of the theory altogether, provocatively sending it off to "R.I.P."[28] Where a writer like Casanova addresses the issue relatively dispassionately, Stark aggressively notes that the facts have always been at odds with "three centuries of theorizing" and that the discipline has only recently begun to emphasize careful empirical research unhindered by "the assumption that religiousness is a sign of stupidity, neurosis, poverty, ignorance, or false consciousness, or represents a flight from modernity."[29]

One of Stark's most interesting themes deals with the question of history and its relationship to secularization theory. He maintains that sociologists have wrongly assumed the existence of a golden age of faith that has been steadily eroding like a seashore before the ceaseless waves of secular modernity. According to Stark, the pious Age of Faith is mythical.[30] Historians are perturbed at the unhistorical belief of sociologists in an age of faith, which does not do justice to the mass apathy, heterodoxy, and agnosticism that existed in Europe for centuries. Stark endorses the idea that there could be no de-Christianization of Europe because there never was a Christianization.[31] Instead of modernization interacting with religion to the detriment of the faith, Stark sees religion rising and falling in accord with its place in a society's religious economy. To oversimplify, religious institutions established by government stagnate and ultimately fail while those that develop independently and maintain their independence work to survive and often thrive.[32] This mechanism, rather than anything having to do with science or modernity, explains the differing fortunes of the Christian churches in Western Europe and their American cousins.[33]

David Martin has intriguingly proposed that we may actually be witnessing a series of successive Christianizations rather than a history of secularization. Martin sees an inherent tension between the Christian faith and the power of worldly rule. Thus, the Christian faith evangelizes, gains great influence, and falls into a terrible struggle (each time enduring slippage) with the problem of reconciling the poor man of Nazareth with the prominence of rule, not in heaven but here on earth. However, the successive Christianizations solve different problems each time and may represent a form of progress toward something quite apart from secularization. Each time, however, the projection of the faith results in recoil. Martin contends we may have been living in a period of recoil from Protestant advance.[34]

Thus, the Reformation itself represents a reaction by some Christians against what they viewed as an unacceptable accommodation of the church to worldliness. In other words, men such as Martin Luther and John Calvin were protesting against secularization. *And the Reformation is not the only instance of this sort of thing happening.* The spiritual movement led by Saint Francis of Assisi is another example. The institutional church repeatedly pushed toward becoming more and more like a political authority or a business, and Christians would object and push back toward piety. The United States can point to the two Awakenings as evidence of the same thing in reaction to a spiritually deadening public cult. The recent American upsurge of Christian efforts in politics, journalism, higher education, and entertainment may be part of a similar process. The tension that continually intervenes is that renewal has a habit of breaking up social unity around the Christian faith because it demands purity over accommodation. Social comprehensiveness is always at odds with an emphasis on regeneracy based on individual religious faith and experience.

Part of the point in bringing Martin's theory forward is to demonstrate that a prominent sociologist of religion can write in this vein with the expectation of being granted a respectful hearing. That fact alone shows that things have changed and that the dominant theory has yielded a great deal of real estate. The other point, however, is that Martin's idea of successive Christianizations has a great deal of intuitive appeal. Certainly, the notion captures the sense of patterns in history rather than a progress toward a particular point in the way old-line secularization theory did.

Peter Berger considers the case against secularization and suggests that what it all means is that secularization may not represent some kind of ultimate destination for humanity but rather a recurring phenomenon that is prominent at some times and not so prominent at other times. Interestingly, his view of secularization mirrors Martin's idea of Christianizations' gaining and losing force. We have been living in an era in which secularization is more prominent, but, on some levels at least, it is now receding. Perhaps a better thought is that secularization needs explanation rather than religiosity. It is arguably the more puzzling phenomenon.[35] There is no reason to think that the twenty-first century overall will be less religious than today. Berger suggests the species would have to mutate to lose the religious impulse. In addition, it appears the Christian faith can itself be modernizing. For example, evangelical congregations often serve as schools for democracy and social mobility.[36]

A Poor Strategy for Common Ground

Whether or not the theory of secularization is accurate, the secular liberal perception is that religion must remain privatized lest it force itself upon all in the form of an established church or bring to bear "extraneous conceptions of justice, of the public interest, of the common good, and of solidarity" inaccessible to occupants of the rightful neutral zone of the public square.[37] The broad thought advanced by advocates of secularism is that there exists a common court of reason from which religious reasons deviate so greatly as to render their deliverances extraordinarily difficult to understand and accept by persons not similarly situated in their hearts and minds.

Robert Audi's work represents the extension of this common-ground logic. He asserts that common-ground secular reasons are available to support political decisions and actions. Given the existence of those common secular reasons, the religious person who wishes to act virtuously will find an independent secular reason to support his political activity (including voting) rather than bring his particularist religious feelings or thoughts to bear.[38] Audi's argument relies on the premise that there is a neutral secular ground of reason from which we may all draw in the political sphere. Audi's premise is a common one. This portion of the analysis aims to show that premise is incorrect and should not be relied upon by fair-minded persons sincerely interested in social peace and civic virtue.

Prior to lodging her complaint against secularism, Elizabeth

Shakman-Hurd described it as "the dominant language of religion and politics in the West." Further, what is "known" about the relation of politics and religion is "dominated by secularist assumptions." The only problem is that secularistic assumptions and the dominance of secularism are not necessarily warranted. Instead, Shakman-Hurd is convinced that secularism is in desperate need of reassessment in its position "as an organizing model of public life."[39]

Instead of freeing up public space for common access by all and ensuring that public debate and deliberation are as productive as possible, secularism emerges as a power player that "arrogates to itself the right to define the role of religion in politics" and thus "shuts down important debates about the moral bases of public order." The result is resentment and ultimately a "backlash against its hegemonic aspirations." Rather than acknowledging the "contingency of its own assumptions," secularism simply assumes it is the default position of rational persons of goodwill, utterly failing to recognize that it does not stand outside the interaction of religion and politics. Indeed, secularism proposes to eliminate the problem of "theological politics" when it actually occupies a position on that very spectrum.[40]

Citizens with strong religious concerns have often tried to point out the non-neutrality inherent in the claims of secularism, but they have failed largely due to a failure to present the issue properly. When conservative Christians have tried to frame an argument, they have tended to complain about "secular humanism" as a religion and have pointed to groups of persons rallying around that flag. That method does not get the point across, however, for it fails to deal with the secularism that presents itself as the established reality of public life rather than as a specific program. Secularism does not have to dress itself up in the formal clothes of an ultimately enlightened religion of reason in order to become susceptible to criticism. Secularism need not be caught officially tipping its hand in a moment of gratuitous public relations. As a method of ordering public life it is inherently problematic. The point of this section is to expose the partisanship inherent in secularism.

Secularism only makes sense in relation to religion. It is, in fact, a specific reaction to religion, which is the "with" to secularism's "without." Yet, secularism defines itself as the starting point from which it determines what religion means. Which concept is actually prior? Is the reaction somehow more common to man than its inspiration?[41] It may be arbitrary for the secular to set itself up as the neutral common ground. There may be other contenders that would serve better or at least are as good as secularism, in which case the matter could be dealt with more democratically without necessary prejudice to human rights.

Democracy is one of the victims of secularism because it has a tendency to rule certain voices out of court. Secularism acts politically against its competitors and defines them as what it is not. It claims to be the exemplar of justice, neutrality, democracy, common sense, rational argument, tolerance, and the public interest. That claim would indicate the religious is not those things. Though those moves can be fair if appropriate concessions are made to context, "they are not the only moves possible." This is where the problem comes in because most secularists do not concede that non-secular democratic alternatives can be legitimate versus secularism.[42]

Secularism tells a story about its differences with religion that are not necessarily true. For instance, one frequently hears about Christian failures such as the Inquisition, but we are led to believe that secularism represents cooler heads, rationality, and common ground. What often goes unacknowledged is that secularism has itself often been associated with the coercive, the unjust, the violent, and the undemocratic.[43] David Martin suggests the reason for the unbalanced look at misused power may have something to do with the fact that the secular enlightenment has not had an institutionalized presence to accept the critique in the same way Christianity has the church. Thus, secular academics may be quick to assert Stalin was not sufficiently enlightened, but they are less sure Torquemada was not sufficiently Christian.[44]

The "automatic linkage between secularism and democratic public order" should be questioned.[45] Secularism creates resistance right from the start because it automatically labels non-secularists as nonrational, unfree, and undemocratic. The targets of the critique do not recognize themselves in it and therefore resist vigorously.[46] Furthermore, the very idea of "secular neutrality" and its universal applicability to human communities fails to acknowledge "the contested process through which the 'secular' has come into existence."[47] There is an additional problem in the sense that secularism as a common-ground strategy directly implicates Christianity as it can be seen as a Christian view of how the world interacts with the claims of God. In other words, the separation of church and state is a Christian idea. Thus, it ends up being common ground only for people with that heritage.[48]

Secularism and Postmodernity

David Martin refers to the onset of postmodernism as the secularization of secularism in which secularism becomes just another member of the competing orthodoxies vying for public supremacy instead of the eye-in-the-sky judge of all the rest. Even during his time as a secularization theorist, Berger saw that secular ideologies would have to create plausibility structures just as religious communities had.[49] Instead of the future coming to a head with a secular plausibility structure killing off all the rest, as Berger once thought might happen, we have arrived at a time when many rival plausibility structures contend and thrive battling against one another, sometimes waxing and other times waning.

During the past several decades, the secularist reading of history and reality has bid with some success to become the reigning structure of plausibility. Part of the strategy in so doing has been to secularize Christian values into the values of a liberal democratic society and to fail to acknowledge the source. Thus, we arrive at the irony that traditional Christianity has weathered potent attacks on its character in the name of "what amounts to a secularized Christian morality" claiming "the high ground" of greater humanity, justice, and compassion.[50] Secularism and the story of secularization tend to leave out "the distinctive character of Christian civilization as compared with any other" and forget "Christian sources of cherished modern ideas."[51] Secularism itself acts like a reporter reserving "the right to question without itself being questioned." With the advent of postmodernism, the license to question without being questioned and to have one's own position left unexamined for personal prejudice and interest has been revoked.[52] One need not purchase the entire package of postmodern theory in order to see the wisdom of the new scrutiny, the secularization of the secular.

The avowed antifoundationalist[53] Stanley Fish sets forth a potent critique of secularism and church-state boundary-setting based on his conclusion that there is neither neutral principle nor unimpeachable authority to establish either social practice as legitimate.[54] Fish instead claims Western liberalism has been performing an elaborate shell game for a few centuries now without anyone really noticing. Fish overstates things when he says that no one has noticed. Many Christian analysts have noticed,[55] as have other religionists, but in the world of the academic vanguard that Fish inhabits his statement may be correct. In Fish's mind, John Locke was the first to complete the maneuver, and what has occurred since his time is merely a footnote. Fish begins his analysis by citing from John Locke's *Letter Concerning Toleration*:

> I esteem it above all things necessary to distinguish exactly the business of civil government from that of religion and to settle the just bounds that lie between the one and the other. If this be not done, there can be no end put to the controversies that will be always arising.[56]

So far, so good. We need a solution to the fact that people are constantly reaching different conclusions as they interpret Scripture and religion. Extreme discord results. But here is where the shell game comes in. We must figure out how to draw lines that institute tolerance. Fish's thesis is that we cannot do so without simultaneously engaging in an act of exclusion, justified by nothing more principled than power.[57] The shell game comes from redescribing "the exclusionary gesture so that it appears not to have been performed by anyone," but follows "from the nature of things."[58] Again, he cites Locke to demonstrate the point:

> But to come to particulars. I say, first, no opinions contrary to human society, or to those moral rules which are necessary to the preservation of civil society, are to be tolerated by the magistrate. But of those indeed examples in any church are rare. For no sect can easily arrive to such a degree of madness, as that it should think fit to teach, for doctrines of religion, such things as manifestly undermine the foundations of society, and are therefore condemned by the judgment of all mankind.[59]

Fish sees Locke making two important moves. Locke dismisses views "so subversive that no society could allow them to flourish" and condemns them by some authority referred to as "the judgment of all mankind." How can it be, Fish asks, that Locke gets away with "declaring [that] differences are intractable because every church is orthodox to itself" and then manages to appeal to a common judgment of all mankind? The notion of common ground is nonsensical "if the entire project of toleration is a response to the bottom line fact of plural judgments issuing from plural orthodoxies."[60] To make the situation clear, let's look at Fish's own summation:

> The strategy of finding common ground assumes a capacity that *has already been denied* (italics mine) by the framing of the problem. Indeed, if that capacity (to identify uncontroversially what is and is not essential) were available to you or to me or to anyone there would be no problem and the lawful configurations of the state would arrange themselves. If general truths were perspicuous and easily applicable to specific situations, or if there were agreement about which policies and practices are beyond the pale, or if procedural rules that respect no persons are fair to all were easily identifiable, tolerance's limits would be self-establishing and no coercion would be required since everyone would readily agree to what they already agreed about.[61]

Fish's point is that while we pretend to have something of a neutral process for adjudicating claims between groups, institutions, and persons based on common ground, the common ground does not exist and we do not want to admit it does not exist. A doctrine of toleration "is always a question of who is tolerating whom, for it is from the perspective of the tolerator that the limits to toleration will be set."[62] Once the very first move of separating the civil from the religious has been made, "the claim of a religion to have precedence in every aspect of one's life will seem prima facie absurd." The next move is to simply draw "a line around religion, supposedly to protect it from state interference, but actually to constrain its exercise in ways the state finds comfortable."[63]

In other words, liberal secularist democracy might be guilty of treating religion the same way men treated women in the late nineteenth century, putting it on a pedestal and "protecting" it from vulgarities like voting and participating in public policy. Again to quote Fish, "There is a very fine line, and sometimes no line at all, between removing religion from the public battlefield and retiring it to the sidelines where it is displayed only on ceremonial occasions marked by the pomp and circumstance we often accord to something we have trivialized."[64]

It is here that one cannot help but think of Michael McConnell's comparison of Nietzsche's hermit to the religiously minded person of today. McConnell retells the story of Zarathustra, who brings the news that God is dead. When he encounters a hermit who sings, laughs, weeps, and mumbles so as to praise God, Zarathustra "leaves the old man to worship in peace." The hermit has been spared because he lives alone in his self-constructed reality. "If the hermit left the forest and attempted to enter into public discussion and debate, he would be given the news of God's death like everyone else." The lesson to be drawn from the story, McConnell suggests, is that "religious freedom is to be protected, strongly protected—so long as it is irrelevant to the life of the wider community."[65]

Is Fish right in his assertion that secular liberalism can offer no truly common ground that justifies segregating religion on the private side of the public/private distinction? It appears unquestionable that tolerance may only be instituted as a driving social paradigm by immediately ruling out or segregating views that differ. But even if we take that as a given, are there no hard-rock foundational principles to which we would all willingly submit regardless of our differing viewpoints?

Fish would argue there are not. He suggests an examination of the apparently broadly accepted principle of fairness to make his point. Americans are big fans of fairness. Virtually everyone can agree that procedures and policies should be fair. The priority of fairness is so great that the concept is often used as a trump card in political rhetoric. Office holders and seekers wish to convince us that they are fair-minded and that their opponents do not care about fairness. But Fish insists that a peek under the edge of the big tent will prove we are not even sure what fairness is. We are incapable of accepting or rejecting a course of action as fair or unfair until "fairness is filled in." He goes on to demonstrate:

> I think it is fair to distribute goods and privileges equally, irrespective of the accomplishments of those who receive them. You think it is fair to

reward each according to his efforts. I think it is fair when everyone has a chance to speak. You think it is fair when everyone who is qualified has a chance to speak. The disagreements between us cannot be settled by the invocation of fairness because what divides us are our differing views of what fairness really is. (Mine is roughly egalitarian, yours meritocratic.) Those differing views are substantive—part and parcel of some contestable vision of what the world should be like—and unless one of us persuades the other to his or her view, persuades the other to exchange one vision of what the world should be like for another, the distance between us will not be bridged.[66]

Fish also points out that virtually all the other noble abstractions (equality, justice, autonomy, etc.) seem to fall prey to the same interpretive problem. Whoever seeks to fill these vessels fills them with "partisan, interested guidance." The result is that "if you are looking to ground your beliefs and convictions in some norm or principle or rule of authority independent of them and independent, too, of the beliefs and convictions of anyone else, you are bound to fail."[67] Common ground is not so easily obtained. It certainly cannot be obtained by the simple expedient of removing considerations of God or religion from the mix. Where does this leave us? Fish does not think his antifoundationalism (or whatever other postmodern label we apply) leads to nihilism. Instead, we all have what we had before: beliefs, instincts, ideas, and interests grounded in our life experience, traditions, and learning. All we have lost is the idea that some neutral authority is capable of proclaiming victories and defeats through appeal to abstract principle.[68]

Bracketing off religion does not solve the problem of toleration. It just disadvantages one set of orthodoxies from interacting with the many secular orthodoxies roaming free in a liberal society.

If one accepts Fish's diagnosis of a secular liberal shell game in action, then the public square can be reconceived as a place full of many competing orthodoxies vying for adherents, perhaps including secular political liberalism at the same level as religious alternatives instead of standing above them. Thus, secular liberalism takes a more honest position as the ideological embodiment of tolerance and the exclusion of divisive religion from public affairs. Instead of being a referee, liberalism becomes the advocate Fish insists it has been all along.

But can we rally around some kind of agreed-upon set of rules written into law embodying our agreement? What about the Constitution, for example? Surely, it can stand as the independent source of authority we need to decide our disputes, especially given its centrality to our government and way of life. Fish says it cannot. The Constitution is a text that must be interpreted and in the process will fall prey to some partisan agenda.[69] A simple review of the vast disagreement between well-trained Constitutional scholars over many of the Supreme Court's biggest cases indicates Fish may be right.

What is the implication for church-state separation? Fish believes Christians should refuse "to traffic in liberalism's vocabulary (fairness, equality, mutual respect) but to reject it and try, instead, to 'rout liberalism from the field'" in order to be true to their beliefs.[70] They should not "bring [their deepest convictions] to the table of rational, deliberative, and open inquiry, because to do so would be to make rationality, deliberateness, and openness into their gods."[71]

When Fish is criticized for recommending a course that would be damaging to the "pluralistic body politic," he replies that the criticism assumes that a pluralistic body politic is a good thing and uses it "as a club against those believers who harbor monistic hopes."[72] In other words, to say that all beliefs should be respected equally is to do nothing more than embrace one of the competing orthodoxies making a play for the power to guide the body politic. In addition, it should be clear that Fish is not actively hoping Christians or any other religious group will use the newly level playing field to press their cause to the point of domination.[73] He is simply expressing his conclusion that hegemony is the right goal for a Christianity no longer cordoned off by a fictitious and nonsensical separation of church and state.[74]

It is one thing for Fish to demonstrate the ways religious views undergo unfair segregation in the public square; it is another for Fish, the nonbeliever, to deliver his analysis of what the believer should seek and demand. Is he right that the natural conclusion of liberal rationalism's fall from dominance is that numerically strong conservative Christians will feel a need to exercise their own will to power? Is power even a proper goal for the Christian? A proper conclusion of the fall[75] and warnings not to judge lest one be judged[76] might be that the Christian should be very cognizant of his limitations and should not be quick to exercise power and judgment over others, particularly not by way of some domineering hegemony. I think this notion of pressing one's claims from humility and goodwill is what Steven D. Smith is aiming at with his ultra-Protestantism. One moves into the public square arguing from sincere belief, but at the same time recognizes the possibility of one's own fallibility and misunderstanding. That is a hedge against the theocratic turn.[77]

Regardless of the incorrectness of Fish's assumption that monism should be the goal of the Christian contestant in the public square, his central point remains true. He is certainly correct that a postmodern, competing-orthodoxies framework has the potential to provide new breathing room and access to public institutions for religion that the secular Enlightenment model has not. If secular liberalism joins a host of other competing orthodoxies clashing in the public square, the purposeful decision to segregate or exclude religion in any way begins to lose credibility.

Though neither a postmodernist nor an antifoundationalist, the Catholic scholar Francis Canavan had a keen eye for the operation of orthodoxies at work and was just as critical of the common-ground assertions of secularism as Stanley Fish has been. Canavan appreciated the genius of liberal pluralism in seeking to avoid matters of fundamental philosophy where possible, but he took offense at the pretense that "more profound" questions could be dealt with "by plain, blunt common sense without resort to premises of a higher level." Drawing a hard line between the religious and the secular and insisting upon the unreal power of common sense is the core of what Canavan attacked as playing "the pluralist game with a stacked deck."[78]

The Secular Rawlsian Defense

Though Fish makes John Locke his proxy, John Rawls might be a better target. Rawls is the scholar widely believed to have offered the strongest argument for a religion-free public political sphere.[79] Rawls does not make the obvious error of attempting to segregate religion from the political process while allowing an army of metaphysical "isms" to run free.[80] Instead, he sees political liberalism emerging as a *modus vivendi* (way of life) from the brute reality of the wars of religion. This political liberalism is not metaphysical. It is simply a "free-standing" and "overlapping consensus" that involves a "reasonable" mix of political values whereby we all agree to be bound.[81] Political liberalism is procedural in nature. "Comprehensive doctrines" such as religions and other metaphysical worldviews do not play a part in political deliberation. As with the modern secularism I set out at the beginning of the book, religion is privatized. The difference with Rawls is that the privatization he proposes is a bit more fair. All comprehensive doctrines are privatized. Thus, citizens "are to conduct their public political discussions of constitutional essentials and matters of basic justice within the framework of what each sincerely regards as a reasonable political conception of justice." This conception of justice is bound to express "political values that others as free and equal also might reasonably be expected to endorse."[82] The type of reason that will characterize political dispute and deliberation under these constraints is what Rawls calls public reason which is theoretically available to all.[83]

The question, of course, is whether Rawls is right about the superiority of a public discourse free of comprehensive doctrines (including religion). Though comprehensive doctrines are kept out of public deliberations (at least with regard to constitutional essentials and matters of basic justice), Rawls does not attack any of them in the way skeptical enlightenment advocates might. He is simply keeping them out in the name of fairness and prudence. The idea is that reasonable religionists should be able to participate without qualms. They will be leaving out some of their own cherished convictions, but for a good cause, so to speak. Rawls's framework depends on convincing readers of the virtue of a particular kind of cooperation and reciprocity as proper responses to the fact of reasonable pluralism. Political liberalism, as understood by Rawls, is how free and equal persons treat each other when they understand their situation.

What flies under the banner of public reason? One of the problems we encounter immediately when we accept Rawls's scheme is that we cannot necessarily imagine how various public debates would be resolved. It is one thing to say that we should offer only arguments that other free and equal persons can accept, but it is quite another to determine what those arguments would be. One also wonders about the justice of treating all comprehensive doctrines equally. I can imagine a situation, for example, that seems to me to satisfy the dictates of public reason, but to which Rawls would almost certainly object. Suppose that I want to argue for a massive program of governmental assistance to the poor. This program may even seem less than prudent because I am calling for sacrificial giving from citizens. My reason is that Jesus said whatever you do for the least of them, you do for him (Matt. 25:40). I have some evidence to believe he said such a thing. I further believe that he rose from the dead and also have some evidence to support that position. Still further I believe that he claimed to be the Son of God (some evidence for that, too) and that his apparent resurrection was the proof of that relationship. Therefore, I think I have it on strong authority that I should advocate for substantial relief to the poor. Is the case a slam dunk? No. But do I have some evidence of all of the above? Yes. It seems to me that I should be able to take this completely Christian case to the public square. Why should the fact that Rawls would label it a comprehensive doctrine stop me? Isn't this case something any free and equal person could conceivably believe? It may not be likely, but surely there is a chance any free and equal person could consider the evidence and agree with me on part or all of it.

On these facts alone, I would submit that we have good reason to find Rawls's version of public reason wanting. Many comprehensive doctrines, including Christianity, have a variety of accessible evidences to back them up. Of course, it is possible for free and equal persons to disagree with even rationalistic deliverances of the Christian faith or of various other comprehensive doctrines, but their possible agreement would seem to be a virtual given. After all, these comprehensive doctrines gain adherents.

Beyond this question of the validity of sequestering various comprehensive doctrines from the public political sphere, Rawls's work also suffers from indeterminacy. How would his philosophy play out for even a matter of very basic justice? The classic example raised in critique of Rawls has been with regard to abortion. Here is what Rawls once wrote on the matter:

> Now I believe any reasonable balance of these three values (respect for human life, reproduction of political society, and women's equality) will

give a woman a duly qualified right to decide whether or not to end her pregnancy during the first trimester. The reason for this is that at this early stage of pregnancy the political value of equality of women is overriding, and this right is required to give it substance and force.[84]

Consider a similar formulation presented by Paul Campos: "The reason why abortion must be prohibited is that at every stage of the pregnancy the political value of the due respect for human life is overriding, and this prohibition is required to give that value substance and force."[85]

Looking at those two statements, it is extraordinarily difficult to imagine how Rawls could see public reason compelling the first rather than the second. Per Campos, reason becomes a "god term" and "invoking reason becomes equivalent to giving reasons."[86] The other conclusion one might form from looking at those two statements is that Alasdair MacIntyre (who is completely ignored by Rawls) gives a far superior account of the public deliberative situation in *After Virtue* than does Rawls in *Political Liberalism*. We reason from premises. The premises Rawls uses to set up a public deliberative space are too thin to give substance to necessary public debates. MacIntyre was right when he said that we offer reasons from different moral frameworks that actually shape those reasons.[87] We cannot simply send them out free-floating as Rawls seems to suggest.

Though "political liberalism" and "public reason" are presented as parts of a theory that is not metaphysical but is rather designed to be a realistic way of responding to pluralism, realism is perhaps the aspect most lacking in Rawls's theory. Though it would be nice (perhaps) to have a theory that would give us "an internally consistent set of principles capable of generating answers to questions of religious freedom," the modus vivendi upon which Rawls seeks to build is the reality. It wasn't a Rawls or a Rousseau who solved the problems that arose from religious pluralism in Europe and thus ended the religious wars. The French Revolution, notably, was an attempt to put Rousseau's notion of the general will and civil religion into effect with disastrous consequences. Rather, the answer to the new social fact of religious pluralism was "a negotiated, and perhaps messy, truth."[88] Rawls's key question is how is it possible to have a just and stable society of persons who are "profoundly divided by reasonable religious, philosophical, and moral doctrines." The answer may be better found in history than in philosophy, because despite the antagonism of our current disagreements, Western society is remarkably stable in the wake of its incremental adaptation to plurality.

Rawls seeks to build upon that negotiated reality with his theory, but one might wonder why citizens (particularly the majority of religious citizens in the U.S.) would give up freedoms they currently have in order to migrate to his system. The fact is that Rawls's "overlapping consensus" is not really overlapping because the sources of the ideas that make up the supposed consensus are important to those who hold them. Further, those sources certainly impact the way citizens view "constitutional essentials." The incommensurability of the abortion debate is a prime example, as demonstrated above. The comprehensive doctrines are never simply a potential source for shoring up constitutional and democratic values. They are intertwined with the political system in such a way as to be at least partially inseverable. The reason persons bring their comprehensive views to bear upon the political process is that they have integrity. They are undivided persons. They agree to be bound by democratic outcomes but not by a system which would bind their participation in the way Rawls proposes. Indeed, the truth is that were a Rawlsian party to manage to impose his views as a sort of "Robert's Rules of Order" for the republic, the resulting antagonism would likely represent a step back in the progress made to date. Taking the above analysis in consideration, it is fair to say Rawls's case does not break the teeth of Fish's complaint.

The foregoing analysis demonstrates that the oft-raised concern of "inaccessibility" of public arguments and assertions having some connection to religion is a chimera. There is no neutral view from nowhere, and thus we speak to each other from different Bergerian structures of plausibility. Worldviews—philosophical, religious, nonreligious, antireligious, gender-focused, race-centered, class-based, environmentally directed, Marxist, etc.—contend freely with one another in the public square. To single out one of those plausibility structures, the religious, and to treat it as uniquely inaccessible to those outside of that structure is to attempt to win a game by controlling the rule-making function. Robert George writes tellingly on this point when he notes that secularism has no more claim to neutrality than a starting pitcher of a baseball team who anoints himself umpire in the middle of the game and begins calling balls and strikes.[89] Much of what others propose to us is "inaccessible" in the sense that we simply cannot buy into it and would probably never do so. Inaccessibility, posed as a unique feature of religious argumentation and assertion, is a public relations stunt, not a reality.

11

Purpose-driven Secularism

George Marsden has written about the enormous gulf between the two dominant views of reality that contend for the American mind. The first begins from the notion that "there is a being great enough to produce and to oversee the universe," whereas its opposite declares "things operate sheerly through impersonal forces." If one takes the first point of view, that which includes a creator/maker "of immense intelligence, power, and concern for us," then "every other fact or belief will have some relationship to that being."[1] To attempt to ignore this theo-political difference and many others through an emphasis on secular liberalism essentially results in victory for a naturalist worldview by ruling competitors out of court. Anti-foundationalists see it. Catholics see it. Evangelicals see it.

That victory works to the advantage of certain parties in various aspects of political and cultural life. In his celebrated book *The Naked Public Square*, Richard John Neuhaus observed that the American people are largely religious, broadly Christian, and resentful of the movement toward secularism. It was a change in public life about which they were not consulted, and it rankled them. Secularism seemed to have been imposed upon the society in which they live.[2] The question is, did the movement toward public secularism occur in an organic way as has typically been portrayed by the theory of secularization or was it the result of human interest and human agency? Christian Smith affirms the latter state of affairs. If he is correct, then the critique of secularism as the basis for the American public order gains increased salience.

Secularists and Their Revolution

Christian Smith, a rising star in the field of sociology of religion, has set out to study secularism and secularists critically, in the same way scholars have typically studied religion. That means not taking things at face value but instead examining human motives, agendas, and actions. He notes that secularization theorists have sometimes paid attention to how Christians were responsible for causation of secularization, as with the Reformation, but have failed to look toward irreligious or nonreligious actors with a secularizing agenda.[3] What Smith has discovered gives fresh legs to Stanley Fish's discussion of the "partisan, interested guidance" of values.[4]

Smith's conclusion, with regard to the United States, at least, is that public secularism achieved dominance by agency rather than by some natural movement of history. Thus, the secularization of American institutions in the late-nineteenth and twentieth centuries was not a mere by-product of historical trends but was, rather, "the outcome of a struggle between contending groups with conflicting interests seeking to control social knowledge and institutions." Stated bluntly, the secularization of institutions in America was the result of an intentional revolution.[5]

The secularization of the public order was the result of an intentional program by secular activists. These activists "were largely skeptical, freethinking, agnostic, atheist, or theologically liberal" well-educated persons "located mainly in knowledge production occupations" and "generally espoused materialism, naturalism, positivism, and the privatization or extinction of religion."[6] This group successfully changed the dominant understandings of science, higher education, primary and secondary education, public philosophy, church-state doctrine, the model of personhood (from the soul to a psychologized self), and journalism.[7]

Part of the reason why we have failed to consider the advent of secularism in America as a purposeful revolution before is that the historians primarily responsible for narrating the story tended to encourage thought about the process as a "natural and inevitable" one.[8] Religion was presented as a reaction to ignorance about the world that prevented and restrained the development of scientific knowledge. The warfare model between science and religion was "one of the ideological moves of late nineteenth century activist secularizers."[9] Eventually, it became common for academics to assume religion would be crowded out of life by the rightful encroachment of the physical and social sciences. Christianity supposedly drifted into irrelevance in a world "ordered by conveyor belts, time-and-motion studies, and bureaucratic organizations." Rational thinking about rational processes blotted out any place for "the operation of the divine."[10]

Yet as late as 1892 the Supreme Court wrote in a unanimous decision that all through American life it is manifest "that this is a Christian nation."[11] Something changed radically. That something has been missing from accounts of secularization and includes "things like agency, interests, mobilization, alliances, resources, organizations, power, and strategy."[12]

"Activist secularizers" tended to represent either the "skeptical or revolutionary Enlightenment traditions" and thus carried a brief against religion based on witty irreverence of the Menckenesque mode or the Thomas Paine-style hope for a "new, rational world" obtained at the price of the destruction of the "old, traditional" one. In either case the influence was antireligious rather than driven by a desire for common ground and social peace and the hope was that science and reason would liberate a new society "from the myths and ignorance of traditional religions."[13]

What of liberal Protestant clergy and the charge that they were the real secularizers, and thus it was not anti-religion but liberal religion that caused secularization? Smith sees the liberal Protestants as mere responders to the activist secularizers and not leaders. They were trying, however unsuccessfully, to save religion through compromise and reform.[14] Liberalized religion was a reaction to secularization, not the root cause of it.

The secularist campaign was helped along by the rapid expansion of American higher education throughout the twentieth century. The result of the explosion of the academy in size and economic priority led to a "critical mass" of Americans "being exposed to . . . secular Enlightenment ideology."[15]

Smith's primary argument and that sustained by other contributors to *The Secular Revolution* is that American secularizers felt their prospects were limited by the Protestant establishment. In order to overcome that artificial limit, rather than pursue a merely "neutral public sphere" they sought "a reconstructed moral order which would increase their own group status, autonomy, authority, and eventually income."[16]

Protestants, to a "shocking" degree, failed to "step back, take stock of the intellectual threat, and formulate a more defensible rationale for its influence in public life."[17] Of course, in the critical period, Protestants had been rocked by the debate over slavery, the Civil War, revivalism, and the fundamentalist-modernist controversy.[18] They were also thoroughly divided on how to respond to secular modernism. In addition, Protestants were not able to seek help from available allies because of still-existing antagonisms with the most obvious ones, the Catholics. In fact, most Protestants saw an equal or greater threat from Rome than from secularism.[19]

The Protestant establishment had viewed illegal establishment of religion as government enforcement of sectarianism rather than as a common-denominator Protestantism that a large majority of Americans could affirm in some way. Activist secularizers turned the logic of sectarianism against the Protestant establishment and all other "religious views and practices." Thus, the formerly Protestant tool was employed to "expurgate religion per se from the public sphere." Ironically, the Protestant big-tent strategy of "superficial commonality" over "pluralistic particularity" rendered Protestantism politically vulnerable to the challenge of secular activism.[20]

In some cases, the agenda for secularization was blunt and obvious. In 1905 Henry Smith Pritchett administered a Carnegie grant of ten million dollars for professors' pensions. Pritchett was himself a secularizer with a personal "faith in science." Pritchett refused to include schools with religious ties in the program.[21] Within the first four years of the new Carnegie fund plan's existence, twenty colleges ended their relationships with sponsoring religious denominations. This result was the explicitly intended policy of the pension fund. Carnegie, Pritchett, and a board including major university presidents such as "Charles Eliot [Harvard], Nicholas Murray Butler of Columbia, Arthur T. Hadley of Yale, David Starr Jordan [Stanford], and Woodrow Wilson [Princeton]" approved the policy with the purpose of "standardizing American higher education" at least in part by secularizing it.[22]

Perhaps no other academic discipline demonstrated the existence of an agenda for secularization as well as that of sociology. Smith, a well-known sociologist of religion, characterizes his predecessors as "men who had personally rejected their own traditional religious faith, were antagonistic toward historical religion, viewed science as supplanting or subordinating religion, and intentionally sought to diminish the authority and influence of traditional religion in American social life." These influential groups of academics "were personally committed apostles of secularization."[23]

In furtherance of his case, Smith provides a useful summary of ten thematic claims regularly found in early sociological texts:

1) Science and religion are different ways of knowing, concerned with different orders of reality, but they are actually absolutely incompatible and antagonistic sources of knowledge. As part of his discussion of this first theme, Smith adds, "The two knowledge systems are perpetually engaged in a war that religion is always losing."

2) Sociology is an immature science, but it will surely deliver the knowledge necessary for social salvation.

3) Religion is concerned with the spiritual realm, which is beyond sociology's ability to examine, but all religions are finally reducible to naturalistic, material, and social causes, and are clearly false in their claims.

4) Modern religion has advanced well beyond primitive religion, but all religions are essentially identical in being based on the fear and ignorance of savages.

5) Religion remains intrinsically important to the mass of humanity, but religion's only real potential value is in instrumentally promoting social harmony.

6) Religion is in the business of promoting morality, but in actuality religion has been history's primary source of oppression, immorality, conflict, and error.

7) Religion has always been an important force in social life, but its influence and credibility in the modern world are for good reasons rapidly declining.

8) Religion has historically been engrossed in politics and public culture, but true religion in the modern world should confine its social role to the private life of individuals.

9) Sociology is indifferent to religious concerns per se, but the modern church must renounce the making of truth claims and

instead emphasize positive, subjective individual feeling and human idealism.

10) Religion is a well-meaning agent of social reform, but it is dangerous and irresponsible unless it submits itself to the knowledge and authority of the social sciences.[24]

It may be an understatement to say that a review of these sociological themes offers ample evidence of its practitioners bearing a powerful brief on behalf of secularism.

What Smith describes in sociology was true of the academy at large during its boom period in the twentieth century. George Marsden has described mainstream academia's evolution of a rule requiring acceptable practitioners to lay aside their religious faith. The problem with the rule is that that empiricism utterly fails "to unite people on the larger questions concerning society and human relationships." With regard to these larger questions, empirical science is incompetent to give authoritative answers and thus "academia is ruled largely by secular sects motivated by political interests."[25]

The bottom line of Smith's analysis, which is supported by George Marsden's distinguished study of the secularization of the academy, is that secularism triumphed in a "power struggle between contending groups with conflicting interests and ideologies." The result was that secular forces displaced culturally established Protestantism and gained control of "institutions governing the production of socially legitimate knowledge."[26]

The claim of secularism under attack in the previous chapter and here is that it promotes superior levels of social harmony to alternatives that might make more room for religion or might even be in some way based upon religion. If Christian Smith's portrayal of a secular revolution is correct, then the reality is that a group of determined elites executed a hostile takeover of sorts to control institutions that produce socially legitimate knowledge. Given that scenario, it is hard to see how a national community full of religious persons would necessarily find themselves in a more harmonious state. The early stalemate among religions in the immediate wake of secularization might seem refreshing, but it could also create resentment and a sense of unfair censorship over the nature of public and institutional expression and the types of education that have gained favor versus those that have lost favor. This is in fact what has happened. Secularism is what has caused conservative Catholics, Jews, Protestants, and some Muslims to join together in decrying the hostility toward religion in the public square. This protest indicates displeasure, discomfort, and a desire for something different.

The Under-acknowledged Secularist Demographic

The reality of the secularism movement is that after it deprivileged the Protestant establishment and evened the score between various religious competitors in the United States, it began to privilege itself. Rather than simply meaning that no religious group could control the public square and the reality-making institutions of the culture, secularism began to mean that only its point of view was valid, particularly in the realm of politics. The result is that a particular type of person, the secularist or the religious liberal with powerful sympathies toward secularism, is far more comfortable with his or her lot in the public culture than the religionist counterpart who thinks his or her faith is directly relevant to the content of political thought and action.[27] If this state of affairs is intellectually justified, then it may be for the better. The next chapter will address that point. For now, the question has to do with secularism and social harmony. The picture of one group having overthrown another for social power and influence looks less like a harmonious situation and more like the hopeful description of a victor trying to maintain control. "We're all satisfied, aren't we?"

Outside of the literature of various religionists, it has not been common to see much talk about secularists as a group with particular preferences about the social order. However, an awareness of secularists as a demographic reality has just begun to dawn. The work of political scientists Louis Bolce and Gerald De Maio is particularly helpful in understanding the place of secularists in American politics.

Consider, for instance, Joseph Lieberman's candidacy for vice-president as Al Gore's running mate. Although there was much talk in the media of Lieberman's potentially alienating conservative Christian voters because of his religious and racial status as a Jew, the real disapproval of Lieberman came from secularists who demanded and received significant changes in Lieberman's portfolio of positions on school choice and partial-birth abortion.[28] Lieberman's political situation in the Democratic Party demonstrated the power of secularists within the organization. Thus, Democrats have worked hard to keep secularists while not appearing too hostile toward religion.

It is fair to say that secularists play a role within the Democratic Party similar to that which evangelicals play within the Republican Party. One does not go too far by asserting that the Democratic Party needs the secularist vote.[29] This antireligious element comes through particularly clearly when one looks at the thermometer ratings Democratic convention delegates assigned to groups of people based on how warmly they felt about them. The delegates assigned fundamentalist Christians the lowest rating of all the groups tested, and, in fact, the lowest rating possible—a zero.[30] Antifundamentalism (anti-Christian fundamentalism, more specifically) is an organizing principle of the modern Democratic Party.

Considering these religious/antireligious dynamics at work in American politics, it is surprising that the media frequently covers the religious dynamic in the GOP but not the secularist one in the Democratic Party. There is a far larger religion gap than there is a gender gap, but only the latter has been extensively covered. Christian fundamentalism is frequently emphasized but secularism completely missed.[31] It was only in the 2006 election cycle that the "God gap" received significant attention and then it was to emphasize that religious voters were coming back to the Democratic Party. Coverage has lacked attention to secularists, focusing instead on the movement of religious voters.[32]

One explanation is that the media closely identify with secularist thought patterns and thus do not recognize those patterns as an outlook so much as just how normal people think. One study showed that eight out of ten in the elite media do not attend religious services of any kind. People for the American Way is regularly characterized by news outlets as a civil-liberties organization rather than as a secularist organization, despite the fact that their agenda is predictably the opposite of a group like Focus on the Family (James Dobson's evangelical organization). Portraying secularists as an ideologically distinct and aggressive political group would have major consequences for reporting and would legitimize the activity of religious traditionalists. Journalists are unlikely to treat secularists that way because of dislike of the political consequences. Media elites know that characterizing the Democrats as the secular party would not have favorable ramifications for the left with which they more closely identify. It may be for this reason that one never hears about how the Democrats "have shorn up their base among the unchurched, atheists, and agnostics."[33]

The point of reviewing Bolce and De Maio's findings is to underscore the theme already present. Secularism is not a neutral formulation that is uniquely disposed to make peace in the general society. It is a particular view of how religion and politics should interact (or not interact) and has the tendency to please one segment of the population while alienating others. How exactly such a state of affairs would constitute a recipe for social harmony is difficult to understand when considered in this light.

12

The Non-uniqueness of Theocratic Danger

It is not enough, in lodging a complaint against secularism, to demonstrate the inherent partisanship in its preference for the public thought and behavior of one group of citizens over the others. After all, it would make sense to embrace secularism despite its difficulties if it were uniquely protective against certain dangers. Secularism is often proposed as a desperately needed wall against the evil of theocracy, for example.

If the French Revolution did not establish the principle firmly enough, the "scientific" dictatorships of the twentieth century successfully proved that secular ideologies could also flagrantly violate human freedom in the service of bringing a bold, new world to pass. Instead of conformity to a particular religious vision, the allegiance required was to detailed ideologies.[1] The danger of secular totalitarianism appears to be as great as that of religious totalitarianism. Douglas Laycock once expressed his fear of being ruled by the Christian Coalition but then immediately added that he would be equally concerned by the domination of environmentalists or feminists. His point is that religion does not present a threat unique from that generated by any other organized human endeavor based on strong convictions.[2]

But forget totalitarianism. What about religion in a democracy? Is it true, as Robert Audi suggests, that the exercise of religious belief in the formation of public policy presents a unique harm to the unbeliever as he or she is forced to succumb to the coercion of the law?[3] Perhaps it is this less dramatic but still real threat that secularism will protect against. Audi's idea is easily challenged, however. The simple fact is that coercion never feels good. One need not be forced to live under Christian or Muslim values to feel severely put upon. Equally negative emotions may arise when socialists, feminists, or ethnic groups find channels for imposing their will.

In fact, it is easy to envisage situations where thoroughly secular public policy will do more psychic harm by coercing individuals than religiously inspired coercion might. Imagine the pacifist libertarian who is horrified by almost everything the United States government does, whether Democrats or Republicans rule, but is still compelled to fully participate financially. Contrast a mainstream secular citizen whose children have the option to sit passively while other children are led through a nonsectarian prayer at school. Given the comparison, one is hard-pressed to justify Audi's unique harm analysis. It is here that we see one of the main problems of Audi's scheme. He gives no consideration to the stakes involved. A publicly funded religious display (such as the Ten Commandments) is almost certain to create less resentful feelings than a decision to substantially raise taxes on gasoline. The essence of the problem is that law involves coercion and being coerced is unpleasant and possibly even tortuous. Whether that coercion is religious, philosophical, or even based on a radically different reading of the available facts, the harm is the harm is the harm. Secularism and secular rationales do not solve the problem. Coercion is the problem.

It is a problem that is not likely to become less troublesome, particularly in the interaction of religion and government. The lack of significant federal jurisprudence on the religion clauses prior to the middle of the twentieth century is no accident. As government has increased its grasp through a combination of technological competence and changing philosophical paradigms, the growth of the regulatory state and the sheer number of governmental functions guarantee that problems will arise. Again, this is not a complication that secularism solves.

Michael McConnell notes that the rise of the "welfare-regulatory state" dissolved the old paradigm in which religion and government had clearly demarcated functions in American life. Government had once been limited to "commerce and civil order" while churches focused on "charity and the inculcation of goodness and truth," but that changed when the state began to grow into areas of life that were previously "private and frequently religious." The natural result has been conflict with both "religious institutions" and "the religiously motivated activity of individuals."[4]

As the government's role expands, the territory for religion in public life goes through a corresponding contraction, almost of necessity per a strict separation view of the Establishment Clause. According to McConnell:

> When the state is the dominant influence in the culture, a "secular state" becomes equivalent to a secular culture. Religious influences are confined to those segments of society in which the government is not involved, which is to say that religion is confined to the margins of public life—to those areas not important enough to have received the helping or controlling hand of government.[5]

Thomas Berg identifies the same tendency of the secular state, writing that a government holding itself separate from "religious influences" is far more tolerable when the government's role is tightly limited. The same dynamic does not hold when the government significantly expands, as it has in the wake of the New Deal and the War on Poverty, into a nearly omnicompetent state.[6]

The problem comes to its clearest focus when we consider public education. McConnell sees public schools promoting "a new set of values no less sectarian than the old: environmentalism, safe sex, opposition to whatever is thought to be racism and sexism, sexual freedom, and a critical posture toward the role of the West in the oppression of the rest of the world."[7] His critique reaches a level of poignancy when he relates the frustration he feels with regard to the educational experience of his own children:

> One can still go through elementary and secondary school today and not be aware that religion has played—and still plays—a major role in history, philosophy, science, and the ordinary lives of millions of Americans. I sense the effect in my own elementary school-age children: they wonder how I can think God and Jesus Christ are so important to the workings of nature and history when they never hear about such things in school.

A secular school does not necessarily produce atheists, but it produces young adults who inevitably think of religion as extraneous to the real world of intellectual inquiry, if they think of religion at all.[8]

Here again, Thomas Berg draws a similar conclusion.[9] He sees that when government funds and operates a system of public schools that carefully separate church and state but "teach competing ideas ranging from secular moral theories to patriotism to evolution," the result is a strong bias in favor of secular viewpoints.[10] The charge rings more powerfully true when we consider that "financial pressure on families to choose low-cost public schools over a religiously informed education does work a powerful discrimination against (at least some) religious ideas and in favor of the secular teachings in the schools."[11]

Francis Canavan made many of the same points well before either McConnell or Berg. Before anyone really applied the insights of postmodernism to the church-state question, Canavan declared "secular monism" to be "increasingly out of date" for any welfare state hoping to maintain real pluralism. Keeping education and other social services strictly secular would fail dramatically at achieving neutrality between the available options. Rather, such a state could only avoid the problem of an expanding, crowding-out mechanism of secularism by permitting and encouraging "private, including religious, institutions of welfare to serve the public as effectively as state institutions do."[12] Such ideas have been entertained in the last decade, but not much acted upon. Faith-based charity regulation continues to be a contentious morass.

System versus Lifeworld

In the light of this problem of a secular state overgrowing other ways of life and other perspectives through inertial force reminiscent of the old "bracket-creep" problem of the federal tax code, religion is increasingly seen as a protector of what is sometimes termed the "lifeworld" (family, tradition, faith, ways of life) against the "system," which represents a combination of secular big-government bureaucracy and international capitalism. It took the Cold War and a century of brutal dictatorships around the world to reestablish the image of religion as a force for righteousness and the limitation of grasping government.

In his distinguished study of public religions and their role in a world characterized by modernity, José Casanova takes up the following questions:

1) Is there a legitimate religious resistance to secular worldviews that is more than a refusal to accept the consequences of the Enlightenment?

2) Is there a legitimate religious resistance to de-politicization, a resistance that is more than a clinging to inherited privileges?[13]

Casanova returns affirmative answers to both questions. Religion serves as "a protector of human rights and humanist values against the secular spheres and their absolute claims to internal functional autonomy."[14] Religion need not and should not allow itself to be secularized out of politics.

According to Casanova, the normative claim of modernity on religion is that it accepts rights of privacy and conscience. But religion does not run afoul of those prescriptions when it goes public to protect its own freedom and other modern rights and freedoms against an authoritarian state, when it questions and contests the freedom of various social spheres to operate utterly free of moral regulation, and when it protects "the traditional life-world" from encroachment by the state.[15]

In accord with this framework, Casanova sees an active counter-movement forming against the secularizing tendencies of the modern state. Religions are refusing to be privatized into social irrelevancy. For example, in many Latin American countries the Catholic Church has taken an active role as a champion of the people against the state. This turn of affairs is somewhat remarkable given the history of the region and the Catholic Church's traditional alliance with state power via establishmentarian arrangements. In like manner, American fundamentalist Christians have emerged from virtual social isolation to make a substantial impact on public affairs. Although it may be the case that the somewhat more "respectable" evangelicals and Catholics are now at the forefront, it was the former outsiders such as Falwell and Robertson who got the ball rolling with acts of almost gauche deprivatization that gave nightmares to secular social elites who in turn wrote prose suggesting new Inquisitions are around the corner. The fact that a man like John Ashcroft, who combines Ivy League education with real and open Pentecostal belief, could be appointed attorney general during a critical period in American history shows how correct Casanova is in his analysis of de-privatization. Despite these developments, the question remains as to whether deprivatization will halt or even reverse the established trend of the system growing into space once occupied by the lifeworld.

William Swatos extends the system and lifeworld framework specifically to the public school. Swatos views the public school as the system's representative encroaching upon the lifeworld, which has a strong organic claim to raise children in a way conducive to the parents' desires. The public school, as a system agent, develops the child in a way suitable to the wishes of the system with scant regard for the desires of the parent. Now, it continues to be the case that parents can remove their children from the public school system, but private schools are not beyond regulatory reach and the resort to them represents a double expenditure for those who are already paying taxes to support the public school. Into the situation steps the conservative Christian who contests many things about the public school with regard to the place of religion in ceremonies, whether children may voluntarily focus on religious themes in their assignments, whether children may bring a Bible, wear religious jewelry, and witness to their faith, and whether they should be exposed to curricula that are expressly at odds with the Christian faith such as the content of sex education courses. The conservative Christian becomes, intentionally or not, the champion of the lifeworld.

This is a development Swatos applauds because of his desire to see human diversity maintained against the system.[16] The verdict is that religion is a crucial bulwark in the protection of human rights, such as the right to raise one's children without excessive interference or overregulation. The tendency of secularism to push religion into private space works in like manner to knock over checks on institutions such as church and family that preserve a space for life outside a growing governmental apparatus that wrongly perceives secularism as necessarily freedom-enhancing.

Conclusion

Inherent in the nature of secularism as a basis for the social order is the idea that leaving religion and religiously influenced ideas out of the political process is the best way to broker harmony in pluralistic communities. By focusing on our common reason, the speculation goes, we will avoid the divisiveness of religion in public affairs. The sociological theory of secularization has walked hand-in-hand with the argument for secularism with the former being the engine that helped drive toward the latter. Today, the theory of secularization is in retreat and/or is being substantially reconceived in more modest form. The notion of secularism is being secularized (to use David Martin's phrase) by a postmodern analysis that skeptically questions the claim of secular liberalism to be a neutral broker for the polity's political process. This dual assault on secularization and secularism drops a giant question mark at the end of any aspirations toward a wholly secular public order.

The postmodern analysis damages anyone's ability to easily give credence to claims of neutrality. Instead, the hermeneutic of suspicion leads the inquirer to look for interested parties. Has secularization really been a naturally occurring process? Has it really been as dominant in the life of Americans (or other world peoples) as the theory would suggest? Is secularism really to the benefit of everyone without privileging anyone? The answers in this chapter undermine the façade of peace and neutrality. The theory of secularization has been overstated. The notion of secularism as a neutral basis for the public order has been sharply disputed, particularly when one throws in the variable of an expanding social-welfare state and public education. There are such things as secularizing agents with real intent to secularize and therefore shape institutions and the public order in their own image. Secularism is just another position on the theo-political spectrum, perhaps better than some options but not necessarily superior to others. It seems quite possible, for example, that political liberalism need not be secularist in nature.

13

The Department of God

A common argument presented in favor of secularism as a preserver of pluralistic harmony is that it prevents the strongest religion (in America, Christianity) from imposing its need for support and its doctrinal orthodoxies upon the nation at-large. The argument raises the question, is Christianity, particularly in America, likely to take advantage of current critiques and strong challenges to secularism by rebuilding religious establishments and refusing to honor religious liberty and rights of conscience?

Christian Self-interest and Lessons Learned

William Swatos and José Casanova both argue for the de-privatization of religion (versus the privatization envisioned by secularism) as a counter to the seemingly ever-expanding reach of government and corporatism. They condition that advocacy on religion's acceptance of basic human rights and freedom of conscience for all. At the same time, scholars like Stanley Fish and Francis Canavan argue that secular liberalism is ideologically bankrupt because it is unable to bear the weight of its own claim to neutrality. What to make of all this? If Swatos and Casanova are right in their positive assessment of religion's role in the social order, and Fish and Canavan are right in their crippling critiques of the purported neutrality of secularism, then the question is whether religion is willing to pay the necessary tribute to pluralism in order to supersede secularism in the public square. Notwithstanding Stanley Fish's go-ahead for obtaining power in the postmodern marketplace, Western Christians, at least, have every reason to find it in their self-interest (and in the interest of the church) to respect religious liberty. Placing a premium on religious freedom allows Christians to transcend the cramped confines of secular liberalism by solving the problem of pluralism without secularism.

Religion (specifically Christianity) can serve a useful purpose without ruling other voices out of court or forcing conformity. Christianity, for example, raises questions about the ability of spheres to function without moral constraint, forces debate about core convictions, and mobilizes people against pretensions of value-free analysis.[1] Given these facts, it is true that Christianity can have full social expression in the United States, including in politics, without any need to retire into the private lives of adherents. The case for secularism as a mechanism for achieving social harmony is crippled if Christianity can accept Casanova's bargain. That bargain is one the faith can easily accept and that actually fits quite well into the Christian church's hard-won self-understanding.

The church was born into a situation where it was merely one spiritual actor among a great mass of others. Despite the inauspicious beginnings, the church made great strides and grew to a large size. As Rodney Stark has observed, it was a mass social movement that prospered through simple persuasion and relationship-building. Before it ever gained the helping hand and the protection of the state, Christianity was vital and influential in the lives of people and their ethics.[2] For example, Christians placed a premium on protecting life (as with their efforts to save exposed infants) and made mercy into a virtue in a culture that tended to hold it in contempt.

Rodney Stark's work with regard to secularization, how it happens, and what works against its happening transmits critical lessons to Christians and the church. Stark has demonstrated that the age-old practice of the church's being established by the state is almost always extremely damaging to the religious group or tradition that embraces it.[3] In Christian theology, the church is not understood to run its priorities by the state on the way to accountability to God. The members of the church are to render obedience to the state short of impiety or perhaps injustice, but they are never to surrender the priorities of the church to state approval. That is Erastianism and it is a heresy. In the situation of state establishment, regardless of what the church tells itself, it has submitted to state supervision. Instead of having its priorities aligned toward the people it serves and the God to whom it answers, the church is naturally going to be concerned with satisfying the state. The foregoing is a simple economic analysis, and Adam Smith knew it[4] before either Rodney Stark or Anthony Gill. Theologically speaking, the established church renders to Caesar much more than Christ recommended when he said the money bearing Caesar's image belongs to Caesar in taxes. The established church is in real danger of violating the admonition against having two masters.[5] Christ's church was not born in thrall to the state.

Stark's work serves as an excellent politico-theological lesson to Christians who would rather return to the old model of maintaining a confessional state than to run an independent church. Though separation of church and state often seems like an insult to the believer who perceives it as exile, it is actually the greatest guarantee of further participation in the life of a society. The lessons of economic analysis that show the powerful effect of structural incentives do not mean that the church is a purely material entity. They do mean that the church and its members are not immune to the effects of sin and that Christ was inestimably wise to build a (seemingly weak) church apart from a political kingdom.

The Cautionary Tale of Sweden

The effect of establishment is invariably to sap the energy of the church, to reduce its impulse to evangelize, and to diminish its desire to give pastoral care to the people. The implication of this discovery for a democratic nation like the United States that has a strong religious concern among the citizenry is that establishment should be avoided and that the church should be wary of almost any entanglement with the state lest it be used, wrongly incentivized, and made ultimately irrelevant as other than a symbol and event marker. There is a darker implication here. Those who desire the active decline of religious influence might note that establishment is key. Marx supposedly said that American churches would resist decline because of their freedom from establishment.[6] He was prescient in that regard. The person who looks too far past this darker implication should consider the situation of the church in Sweden.

Besides the growing empirical certainty with which it appears government establishment is damaging to the vitality of the church,

Christians might reinforce their commitment to independence from government by considering the recent history of the Swedish national church, which shows that official alliances with power can lead to a debilitating existence for the church as little more than a captured lapdog of the government. In order to flesh out the point, I offer a brief summary of that national church's experience:

> Because liberals were their primary opponents during the nineteenth century, the Swedish national church allied itself with the traditional, hierarchical, agrarian society, which was being challenged by progressive egalitarianism. The Church's resistance engendered significant hostility from Social Democrats and Liberals who were gaining power. They criticized the clergy as overpaid, lying spokesmen for an unjust order.[7]

In some ways the clergy were a ripe target for the criticism of secular reformers. They enjoyed tremendous influence in their communities, supervised tax-exempt church property, had a steady income from the taxpayers' purses, and looked every bit the elite class. The Christian faith makes no obvious case for comfortable, state-supported clergy who end up looking like kept men. Sweden's clergy were collectors of government statistics such as births, deaths, marriages, and relocations.[8] Their bureaucratic status and government income did not serve them well in times of attack. The combination of perceived "soft living" while others faced economic uncertainty and an inability to creatively engage new political movements made the church look like a stagnant organization that was being left behind by the times.

At the beginning of the twentieth century, the church began to moderate its stance in accord with the rising fortunes of political liberals. Nathan Soderblom, appointed as the new archbishop in 1914, pushed the church to disavow allegiance to any particular economic or social order and to embrace greater political tolerance. The perception of the church's prior commitment to the old order had damaged its credibility with some segments of the population and led to its increasing marginalization.[9] Soderblom's action eased tensions with up-and-coming Social Democrat reformers and enabled the church to coexist peacefully with the type of secular-minded, welfarist governments that came to dominate Sweden.

One plank of the Social Democrats' platform was stillborn

through much of the twentieth century. The soon to be dominant party insisted on the disestablishment of the state church. Many of the party's leaders were professed atheists. Soderblom's re-characterization of the church as a nonpolitical entity seemed to pave the way for the church to exist as a folk church, one that all could participate in at some level regardless of adherence to doctrine. Social Democrats ended up having their children baptized and used the church for weddings, funerals, etc.[10] The long-ago mighty church settled into an existence as a harmless lapdog for the state's new managing elite.

With social values, education, and government moving strongly toward secularization, one agenda item remained on the list for Social Democrats. Despite calling for disestablishment over a period of decades, the Swedish people and the national church resisted the idea of formally severing the relationship between church, state, and king. Eventually, however, the logic of disestablishment became irresistible. The king no longer had any power. The church was a cultural eunuch. In the year 2000, after several rounds of reports and committee discussions, Sweden cut ties with its national church.[11]

The primary consequence of the new relationship has been that the Church of Sweden no longer receives tax money to support its activities. However, the Church of Sweden and other Swedish religious groups are able to collect membership fees through the tax system. Only official members will be expected to pay. The government will perform this service for a religious community that contributes to maintaining and strengthening the fundamental values upon which the society is based, is stable, and plays an active role in the community.[12]

One might immediately note that these two rules (particularly the first) could prove somewhat perilous to the religious liberty of any "religious community" that accepts the deal.

Employees of the Church of Sweden are no longer civil servants. The church is on its own with regard to maintaining an adequate number of dues-paying members to survive. Swedes are accustomed to high tax rates and are unlikely to see the membership fee, which they used to pay as a tax, as excessive. Whether or not the people attend the church or participate in its services regularly, they have an attachment to the ceremonial aspects of baptism, marriage, and burial. About 76 percent of Swedish children are still baptized into the church, 57 percent are confirmed, 62 percent marry in the church, and 90 percent of burials are performed through the church. Those high numbers are astonishing given the very low numbers (perhaps 2 to 4 percent) who actually attend.[13]

Although the Swedish Church has witnessed no mass exodus in the wake of its separation from the apparatus of the state, and the core membership remains intact, it is not clear at all that the church will survive the transition in the long term. Between 2000 and 2004, the church has lost 200,000 members, a loss which represents approximately a 1 percent reduction each year. Members pay about 1 percent of their income as a fee for belonging. If the trend continues over a decade, church financial officer Gunnar Nygren cautions that serious consequences will follow. About 80 percent of citizens are still members, but deaths are outpacing baptisms.[14]

Here we reach the insidious element in the story. In the midst of separation, the state has acted to keep a fairly short leash on the Church of Sweden. One strong objection to separation was that active church people would gain more influence on church affairs and make them "less open and democratic." Parish councils have not been and are not elected simply by churchgoing people. The political parties mobilize voters and ensure that church government is not controlled by worshipers within the church. Many parish council members attend church rarely, if at all. Some consider themselves atheists or agnostics. The effect is to create significant tension between believers and their fellow council members.[15]

The church is in the desperate situation of being largely controlled by the state and political parties and has been deprived of its financial guarantees and full official status. Arne Rasmusson points out:

> The new law is not neutral and has not made other churches equal to the CoS [Church of Sweden]. The law states that the CoS should be an evangelical Lutheran open "folk church" which covers the whole territory of Sweden, and which is episcopal and democratic. Under these terms, the government guarantees the future development of the CoS and retains the right to intervene if the CoS develops in an undesirable direction.[16]

The Church of Sweden's situation is essentially worse than ever. It had already been intimidated or beaten into submission by the Social

Democrats' political program and values. With separation, one might expect the church to go through the fire of losing government support and have a chance at regaining a distinctive voice, perhaps even becoming a challenger to the government as an articulator of values. What has happened instead is that the church is trapped in a rigged system where it can only lose. Because the government guarantees the church's "open and democratic" nature going into the future, it is prohibiting the church from assuming a new, more independent role (i.e., fearlessly preaching the Bible). A story in *Christianity Today* after the separation confirmed the existence of the problem. *CT* reported, "Theologically conservative seminary students in Sweden find the path to Lutheran ordination has insurmountable obstacles. Evangelical Lutheran pastors are all but locked out of senior positions in the Church of Sweden." The political parties continue to "hold the upper hand in church affairs." One pastor reported, "There is very little change."[17]

It appears the church will be forced to live or die as a pale mirror of dominant attitudes and mores. The state secularizers prefer a church under their control to a free one and are loathe to see it change. As long as the CoS is constrained to the role of a "folk church" that simply adds a religious aura to selected cultural events, it is destined for a meager existence. Some pastors have already drawn the obvious conclusion and have left the church. Anders Lindstrom, the former vicar of Munkedal and a fourth-generation Lutheran pastor, believes the modern period has left the church "unreservedly" handed over to the political parties. When he showed a pro-life video to teenagers at his church's youth meetings, he was attacked by the media and by the community's church politicians. Ultimately, he concluded the Church of Sweden can "no longer be called a Christian church" and resigned his pastorate.[18]

Other religious institutions, such as the Swedish free churches or Muslim mosques, are not equally constrained. However, it should be noted that if they accept the government's aid in collecting membership fees, they will have to accept the conditions of "maintaining and strengthening fundamental values"[19] mentioned above. Thus, the door is opened for them to lose their voices, as well.

Even if other Swedish churches eschew governmental help in collecting tithes or membership fees from parishioners, there are significant threats to their independence by the state. In 2002, the Swedish parliament approved a law criminalizing hate speech against homosexuals. Although the bill targeted Nazi and racist hate campaigns, it also addressed church sermons. Penalties for breach of the law include imprisonment for up to two years. A Finnish Lutheran pastor who was also president of the Religious Liberties Commission of the World Evangelical Alliance criticized the bill, saying it would "place Sweden on a level with China" where the state can define what theology is permitted.[20]

A look at the history of Sweden's state church suggests that the church long ago ceased to be a church but, rather, became akin to something we might refer to as the state's Department of God. The vital, politically active, confrontational Reformation Church of Sweden has virtually nothing in common with the church of today. The old church engaged in disputations, preached before large congregations, confronted kings about the proper roles for church and state, even at the risk of lost status or perhaps lost life. The modern Church of Sweden, on the other hand, has long been a keeper of statistics, an official morgue, a body in which doctrine and personnel are carefully regulated by the government under the guise of maintaining some useless identity as a "folk church" that is "open and democratic." This is not a church as most Christians would recognize it. Nor is it a natural self-understanding for the church. The spiritual/ceremonial welfare of the people has been little more than a governmental function funded by taxpayers, virtually all of whom belong to the church but very few of whom actually care about the church or invest it with any authority.

With the advent of separation, policymakers have effectively spun the Department of God off into a governmental corporation like the U.S. Postal Service, which it will help in the collection of fees. Thus, the ideological goal of removing church from government is finally crossed off a long-kept list. Ordinarily, such a change might prove risky. Perhaps the newly separated Department of God would engage in self-examination. Possibly, the minuscule portion of people actually involved in the life of the church would reflect, reform, and engage their culture. *Sweden's policy elite anticipated that possibility and moved to formally prevent it.* As has been demonstrated, the new "freedom" comes with precious little actual liberty. The church has all the burden of maintaining its members' allegiance with none of the guaranteed income and no ability to embrace a new (or older) self-understanding and/or a contending role with the state. Sweden's church is unable to choose its own course or its own leadership. It can only lose. Either it will serve with an identity that pleases the state or it will fade into oblivion.

The putatively Lutheran nation of Sweden should consult Luther in order to move toward a better reconciliation of the two kingdoms of church and state. Luther railed against churches that wished to brandish the secular sword and princes who would rule over souls by attempting to set church doctrine. Each kingdom should hew to its core competency. The Swedish government should continue to seek after a just and efficient economy. It should set a foreign policy. It should protect citizens by providing a police force. However, it has no special skill in theology or warrant to practice it. The notion of controlling the church by the election of atheists and agnostics to parish councils in order to maintain an "open and democratic" church is a smokescreen for the same sin many kings of old wished to commit. They wanted to control the church to keep it from challenging and critiquing them and their policies. That is what is happening today in Sweden and the fact that it is being exercised on behalf of an enlightened socialist state makes it no less offensive to God or the church than if it were being done by a ruthless monarch.

Secularizing reformers of the left do not bear all the blame in this unfortunate situation. The Church of Sweden allowed itself to be domesticated by state support. When the state began to breach reasonable limits, such as placing atheists and agnostics in positions of church influence, faithful clergy and members of the national church should have left the state-sponsored entity en masse. Some clergy have taken the hard step of exiting the only church they ever knew. Other clergy should follow, as should the believing laity. They will have to give up the largely empty but grand historic buildings in which they have been accustomed to worshiping. One imagines, however, that the carpenter they follow would happily welcome them in humbler confines. Faithfulness is more important than spires and stained glass. That much is surely clear from the founding documents of the faith.

What Christian can read the story of Sweden and wish to see their church's fortunes tied to the largesse of the state? The experience of history shows convincingly that establishment has been bad for the church. The longtime knock on establishment was that it involved the church unsavorily in politics, not to speak for justice but rather to work its own worldly advantage and to forcibly institute religious conformity at the point of the sword. Rodney Stark's work and the example of Sweden show that even if the established church gets beyond those problems, it may end up worthless, irrelevant, and in the service of a temporal master in the form of the state. The record is clear. Sincere Christians should choose something better than state sponsorship for their churches.

Separation of Church and State versus Secularism

What the lesson of Sweden (and many other state-established churches) shows us is that the separation of church and state is a good and necessary thing. When the church is provided for by the state, it becomes concerned with pleasing the state and gains a second master. Though Christians often bemoan the separation of church and state and claim angrily that the separation of church and state is not in the Constitution, they are actually expressing their frustration with secularism as the preferred ideology of many elites in politics, media, and education. Christians should absolutely bring their faith to bear in the public square. They should reject the influence of secularism urging them to keep their faith private and not to argue for a Christian perspective in areas like politics and education. What they must not do is to repeat the mistake of mingling the church's future with that of the state. Temporal kingdoms have no eternal destiny. The church does.

14

The Legend of Warfare between
Science and Religion

Previous chapters demonstrated the non-neutral nature
of secularism and thus disputed its ability to fulfill its reputed function as the guarantor of social peace. Even if those chapters are fully
correct in their critique of secularism, there might be another reason
for choosing a secular social order. The advocates of a secular social
order in which citizens virtuously exchange secular rationales for all
public deliberations tend to see secularism as the method of organizing public life to be most closely aligned to a scientific outlook that
deals in facts and reality. If secularism is, in some organic way, the true
ally of science and reason, then we might do well to foster a secular
order despite some cost to citizens not so inclined. Thus, the question
faced in this chapter is whether secularism somehow follows from
science and hard reason and thus compels our assent. The truth, this
chapter aims to show, is that secularism does not follow from science
and is not necessary for enjoying the fruits science offers to a society
gifted in its practice and outlook.

Presenting Warfare between Science and Religion

One of the key contentions of this book is that secularism has been
advanced by partisan agents seeking to remake the social order in
their own image. To use Peter Berger's language, advocates of secularism have sought to ensure that their structure of plausibility will
overcome the broadly religious plausibility structure that preceded
it. One of the key ways to change public opinion and commitment is

by the telling of stories. Postmodernists speak in terms of a contest of narratives. Secularists have employed a compelling narrative in their efforts to displace the religious influence in society. One of the forms that narrative takes is the legend of the war between science and religion. It was popularized in the late nineteenth century and is still often invoked today.[1]

John William Draper contrasted a "pagan party" concerned with obtaining knowledge "only by the laborious exercise of human observation and human reason," with a Christian church that held revelation sufficient for "all that he [God] intended us to know." This church made itself the depository and arbiter of knowledge and "became a stumbling block in the intellectual advancement of Europe for more than a thousand years."[2] Before I go on, I have to stop and marvel at Draper's interpretation of the facts. True science developed in Christian Europe and nowhere else, *yet we are to believe that the faith prevented its flourishing?* In *The Conflict between Religion and Science* Draper popularized a story about the history of the interaction between science and religion that would become dominant in Europe and the United States.[3] Draper's book was translated into "French, German, Italian, Spanish, Polish, Russian, Portuguese, and Serbian." His key theme was that a revelation from God is unchangeable and therefore is at odds with human knowledge, which is always expanding. Thus, science and religion are at war with one another.[4]

While Draper's presentation has proven popular and durable, it suffers the defect of carrying along with it a great deal of assumption and overstatement. Draper's book, for example, contains a detailed list of technological achievements such as telescopes, thermometers, batteries, photographs, and many more, all designed to highlight the value of science versus the value of, say, Catholicism. But the problem is that Draper failed to consider exactly why "anyone who invented a camera or possessed a barometer might be led to think his faith in the God of the Christians [is] shaky."[5] The one simply does not naturally follow from the other. It is not as if the Bible issues some command of Luddite-ism.

Andrew Dickson White published his own blockbuster history on the subject, which is still in print. White's thesis looked impressive with its numerous sources and endorsements by strong scholars, but it was actually a serious distortion of history, perhaps affected by his own experience at Cornell.[6] Together with Draper's, White's case against Christianity boiled down to two primary complaints. First, it charged that Christians devalued the investigation of nature because the kingdom was ever nigh. Second, scientists and their predecessors gained knowledge "through patient observation and reasoning" despite the miserable oppression of churchmen who forced real truth to submit to "puerile opinions . . . extracted from sacred writings." Per White and Draper, a tyranny of ignorance and superstition thus reigned over true science struggling to offer the world real redemption.[7]

White, in particular, successfully created an enduring roll call of shame designed to bring Christianity into disrepute for its supposed bullheadedness and real animosity toward science. Historians David Lindberg and Ronald Numbers have addressed some of the most infamous examples:

1) Counter to White's charge, Christian thinkers did not attempt to construct their worldviews purely from Scripture. The idea is "ludicrous."

2) White's presentation of Christians holding tight to the flat earth idea was also untrue. Christian scholars in the middle ages understood the correct shape of the earth and its approximate circumference.

3) Copernicus did not suffer persecution for his promulgation of heliocentrism in the sixteenth century. He was encouraged in his work by various churchmen.

4) Galileo got in trouble "not from clear scientific evidence running afoul of biblical claims to the contrary (as White tells the story), but from ambiguous scientific evidence provoking an intramural dispute within Catholicism over the proper principles of scriptural interpretation—a dispute won by the conservatives at Galileo's expense." What happened with Galileo was not the war between Christianity and science, but a dispute among Christians who "all acknowledged biblical authority." Galileo offered a form of biblical interpretation in addition to his scientific theory, and that is where the trouble began. He was in conflict with the Council of Trent, but the doctrine he propounded has predecessors in the church, too.

5) White showed Christians fiercely resisting Laplace's nebular hypothesis only to back down and harmonize after the theory was

proven respectable. In reality, the theory was rapidly embraced and harmonized by distinguished American scientists James Dwight Dana and Arnold Guyot.

6) Finally, White was also guilty of ill-treatment of the early critics of Darwin. He repeats the famous untruths about the learned clergyman Samuel Wilberforce's encounter with the famed "Darwin's bulldog," Thomas Huxley. Though often presented as having argued in bad faith with Huxley, the truth is that Wilberforce objected to the science, not the religion, and professed willingness to accept the theory if better demonstrated. Contemporary records indicate Wilberforce actually had the edge on Huxley in the encounter, gaining the support even of "eminent naturalists." White was blind to the fact that critics of Darwin could have scientific reasons and supporters could have theological reasons. Thus, he psychologized the objections of Louis Agassiz and William Dawson rather than dealing with them in good faith.[8]

Looking back on the popularization of the warfare thesis by Draper and White and their subsequent progeny, Lindberg and Numbers conclude:

> For more than a century historians of Christianity and science have wasted their time and dissipated their energies attempting to identify villains and victims, often with polemic or apologetic intent, and always within a framework heavily laden with values.[9]

The relationship between the two has been anything but simple, especially when one considers the individuals themselves and the outlook of the particular period rather than our own. For example, commentators tend to assume the objection of various medieval personages to the changed position of the earth in the cosmos suggested by Copernicus and Galileo was due to "a dethroning of the human race," which was "no longer the special darling of God's creation." Contemporaries of the two scientists, however, actually saw elevation of the earth, not a diminishment of it, as the key point. In the Aristotelian cosmic economy, the flawed earth now flew among the "incorruptible heavens." While the work of Newton and Kepler was seen by *philosophes* of the French Enlightenment as a displacement of God from a "clockwork universe," neither Kepler nor Newton felt that way. Kepler even experienced a form of religious rapture at the thought of the harmony of the heavenly bodies as they sped through space. Newton, we know today, was a great student of Bible prophecy and saw God in the system of celestial mechanics. Although polemicists act as if science has always damaged the prospects of religion, there are counterexamples. Louis Pasteur's successful rejection of spontaneous generation allowed him to "launch a public attack on materialism and atheism." [10]

The Success of a Legend

What happened in the matter of science and religion was the creation of a legend. Upon labeling the two antagonists, their "antipathy" could be read back through history with certain events available to punctuate what was assumed to be a continuous battle.[11] The effect is similar to the one Marsden, Noll, and Hatch observed among Christians wanting to turn the American founding into the founding of Christian America.[12] History is thoroughly susceptible to being read through the lens of agenda. There are two major interpretive paradigms traditionally applied to the relationship between science and religion. One views the two through the lens of conflict. The other looks for harmony. The consensus among historians of science is that both are oversimplifications. In reality, there are a wide variety of possibilities for each encounter such as "separation, dialogue, integration, and subordination." As far as how the two influence each other, the dispassionate analyst should consider "presupposition, sanction, motive, prescription," and other modes. Even when conflict is appropriate, the competition could be peaceful in nature. [13]

The Galileo affair has frequently been recycled to underline the validity of the warfare thesis, but it has been too hastily judged to be one of simple conflict between science and religion. In point of fact, Galileo had many allies among churchmen and many detractors among scientists. Members of the Catholic hierarchy played complex roles in the affair. A fair way to characterize the situation would be to say that there were splits both within the camp of science and the camp of religion with regard to Galileo and his work. The real conflict was between "a conservative attitude and a progressive attitude."[14] Interpreting the Galileo controversy in the light of any simple assumptions about either conflict or harmony between science and religion is an untenable project. What the Galileo story may really be about, in the end, is the "origin, diffusion, and development of cultural myths."[15]

Though the Draper/White warfare model has receded significantly among historians of science, and scholarly opinion has become significantly more subtle, popular opinion continues to labor under the broad brush of warfare.[16] The warfare legend has been assisted by the normal workings of the mass media, which tends to eschew complexity for Manichean views. Rather than attempt to understand the history, it is enough to know that there are scientists who say the earth is millions of years old and that there are certain preachers who will say with certainty that it is no older than 10,000 years.[17] Pop history is a lot like gossip. If you don't like the person or people, you believe it. If you do, you dig a little deeper before drawing conclusions. Until content-providers decide to question conventional wisdom, the impression is frozen under glass to be thawed as an evergreen story whenever *Time* or *Newsweek* needs a cover for a slow news cycle.

Religion occupies a vulnerable position in the press. People are very generally for it when "considered vaguely," but statements or findings critical of religion are widely publicized. On the other hand, potential stories favorable to religion—not heartwarming features but items positive with regard to its credibility—are "little remarked." For example, Owen Chadwick observes that during the nineteenth century (surely the same is true today), "if a scholar said that all the gospels were forged in the fourth century, it got wide publicity; the refutation got little." A Catholic theologian making himself ridiculous by saying volcanoes affirmed Purgatory gained massive infamy and became a figure of fun. But when the iconic biologist Ernst Haeckel foolishly asserted the four Gospels had been chosen by the Council of Nicaea from "a heap of apocryphal and forged documents" his error received very little notice, despite the fact that the two silly assertions occurred at the same time and that they were "equally absurd academically." Haeckel had gotten his information from "an exceptionally discreditable English pamphlet" and declared it to be "the work of a learned and acute theologian."[18]

Academic scientists tend to lose their standards when they become "evangelists" for science against religion. Haeckel, for example, was an outstanding practitioner of science, but "careless" and even "scurrilous" as an anti-Christian crusader. Reading Chadwick's critique, one can see the same sort of thing going on today when Richard Dawkins, the evolutionary biologist, and Sam Harris, the neuro-science graduate student and professional atheist, take to analyzing religion.[19] Because of the slanted nature of the social perception of the conflict, however, Haeckel did not pay nearly the price his Catholic contemporary did because of the enormous esteem the public has for scientists, even when they speak as very bad historians, philosophers, or theologians.[20]

The "battle" between science and religion, is and has been a large part of how advocates of scientific idealism gain interest from the larger public. Far more people are interested in religion than physics or chemistry. To join the two is to get attention.[21] This publicity ploy is particularly important for scientific ideologists who resent the idea of science as something that merely serves the community by producing innovation. It should instead, they believe, order society and somehow serve as its basis.

In order to get a better handle on the notion of warfare between science and religion, the next few sections will attempt to present a picture of the real relationship between science and religion in three periods: the rise of the Christian church, medieval times, and the Victorian era. The picture that emerges is significantly more complex than mere warfare, and unsurprisingly, includes nearly as much color and detail from human interaction as it does from the interaction of ideas.

Science and the Early Church

The advocate of the warfare thesis might look at Tertullian's famous question as to what Athens has to do with Jerusalem and consider the case closed. Reason versus revelation. No compatibility. The reality, of course, requires a bit more digging.

Though there was a diversity of opinions among early Christians about the usefulness of classical learning, the most influential figure was Augustine. He has been misrepresented as a voice in favor of substituting faith for reason. Augustine clearly believed in the value of reason and employed it extensively throughout his work. Maybe the best refutation of those (such as White) who cast him as a hater of the human rational capacity is his simple exclamation, "Heaven forbid that God should hate in us that by which he made us superior to the animals! Heaven forbid that we should believe in such a way as not to accept or seek reasons, since we could not even believe if we did not possess rational souls." For Augustine, faith was not the "taskmaster to which reason must submit" but, rather, was the spur to "genuine rational activity."[22]

When introducing the matter of what the church did or did not do to natural science, Lindberg delivers a highly reassuring statement up front. "The answer is not simple." Christianity bloomed in a pagan world that offered "a broad spectrum of attitudes toward the material world." Although critics charge that Christians despised nature and cared only for revelation-based knowledge, Lindberg places them in the center of a spectrum ranging from pagan cosmic religionists, who viewed the creation as perfect and worthy of study and contemplation, to Gnostics, who saw the material world as irredeemably evil. Of Christians generally, it is fair to say they neither worshiped nor repudiated nature. Lindberg invokes Augustine again to demonstrate. Although he can be heard expressing a lack of dismay over Christians' failing to gain knowledge about "the properties and the number of basic elements in nature," he can also be found deploring that a Christian should utter unreasonable nonsense on matters of which "one who is not a Christian has knowledge derived from the most certain reasoning or observation." This middle position was no accident. The instruction of revelation that the creation is "God's handiwork" virtually dictated such a position.[23] Augustine essentially insisted that Christians interpret Scripture in the light of what we know about the creation through disciplines like cosmology.[24]

The charge that the appearance of Christianity somehow led to a millennium-long depression of thought and delay of the march toward science is simply untrue. Ancient societies had few resources to shift toward the pre-scientific study of nature, particularly since it was "rarely seen as a socially useful activity."[25] Social conditions were not disposed toward a flurry of scientific activity. Thus, the accusation that the early church was somehow responsible for inhibiting the birth and growth of science seems motivated far more by polemical goals than by any real evidence. In short, studies of the problem tend to be proxies for religious preference.[26] That verdict, of course, is thoroughly in line with this book's assertion that the advocates of secularism are self-interested and partisan.

Science and Religion in the "Dark Ages"

Of course, the advocate of the warfare thesis might simply shift his case further forward in history and rely on the purported darkness of the medieval period to demonstrate the oppressiveness of the Christian faith toward scientific pursuits. Lindberg describes that point of view as having been "first developed by the humanists of the Renaissance, further articulated by the *philosophes* of the Enlightenment, and given canonical form by a variety of polemicists in the nineteenth century" as part of a project by European and American intellectuals to "establish and explain the superiority of their own cultures."[27] As with the early church, it is Lindberg's thesis that the "powerful old stereotype" of medieval science laboring against fierce oppression from the church needs to be replaced with "a cautious, defensible account of the relationship between the church . . . and the scientific enterprise." He arrives at the conclusion that the church in the Middle Ages was "the primary patron of scientific learning."[28]

If the medieval church is compared in its sponsorship of scientific pursuit to a modern government, then it will surely fail. The comparison is, however, an unfair one. The correct comparison is of the church to contemporaneous institutions. When that is done, comparing the church, say, to the crowns of Europe, then "it will become apparent the church was *the* major patron of scientific learning." Removing the church from the Middle Ages would not have had the impact of liberating science into a community structure supportive of its unselfish development. Take the church out of the equation and "there is an enormous amount of serious intellectual activity that would not have occurred."[29]

Though critics of the church's involvement with science might insist that science as the handmaiden of theology or anything else is not science at all, such a view is remarkably naïve. Scientific enterprises that are "simultaneously the recipient of social support and autonomous" are so rare as to be near creatures of myth. Science has progressed in regular partnership with a host of ideologies, military ventures, social programs, and pragmatic purposes. Lindberg's assessment as a historian of science is devastating to proponents of the warfare model: "The question throughout most of the history of Western science has not been *whether* science will function as handmaiden, but *which* mistress it will serve."[30]

Certainly it is true that science's being considered the handmaiden of theology led to medieval scholars thinking within the broad framework of a Christian cosmology, but the real limitations imposed by that framework were few. Technical subjects such as "mathematics, astronomy, optics, meteorology, medicine, and natural history" experienced essentially no restriction from the church. When new information arrived from the encounter with Arabic discoveries and their portion of the inheritance from the Greeks, medieval scholars easily applied it to their own work. Contrary to popular legend, "The medieval scholar could follow reason or inclination wherever it led and defend almost any position he wished."[31]

Conflict occurred, however, in what Lindberg characterizes as the "broader disciplines" like cosmology and metaphysics. It does not follow, though, that there was coercion of the type and frequency suggested by advocates of the warfare model. Cases produced to demonstrate the repression of science were often about different issues entirely. Some of the trouble Roger Bacon got into, for instance, had to do with theological matters rather than with any "scientific novelties." Yet Lindberg asserts that those who invoke Bacon, even serious scholars, "are extremely reluctant to relinquish one of their most potent illustrations." The reality is that although there were some theological limits set, there was no orthodoxy imposed on matters scientific or philosophical by the church.[32]

Just as Lindberg's assurance that the relationship between the early church and science was not a simple one to portray, so too are his statements about the question of whether Christianity had a positive or negative effect on science in the medieval period. He calls the question a "pernicious" one that invites observers to view the past in terms of "villains and victims" and to grade the period "on a scale of modern values" and with our assumptions about how science and religion should be ideally situated. But it is also problematic because to answer the question is to implicitly accept the warfare model as the way in which to view the issue. There was no monolithic Christianity facing some beleaguered avatar of science. What really occurred case by case between scholars and clergy who often wore both hats was *accommodation*. Warfare is a completely inappropriate model.[33]

Professionalizers of Science in the Victorian Era

The Victorian period in the nineteenth century certainly featured some conflict between science and religion, though it is difficult to view the champions of religion as the aggressors. In England, ideological warriors for science such as T. H. Huxley expressly urged "the authority of critical reason and empirical verification" specifically against belief in the Bible. Notably, Huxley was fond of referring to "extinguished theologians" lying like "strangled snakes" near the cradles of science. In this sense, the conflict thesis may have some real meat on its bones.

During the Victorian period, self-proclaimed spokesmen for science aggressively attacked the influence of religion in England and in the rest of Europe. In order to prosecute that attack more effectively, Huxley and others posited the ideal existence of science disembodied from earthly troubles against the all too human realities of religion. Thus, "good progressive science" bravely struggles forward with "evil retrogressive metaphysics" blocking and hindering. The problem with such a view, of course, is that it ignores the fact that science is practiced by human beings who do not always live up to scientific ideals just as religionists often fail to meet the standards of the faith. Competition, pride in one's own achievements, resistance to change, blindness toward evidence, selfish ambition, and a variety of false starts and failures all characterize the scientific quest in its less ideal manifestations.[34] It is fundamentally unfair to contrast scientific paradise with religious perdition.

The reason for the initiation of warfare surely had to do in part with the sense of opponents of religion, that they held the advantage with both geology and biology producing findings damaging to the cultural authority of Genesis. But the aggressive strategy of warfare had to do with desired outcomes too. The ideology-of-science group did not want to see harmony between science and religion. They wanted a fight that would end with religion on the outside. English research science, well into the nineteenth century, did not command a great deal of prestige, nor was it clearly professionalized. That tradition had been "amateurism, aristocratic patronage, miniscule government support, limited employment opportunities, and peripheral inclusion within the clerically dominated universities and secondary schools."[35] Science was not accorded a great deal of priority. Those young men wanted money to advance their livelihoods and career goals plus greater social respect. They realized they would have to establish "greater public appreciation for science."[36]

The strategy for professionalization and attainment of greater resources and priority was to take a naturalistic approach to science. The "young guard" of English science agreed with scientific positivism (the idea that we can only count on information derived from the five senses, and the material world is all there is), but it was also an effective way to isolate and marginalize the many clergy and other scientists who related their own scientific work to theological insights and beliefs. Such persons had to be removed from the process of evaluating work, arranging funds, and making appointments. Accordingly, the young men of science defined positivism as the only legitimate approach to doing scientific work and as the only way to know anything, really.[37] The success of the scientific revolution naturally implied that metaphysical concerns outside the laboratory were nothing more than useless speculation. One suspects the growth of social science took place at least in part as a way of filling the sudden void that opened up around the question, "How should we then live?"

Making science very specifically positivistic created friction between the scientific crusaders and two segments of the population with whom they desired conflict: "supporters of organized religion" who wanted to see religion continue to be a prime source of moral and social value and the clergymen and laypeople who pursued science in the service of larger goals such as praising God's creation or refining natural theology. These people had once easily fit into the loose arrangement of the scientific community and were now the object of a forced removal by delegitimation. Science and religion would no longer be complementary, not because religionists wanted it so but because professionalizing scientists were moving that way. It was not enough "to ridicule the intellectual problems of the clerical scientist." Rather, men like T. H. Huxley and Francis Galton felt they had to prove that no clergyman could function as a scientist, period.[38]

The Roman Catholic biologist St. George Jackson Mivart worked from the Augustinian approach to the deliverances of science with regard to the creation and proposed that evolution was compatible with orthodox theology. For his trouble, he earned "the most scathing review essay ever to come from Huxley's pen." Mivart wanted to talk about the relationship between the ideas of science and theology. Huxley wanted the two separate and opposed. A harmonious relationship between the two might have preserved the religious presence and influence in the sciences.[39]

Galton, in fact, published a study claiming to demonstrate the unfitness of clergymen for science. Moving them out of scientific positions and bringing members of the new set in was a clear goal. In order to make his data more compelling, Galton did something that may not shock the academic reader. He chose the parameters of his statistical inquiry in such a way as to provide maximum reinforcement to his thesis. Galton set out a definition of what a "man of science" would have attained and then held clergy up to it. Unsurprisingly, most of the hybrid scientist-clergy types compared unfavorably, thus apparently establishing Galton's point that science had to be professionalized.[40]

Other important factors intervened, as well. During the period Galton examined in the second half of the nineteenth century, two movements reduced the scientific activity of clergymen. On the scientific side, Galton and Huxley's group were actively marginalizing and isolating the amateur scientists. On the church side of the equation, the Oxford movement and associated forces were pushing for a stronger theological focus of the clergy and less involvement in "extra-ecclesiastical" affairs. Interestingly, the Christian activity level in England was bristling with energy as the Anglican church added many new parishes and clergy and evangelicals such as Charles Spurgeon, and Americans such as Ira Sankey and Dwight Moody gained time in the national spotlight. The synthetic effect of these developments was to achieve a "reorientation of the scientific community." [41]

The ideology-of-science group had ambitions beyond simply professionalizing science. Seeing the deliverances of religion as mere sentiment, they hoped to make science the guiding light of national life. This theme had the happy effect (in their eyes) of adding force to their argument that the sciences deserved a far greater share of financial resources and public influence than they had previously. By World War I the rift was complete. The amateur clergyman-scientist was a thing of the past, and professional scientists had firm control of the enterprise and a powerful influence throughout the educational system.[42] Soon, the big headlines in science and religion would be made on the other side of the Atlantic.

Darwin in America

When Clarence Darrow goaded William Jennings Bryan into taking the witness stand as a Bible expert (something he was not) in the famed Scopes "monkey" trial, he transformed a local dispute into one of the first major battles of the modern American culture war. With the proud populist politician and orator sitting before him, Darrow picked Bryan's faith apart just as surely as if he had pinned the old man down on a table for vivisection. He asked questions about how Jonah could have survived being swallowed by a whale. He wondered how the sun could ever have been made to stand still. He pushed Bryan to answer whether he believed the six days of creation were literal or metaphorical.[43] In so doing, Darrow highlighted the apparent difficulties involved in maintaining a literalist interpretation of the Hebrew Scriptures.

Bryan could not resist the challenge of taking on the great Clarence Darrow in defense of revealed religion, even if Darrow had all the advantages of an attorney cross-examining a hostile witness. Bryan defiantly announced, "They came to try revealed religion. I am here to defend it. They can ask me any question they please." With that statement, Bryan highlighted something no one ever seems to remember about his famous battle with Darrow: *the famed defense attorney never asked Bryan a single question about evolution.* He was the best trial lawyer of his time and knew better than to stray from the topics that served his purpose best. "We have the purpose of preventing bigots and ignoramuses from controlling the education of the United States," he said.[44] For that purpose, it was enough to make Bryan's religion look silly.

Had Darrow been on the stand instead of Bryan, the former secretary of state would have had a few questions of his own to ask about evolution. He had indicated as much when challenged by Darrow in the popular press earlier. Bryan declared, "Anyone can ask questions, but not every question can be answered. If I am to discuss creation with an atheist, it will be on the condition that we [both] ask questions. He may ask the first one if he wishes, but he shall not ask a second one until he answers my first."[45] Regrettably for Bryan, he broke his own rule and met Darrow on a battlefield distinctly not of his own choosing. It was an honorable but unwise decision. Thus, he had no opportunity to query Darrow about significant gaps in the evolution hypothesis and the many disagreements that exist among naturalists as they attempt to fill in details of the theory.

Accordingly, we have based much of our public discourse about evolution on a milestone clash between archetypes that had a great deal to say about literal interpretations of events in the Old Testament but nothing to say about the positive merits of evolution. America's popular culture has no memory of Darrow's presentation of expert witnesses extolling the explanatory power of Darwin's theory. Instead, we have celluloid moments of the film *Inherit the Wind* flashing across the screens of our minds. One imagines it is the film portrayal that members of federal courts recall when asked to adjudicate the treatment of evolution and alternatives to evolution in public schools.

Where are we now that several decades have passed since Bryan weathered Darrow's formidable storm in Dayton, Tennessee? Evolution is no longer a contender fighting to be taught alongside creationist accounts in public schools but has instead become the dominant scientific account of human origins. The public is scarcely any more settled about the matter than it was during Bryan and Darrow's time, but the scientific-educational establishment has confidently decided the issue for themselves and the nation's public schools.

The public has never strongly embraced evolution[46] and certainly has not accepted the theological conclusions of blind, purposeless, natural selection that tend to lead toward atheism. For that reason, almost any challenge to the now-dominant evolutionary paradigm has been able to garner significant support, particularly in Bible Belt states.[47] The early challenge of creation science has always suffered from its unquestionable link to the Genesis account. Aside from pointing out inconsistencies in Darwinian theory (which is a religiously neutral activity), creation scientists have depended heavily upon Noah's flood to explain their own account of human origins. Their positive narrative is thus indisputably religious, which leaves creation scientists locked in conflict with the Establishment Clause when they try to press their case in public schools.[48]

The creation science group is usually dismissed with great prejudice, but historian Mark Noll thinks their influence has been mixed in nature:

> Promoters of fundamentalist creation-science have been justifiably upset with the way that the academy and, in recent decades, many governmental agencies have transformed scientific speculation about the origins of the universe into quasi-religious conclusions about how everything works. Creation scientists have performed an excellent service by denying that vast cosmological claims about the self-sustaining, closed character of the universe can ever arise from scientific research itself. They are just as insightful when claiming that such grand conclusions are as much an act of faith as any other large-scale religious claim. Furthermore, their resentments are justified at the idea of paying to buy textbooks or support teachers who champion a supposedly neutral and up-to-date science as a better path to ultimate truth than the traditional religions. In a word, fundamentalist and evangelical resentment at how capital-s Science is practiced, funded, preached, and prescribed in our culture could not be more appropriate. It is quite otherwise with the fundamentalist practice of science. Fundamentalist social resentment may be well grounded, but not fundamentalist science.[49]

Though he thinks many of their broader objections are valid, Noll sees creation scientists seeking to prove their own account almost exclusively by exploiting weaknesses in current science and adverting to Scripture rather than by conducting natural investigations of their own.[50]

Avid advocates of evolution, particularly popularizers such as Richard Dawkins who carry a brief for atheism, practice their own brand of partisanship. They value evolution as an instrument for blunting the influence of religionists who hope to employ their faith in regulating public life. Evolution creates enough doubt about religious authority to justify liberalization of social mores. And there is little question that the advent of Darwinism has significantly improved the standing and number of atheists in society. Thus, evolution has its champions because it is the dominant explanation of human origins and also because it carries a vast social and religious significance.

For some citizens, the face-off between Clarence Darrow as the prophet of the Enlightenment and William Jennings Bryan as the withered apostle of a spent Christian faith stands as a holy moment in history. Jews have Mount Sinai. Christians have Calvary. Convinced secularists have Darrow brilliantly cross-examining Bryan in a court-house in Tennessee. In their version of the national myth, people of learning finally overcame the fearsome faithful through the triumph of cold, hard, liberating reason. Moments like that, properly inter-preted or not, are hard to let go. That's why evolution has always been much more than a scientific issue in America. Darwin's legacy is fully bound up in the broader American culture war between the enthusiasts of Promethean enlightenment and those who insist there is something else waiting for us behind curtain number three.

It is this automobile-bumper-sticker confrontation of the Jesus fish (the Ichthys) versus the walking Darwin fish that informs the standard treatment of science versus religion in America. This hack-neyed story is poorly informed by the history of science and ignores the depth and complexity of the relationship between science and reli-gion. It also ignores the broader problem of socially useful knowledge in the broader society. For many, it is enough to recommend a secu-laristic viewpoint to be able to show that highly literalistic accounts of certain portions of the Bible are possibly wrongly interpreted or wrong altogether. The point of the next chapter is to take this little war all the way down to the ground and make a careful examination of where we stand in the knowledge situation and what the conse-quences are.

15

The Knowledge Situation

We have a tendency to speak as though there is a segment of the population that lives according to a purely scientific ethos while there are others who cling to mysticism and reject the deliverances of science. In that shorthand, religion becomes the enemy of science, a jealous rival lashing out desperately at a superior that has bled the faith of its old influence and power. If this is one's frame of reference, then the influence of religion must be continually blunted and prevented from suppressing science.[1] Only by the victory of science might we be able to enjoy ever greater technological innovation, peace, prosperity, and superior rationality. The prejudice against religion that accompanies this worldview can blind its holder from perceiving that there are massive philosophical problems that arise from it.

Appreciating Science

The place to begin is with science. Scientific knowledge gained via the experimental method is surely the most desirable and most confidently relied-upon knowledge that we have. Even before science became the professionalized, standardized discipline that it is today, we were surely using the experimental method with regard to figuring out what worked or did not work with planting crops or determining whether a certain log lying across a creek would hold one's weight or finding out whether certain foods could be eaten without harm. Science in its more and less developed forms has always been important.

The standard perception is that we were once all savages who viewed ourselves as completely at the mercy of magical/supernatural forces, but that does not jibe with common sense or with what one finds when looking at anthropological findings. Primitive people of the last century employed magic and the supernatural as methods of explaining only the things they did not already understand. Where rational explanations were available, they used them.[2] So, I suggest, it likely was with our ancestors. Those workings of the natural world that could be explained by experiment and experience surely were so explained and relied upon. Those workings of the natural world that were beyond understanding were susceptible to explanation by other means such as the pleasure or displeasure of God, curses, and the presence or absence of good fortune. Resort to those other methods was not irrational in the context. At a minimum, those other methods reflected an attempt to understand and respond rather than to be idle. With regard to dealing with the exigencies of the natural world, the Christian religion, for example, might have been (and is) a rival to science in the sense that one could seek prayers for healing, well-being, or a good crop, but in another sense Christianity was not (and is not) really about material understanding or control of the natural world. The true rivals for science in terms of having similar goals (meaning control of the natural world) were things such as witchcraft and alchemy.

In our experience of the natural world, science is the proven best alternative for dealing with a difficult topic. After two or three centuries of incredible scientific advance, there are still innumerable mysteries to be solved. No one, this side of certain extreme types of environmentalists, wants to return to primitivism or leave behind the search for scientific information about the world. Science's claim to being the best discipline by which to engage the natural world is not seriously contested.

Despite the frequent "science versus religion" theme played out in pop culture, pop news, and occasionally in politics, there is little evidence to suggest religious persons resist it or bear any real animus toward science. Christianity, for example, is no reliable indicator of Luddite-ism or negative attitudes toward research. One seriously doubts that regular churchgoers are really any less likely to send e-mail on a Blackberry, have high-speed Internet at home, consult doctors regularly for treatment, count on meteorologists for weather reports, and eagerly follow the results of nutritional or medical studies. And while it is true that a surprisingly large number of Americans do not accept the neo-Darwinian synthesis as gospel, that resistance itself may be quite rational. After all, the story of evolution touches directly on the question of who we are and how we developed with or without God's guiding hand. Given the potential implications of evolution, particularly the purposeless, accidental brand pushed by certain members of the scientific intelligentsia, a certain degree of insistence to see the theory extraordinarily well proven could be seen as the better part of common wisdom.[3]

Limitations of Science

Leaving aside the unique quality of the evolution debate, it is easy to stipulate that science is appropriately appreciated and surely holds sway where it ought to hold sway, particularly in the West. There is little question of that. But as powerful as science is, it is simply incapable of providing substance to any worldview that would purport to offer political ends that the larger society should achieve beyond reinforcing its own value as a method of interacting with the natural world. What is love? What is justice? Is it better to help the poor or to reduce their numbers through the survival of the fittest? Is something like eugenics a reasonable approach to improving society? Should we encourage a society that integrates disabled citizens as much as possible or should we reduce their numbers through genetic screening and abortion? Should science be used to the benefit of all or only for those who can keep its secrets to themselves? Should men be free or should they be managed by the brightest for their own good? Presented with questions such as these, science is insensate. Some of us forget that or conveniently ignore it.

How could we fail to keep science's limits in mind? It helps to offer a short narrative. Our faith in science began its rapid ascent during the nineteenth century, when the scientific approach began to yield benefits sizeable enough for large chunks of the population to notice. Medicine began to emerge from its long period of feeling for markers in a darkened room. (Imagine, for a moment, the difference anesthesia has made in the world and how truly miraculous it must have seemed when first introduced.) Machines began to transform the economy. The natural world yielded more information and predictability than ever before. Perhaps most impressively, science challenged religion by intruding on territory that had been owned lock, stock, and barrel for a long, long time. Darwin proposed to explain the origin of man (and every other living creature) without necessary reference to a creator. In terms of concept and achievement, science began to form and dominate the modern mind. The explosion of science demanded space and deference.

The success of science spilled out all over the culture. In the twentieth century one could find no stronger support for one's ideas than to proclaim them scientific. Thus, we began to see the emergence of and a new emphasis upon "scientific management," "social sciences," "scientific socialism," and "scientific atheism." There was only one way to do anything, and it was the scientific. Science became almost like a much-desired consumer additive.

All of life would ideally yield before cold reason operating on a citizenry carefully controlled and directed. Experts and managers wielding great scientific knowledge about their disciplines would move the masses into a better, more rational world. This was bureaucratic expertise and authority operating scientifically. Max Weber thought the recession of religion would be matched by an opposite movement toward the rule of every discipline by effectiveness rather than by any extraneous considerations.[4] Because the Soviets began organizing their society along supposedly scientific lines in earnest, many in the West feared that a free society could never compete and would eventually be overwhelmed by the centrally planned scientific superiority of the New Men. One recalls Whittaker Chambers's grim personal forecast that by switching sides from Communist to American democracy he was joining the likely loser.[5]

Given the speed and the heat of the revolution, maybe we can understand why it took such a long time to realize that the plans of many to integrate science into every human endeavor were far too ambitious. Marxism, for example, was not nearly as scientific as it claimed to be and came fully equipped with its own end-time eschatology. The weakness of the Marxist system did not become clear until the boosterism of sympathetic Western intellectual elites gave way to stories about serious material scarcity and political repression in the Soviet bloc. Then the image went from Soviet supermen to that of burdened human beings living under a gray totalitarianism ruled by an iron fist.[6]

During the same period we began losing confidence in the social sciences. The image of dispassionate analysis eroded in the face of frank advocacy by some social scientists[7] and the obvious problem that those disciplines could not seal up human behavior in a labeled sterile baggie the way the hard scientists could their liquids, rocks, and gases. Besides, much of the early material contained a great deal of armchair theorizing that was mainly counted scientific because it was an alternative to religious accounts. Freud's children who secretly wished to kill their fathers and Durkheim's speculations about the primitive past serve as notable examples. Even economics, arguably the most rigorous and quantitative social science, exhibited little of the foundational agreement necessary for real science. Having economists who supported socialism and others who prescribed the free market was a bit like physicists arguing about whether gravity exists. Management as a science, too, began to look questionable as contradictory theories of work and organization appeared regularly, each claiming to have uncovered the secret of effectiveness unhindered by old bromides and customs.[8]

This widespread failure constituted the first great chastening of science. Science, it appeared, would not be able to provide the same degree of predictability and control in human affairs that it exercised in other domains. This setback partially explains postmodernism. Science in realms beyond the hard disciplines such as physics or chemistry proved to be much less neutral and objective than its public relations claimed. Skepticism and relativism were natural reactions.

The great chastening did not stop the scientific revolution; it just refocused it on more certain targets. Where the social sciences stumbled, the hard sciences such as physics, chemistry, astronomy, and biology continued their romp. Today, science can take account of almost everything we observe in the universe. It can tell us things we never knew about animals, plants, minerals, the sky, the clouds, stars, moons, and planets. It can gain godlike perspective on massive heavenly bodies and tiny microorganisms that have existed completely unknown for most of world history. It has enabled medicine to progress from a very dicey proposition that probably killed patients as often as it healed them to being so safe we expect millions of dollars in compensation when something goes wrong. Through an alliance with technology it has brought virtually all people into communication with one another. We can even, with some degree of certainty, predict the weather. Science has achieved the paradoxical task of making the world smaller while simultaneously expanding our horizons. There are some, having observed this impressive track record, who believe science will eventually bag even bigger game. Some think it will conquer death.[9] The technological messiah shall rise with the next dawn with nanobite angels following in its wake.

And yet the inability of science to make the human being yield his or her secrets like the table of the elements looms large in a scientific world. G. K. Chesterton once wrote, "One may understand the cosmos, but never the ego; the self is more distant than any star."[10] The first great chastening opens the door to a second. It is simply this: because science is unable to understand the strange uniqueness of the human personality, it proceeds blindly into discovery and subjugation without the benefit of real self-generated moral limits. When limits are proposed, they appear inexplicable when considered against a scientific worldview. Consider the television and film series *Star Trek*. Humankind lives in a highly rational space bureaucracy thriving on technological advancement and a scientific attitude. One rule is held above all others. It is the Prime Directive that requires that the advanced societies of the Starfleet Federation do not interfere with more primitive societies that have not reached certain civilizational benchmarks. Things get sticky rather quickly when one asks why such a rule should be observed. The answer given is that the lesser societies have a right to their natural development. But why is natural development so highly prized? Why not reach out and offer the benefits of advanced technology right away and save countless lives and relieve great suffering? Science lacks any criterion for resolving this question.

Science, Ethics, and Being Human

One of the silly things about scientific projects is their approach to ethics. Typically, a bank of individuals purportedly trained as experts in ethics are consulted about setting limits and doing the right thing.

Sometimes, various religionists will be added to the mix, but they are invariably of the sort who have already yielded to the modern age whatever authority they might have had. Besides, they know that if they make too much noise, they will be thrown off the ship. In the case of either toothless ethicists or religionists, the impact of their participation is unlikely to be significant. Why? Because ethics are dealt with as a tack-on enterprise. The entire idea is laughable to begin with. Physicists for theoretical constraints? Check. Engineers for design? Check. Mechanics for maintenance? Check. Ineffable art of being human? Right and wrong? Throw a mainline theologian or ethicist at it. They won't make trouble.

Science, as currently conceived, cannot come to terms with morality beyond basic utilitarian concerns. "Is there more benefit than cost (a notoriously inexact and biased calculation)? Is the political liability too great? Will we lose our funding? Is there a market for this product?" On the rare occasion when an ethics panel does challenge a scientific endeavor, as has been the case with Leon Kass's leadership of President George W. Bush's Bioethics Council (2001–2009) with regard to embryonic stem cell research, one hears the steady drumbeat that rank ideology is suppressing science.[11] Science suppressed in a scientific age? Unlikely, but if so, perhaps for good reason.

We have to pay attention to concerns raised about science because of its ability to subvert the art of being human. Discovering what can be done through the manipulation of the natural world is scientific, but actually doing those things is a human decision not delimited by the scientific method. Thus, we discover that we can split atoms, harvest cells from embryos, alter human brain chemistry, or implant foreign objects under human skin to create pleasing shapes. Yet, we still face a choice of whether to wipe out a major metropolitan area in a massive explosion, to kill a human at an early stage of maturity for one older and better formed, to control a child via a chemical switch rather than through the exertion of discipline, or to make large breasts and a pouting countenance our sexualized standard of beauty.[12] Science cannot make those choices. To suggest otherwise is to substitute mere ability for considered judgment. These choices therefore revert to the human soul or the conscience, which cannot be accounted for by science and has no place in a purely naturalistic understanding of the universe. Yet, the conscience exists and every person spends a lifetime struggling to make decisions with which they can make peace in their hearts.

Who Owns Science?

Here is the real knowledge situation. We have science to give us unparalleled understanding of the natural worlds. We can gather an astounding array of facts, methods, and theories. None of them can help us formulate political ends. The rest of it, the nonmaterial things that are unquestionably real in our experience as human beings in a material world, things like justice, love, morality, righteousness, charity, and mercy, all lie outside the ability of science to fill with meaning. Therefore, what I propose to the reader is that we stop simplistically contrasting science and faith or science and religion and refer more honestly to science and all other types of knowledge with varying levels of dependability.

A thoroughgoing positivist would look upon the situation I have described and would say there is empirically verifiable knowledge and the rest is mere sentiment. The problem, of course, as Francis Schaeffer and many others have pointed out, is that no one lives as though they really believe that.[13] Show me a positivist and I will show you someone who rages at being treated unfairly. We all believe in justice, fairness, love, and morality. There are differences to be sure, but they are not so great as to render them utterly unrecognizable to each other. For example, in an earlier chapter I quoted Stanley Fish regarding the chasm of understanding between versions of fairness with which he might identify and which others might embrace. Nevertheless, we know we are talking about fairness still, and not aliens or petting zoos or softball. Morality cannot be empirically verified. Justice cannot be proven to exist as other than something we like to prattle on about and demand for ourselves and/or others. But we all believe in justice. If adherence to a scientific worldview means that justice is nothing more than a sentiment, then a scientific worldview is not worth having. The truth is that there is no such thing as a scientific worldview. There is merely a variety of worldviews informed by science to lesser or greater degrees.

The secular Enlightenment worldview is clearly informed by

science, but it has no monopoly upon it. Certainly, we can produce lists of great scientists who were simultaneously devout Christians.[14] We can also produce survey evidence indicating that practitioners of hard sciences (far more so than their comrades in the social sciences) are really quite likely to believe in God and not merely the blind watchmaker.[15] The United States generates more scientific research and technological innovation than any other nation, yet it is one of the most religious societies on the planet. The goods (and potential evils) of science are available to anyone willing to make use of its power to investigate and control. That includes totalitarians and religious extremists. Witness the heavy emphasis on science by both the Nazis and Soviets. Also observe the coming of nuclear nation status to Iran, which appears to be soon. John Gray reminds us, "Scientific knowledge is used to further the goals people already have—however conflicting and destructive."[16]

So, though science is a highly effective tool for knowing things about the physical world and the creatures in it, it is unable to serve as some master decoder ring for ways of life or politics. Those who would present the case of scientific outlooks being oppressed and restrained by religious ones are working primarily from two motives. The first is that revealed by the earlier analysis of the history of science, particularly the section about the Victorian period. Unnecessarily engineering the estrangement of science from religion was a method of gaining social and financial priority. The second motive is to turn science into what postmodernists call a master narrative that trumps and controls the competition. By claiming science for themselves the secular Enlightenment group hopes to characterize their opposition as the enemies of real knowledge. Thus, opposition to something like embryonic stem cell research is cast as some kind of war on science rather than as a valid ethical concern. Because science, as discussed earlier, is unable to generate ethical constraints by its own nature, any attempt to set limits can conveniently be portrayed as unscientific. The success of that sort of story depends mightily upon a lack of critical insight from the intended audience. Because that audience already possesses the handy science versus religion template, it too easily accepts the argument as legitimate. They do not stop to ask how any limits on scientific endeavors that are viewed as legitimate are somehow independently justified outside of some extrascientific view of the world.

Science, Secularism, Politics

Consider two icons of the movement for a more scientific outlook in society. John Dewey wrote about the impact of Darwin on philosophy and insisted that taking a more scientific approach would rid us of the philosophical mistakes we make in consequence of our apprehension of design in the universe. Dewey could write about the chance ordering of life by nature and how we do not solve old questions—"we get over them."[17] But he very quickly followed that thought by insisting in the same volume upon the need to create a more just social order.[18] The reader finds himself breathless. What? We thought you said life has been ordered by chance. Then what is this thing called justice? And why should we care to attempt to bring it about in the industrial order?

One finds the same near neck-breaking turn in the kinds of things Richard Dawkins says. He is a dogmatic atheist and an evangelizer of the strongest possible antimetaphysical conclusions from Darwin's work. Does this turn him into a Nietzschean nihilist of some kind? No. Dawkins has very proudly proclaimed that though he is a "passionate Darwinian" in the academic sense and holds Darwinism as "the main ingredient" for understanding all of life and our existence, he is at the same time a "passionate anti-Darwinian when it comes to human social and political affairs."[19] So, the survival of the fittest and natural selection are the reality underneath our veneer of civilization, but we must actively think differently when it comes to ordering political life. Again, why? If Dawkins is right and blind nature is running the show, isn't that anti-Darwinian stuff in politics little more than cheap sentiment? Why not just follow nature and install a program for culling the weak and breeding stronger, smarter human beings? What exactly is wrong with being a passionate Darwinian in politics as well as in "the academic sense"? It is a question to which Dawkins should address himself. Carefully.

This implicit trouble in the statements offered by luminaries of the science/religion battle such as Dewey and Dawkins, in addition to the already obvious problems raised for any idea of a secular/scientific politics by the existence of the fact/value dichotomy, leads nicely toward a highly relevant example. The ultimate test for the claim of a scientific worldview by secularists rests upon the very great value they place upon equality (as do most of us). Scientifically speaking, it is extraordinarily difficult to argue for the equality of persons. One could certainly rank the individuals in a society based on empirical factors such as physical and mental abilities, potential, and real accomplishments. Political philosopher Louis Pojman notes that if we are to accept the empirical reality of people and their differences, there should be a presumption of inequality rather than the presumption of equality upon which so many political philosophers depend.[20] If we are equal, it is almost surely in the sense of being equal before God, *because we are in fact equal in virtually no other way.*

Pojman has critically examined the emphasis upon equality by political theorists who insist on avoiding metaphysics and present their ideas as secular. He begins the article by pointing out the natural weaknesses of the various secular Enlightenment takes on political egalitarianism. The key weakness is that they make a presumption in favor of equality without successfully grounding their theory. Current theories compare poorly to competing frameworks in favor of inequality that could be equally said to proceed quite reasonably with empirical reality on their side.[21] I fear that I am beating a dead horse when I suggest at this point that the congruency between prized secular thought and the deliverances of science is somewhat strained.

Pojman goes on to state what we know to be true, which is that the ideas we cherish about "equal worth" and "inalienable rights" are products of our religious heritage.[22] They simply cannot be justified by a naturalistic/empirical view of the world.[23] Secular egalitarians, then, "are free riders, living off an inheritance they view with disdain."[24] A divorce from comprehensive views leads to instrumental reason, which in turn is incapable of justifying the basic commitments of the American constitutional order.[25]

The standard trope is to counter Christian claims to having provided the basis for modern egalitarianism by adverting to classical culture or some other source. Pojman freely admits there are a variety of alternatives such as "Stoic panentheism which maintains that all humans have within them a part of God," Islamic and Hindu notions about human worth, and possibly "a Platonic system." The possibilities, Pojman writes, "are frighteningly innumerable," but the multiplicity of possible sources does not relieve the need of "some metaphysical explanation" to ground equal human rights. Even though there are problems with the religious systems in question, that still does not take away the problem secular rights systems face in justifying their own priority for equality.[26]

So-called secular approaches to political thought have gained an advantage over more obviously religious approaches for the simple fact of their lack of ties to religious specificity. The susceptibility to believing that they represent some more rational way is the heritage of the post-Reformation experience of religious pluralism, which featured massive disputes within and between polities over which form of religion would officially reign. For that reason, political thought models that have been seen as divorced from religion have been welcomed as liberators of the polity from the troubles of faith. Now that the secular has become the established mode and the religious has become the critical outsider, these modes of thought become obvious targets for the type of critique and demand for justification posed by postmodernism, and, for that matter, by this book. Secular thought is becoming a subject of study and critique just as religion has been, and the cracks in its foundations are becoming clearer all the time.[27]

If I am correct in dividing knowledge into two areas—the scientific, which we are largely bound to accept, and everything else, which encompasses a great deal of social real estate and is seriously contested—then there are clear implications for political thought. The first, and most important in my view, is that it becomes senseless to speak of the religious and the secular as two utterly different methods of reasoning, one which is private and mysterious and the other which is common and rational. For too long there has been tacit acceptance of the presentation of religion as irrational but perhaps emotionally satisfying, while the secular insists upon hardheaded truth. I think this chapter has demonstrated the incorrectness of that way of distinguishing the secular from the religious. For no reason other than to provoke a few sparking neurons I ask whether it is possible that there is more evidence for something such as the bodily resurrection of Christ than there is for a nonmetaphysical insistence upon human equality or even justice.

The second implication follows from the first. Secular liberals should cease demanding restraint from religious persons who reason from their religious convictions. Arguments that such persons should not offer religious arguments, or should offer religious arguments only in their own community while bringing secular arguments to the public square or should not even vote on a matter without an independent secular rationale, are unjustified. Political theorist Christopher Eberle has written a far more detailed and technical account of the epistemological issues invoked in this chapter. His conclusion is worth repeating here: religious convictions are neither more controversial nor "different in epistemically relevant aspects from some of the moral claims citizens will unavoidably employ in political decision making and advocacy."[28] In fact, what is often ignored in the discussion about accessibility is the simple fact that religious appeals are often more generalizable and universal than purely secular alternatives.

In this connection, I recall talking to a friend in graduate school who was enthusiastic about secularism. Knowing his appreciation of Martin Luther King Jr., I reminded him of King's "Letter from a Birmingham Jail." The letter explicitly appeals to religious sources such as Augustine who claimed that an unjust law is no law at all. My friend's reply was memorable: "King wouldn't have had to do that if he had had access to a higher Marxian critique, which he got later, by the way." I am not poking fun at my friend, but two things immediately occurred to me when he made that remark. First, does anyone think "a higher Marxian critique" would have moved America beyond segregation? It was King's appeal to the quality of persons as God's children, not "workers of the world unite," that succeeded in America. Second, King's appeal was religiously explicit, and it made his message anything but inaccessible. The fact that the majority of Americans are not alienated by religious talk should "count for something" in a democracy.[29]

Secular liberals have misconceived the entire knowledge situation. The practice of politics is far from an organic result of perfect critical rationality. It is in fact a hotbed of ideals, emotion, and stage management.[30] There is no way to formulate adequate political ends scientifically and thus there is no reason to cabin off religion from the political process. The contemporary academic and legal culture has too easily assumed that there are clear differences between concepts like secular, religious, religion, and morality.[31] There is no such thing as metaphysical neutrality for states. They affirm fundamental values with metaphysical foundations in doing and in not doing. A very great proportion of the large decisions made by the state are, to employ an inexact phrase, faith-based. Implicit faith claims deserve no hegemony over explicit ones. To fail to recognize that much is to threaten real pluralism without adequate reason to do so.[32]

Though the rank and file member of the conservative Christian community might not find just these words to describe the problem, the above is a fair explanation of much of the resentment behind the American culture war. There is a feeling that religious convictions are unfairly discounted in favor of other systems of morality without firmer grounding. The analysis offered in this chapter, I contend, is what Christians have been attempting to get at with their perpetual campaign against the "religion of secular humanism" in schools and government.

The best summation of the real knowledge situation and how it sits with reference to politics has been set forth by Robert George. Secularism finds itself in a conundrum, because if it draws the requirements of reason in too tightly, then it is unable to satisfy its own ideal of public reason, just as it suggests religious thought does not. At the same time, if secularism does not insist on essentially scientific, hard reason, then it leaves the door open to full engagement with religious worldviews, something which its attempts to segregate and privatize religion suggest that it is not eager to do. Christians, for example, react to this information in two different, compatible ways. The first is to concede the difficulty of grounding religious and moral claims in rationality but to point out that secularism has the same problem. Thus, the public square must essentially remain open to all comers, specifically religious or not. The second, and George's preferred tactic, is to affirm the demand for public reason and to appeal to "fully public reasons provided by principles of natural law and natural justice."[33]

This book has been far more concerned with the first strategy rather than the second, as it argues against secularism rather than for any particularistic Christian positions. If secularism cannot stand up to highly rationalistic requirements for participation in politics, then a version of public reason that leaves religion out of the picture has little value for deployment in the public square. On the other hand, if we expand our understanding of public reason in a manner that is realistic with regard to what secularism really can and cannot offer, then religious contestants, such as Robert George, have much to say that is potentially convincing.

Conclusion

Just as an earlier chapter sharply criticized the inherent claim of secularism to offer the culture's best chance at social harmony by removing consideration of God from the political calculus, the last two chapters attacked the presentation of secularism as the exemplar of rationality and the partner of science. Taken together, these chapters carefully make the case for considering the secular as the preference of a particular group with a particular worldview as opposed to a neutral and rational ground of deliberation for all parties. The displacement of religion has been a clear program for some groups and cannot be justified purely on the basis of what is rational or what is conducive to successful employment of science.

The history of science dispels the saliency of the discredited and simplistic warfare model directed toward marginalizing religion. A careful consideration of secularism and its interaction with the formulation of political ends demonstrates its reliance on extrascientific values not distinguishable rationally from those provided by certain religious sources, such as Christianity.

There is knowledge available to us via the exercise of science, and there is everything else. Political players both secular and religious interact in the realm of the "everything else." Privilege on the basis of rationality is much harder to justify than members of the secular camp seem to assume.

16

Secularists Sit One Out in the Bible Belt

I have spent several chapters explaining why secularism follows a certain logic as a reaction to the history of church and state in the West since the time of Christ and why that logic only goes so far before it begins to crack under its own weight. The case has been both historical and conceptual. Moving toward the conclusion, I'd like to tell a story that helps demonstrate the selectivity of public secularism. The theocracy alarm seems to ring (or not ring) in an unpredictable manner.

Alabama, Jesus, and the Tax Code

Susan Pace Hamill was once a New York tax attorney helping wealthy people figure out how to pay the least taxes possible. She moved south to become a law professor at the University of Alabama and after a time took a sabbatical to study at Samford University's Beeson Divinity School in Birmingham headed by Timothy George, an editor for *Christianity Today* and part of the editorial board at *First Things*, a conservative journal of religion and public life. It would be fair to call Beeson an evangelical institution with a centrist orientation. For her part, Hamill was and continues to be a mainline Methodist. When she embarked upon her course of study at the seminary, she intended to offer "a theological critique of the degree of deference the law gives to the decisions of corporate executives." Hamill hoped her critique would be suitable for the *Harvard Law Review* when she finished.[1]

Those familiar with this story know that Hamill chose a different subject for her thesis. As a transplanted Alabama resident, she had noticed the sales tax was quite high and property taxes were low. It seemed to her that her children's schoolteachers frequently asked for parental donations to cover expenses not provided for by the state and local budgets. All this percolated in the back of her mind until she saw a newspaper story reporting that Alabama taxed income at levels below the poverty line. As both a student in seminary and a law professor she began to think about the situation in terms of "biblical principles of justice." When she consulted with one of her professors, a New Testament scholar, the two concluded she had an "ironclad" case for a biblical attack on the Alabama tax code. With her professor's encouragement, Hamill left her theological exposé of the business judgment rule behind and decided to focus on the Alabama tax code from a biblical framework.[2]

Hamill produced a master's thesis on the tax code, which she then expanded into a long article for the *Alabama Law Review* titled "An Argument for Tax Reform Based on Judeo-Christian Ethics."[3] The article opened with a quotation of Jesus' found in the Gospel of Matthew: "Truly, I say to you, as you did it to one of the least of these my brothers, you did it to me" (25:40 NIV).[4] Very few law review articles have ever had the sheer political impact of Hamill's work, which resulted in a massive public struggle, a Reaganite governor risking everything to support Hamill's call for biblical justice, a schism between the national and state Christian Coalition organizations, and a statewide referendum.

Hamill's Argument

Professor Hamill spends the first several pages of her article detailing the way Alabama's tax code rests comparatively heavily upon poor citizens while leaving a relatively light touch upon more well-heeled citizens. She considers theories of taxation and what makes for a good tax system and why Alabama has long been out of line with what she considers to be best practices in taxation.[5]

But the real action in the article hits halfway through, where she begins to prophetically condemn the Alabama tax code through the use of Old and New Testament texts. Working through the Old Testament, for example, Professor Hamill explains how our creation in the image of God generates ethical responsibility for our fellow human beings and implicates us in sin against God when we fail to recognize that responsibility. She discusses God's special concern for the poor and vulnerable and his hatred of economic oppression of the poor. Hamill develops these points against a community backdrop in which oppressive economic circumstances were limited by provisions requiring the periodic release of servants, the regular forgiveness of debts, and the return of alienated land. Her analysis indicates that God sets up a system through which even the poor have "at least a minimum opportunity to improve their economic circumstances."[6] In addition, rulers (and government is at issue here) had the responsibility to maintain the general well-being of the entire community, which included the poor.[7]

Moving into the New Testament, Hamill affirms the continuing moral validity of the Old Testament while noting the Christian belief that much of the old law (particularly ceremonial law) has been abolished or set aside. From that beginning she moves to the person of Christ and his identification with "the least of these." To love Christ is to share with those in need, "especially those who cannot reciprocate." Trust in God means that sharing and giving are far more important than the stockpiling of wealth, which can indicate a lack of trust in the Lord's provision. Hamill points to these New Testament standards to once again support her brief against oppression through the tax system and the failure to adequately fund mechanisms (such as education) that could help provide a minimum opportunity for people to break free from cycles of poverty.[8]

Having made her case on the content of Jewish and Christian scriptures and citing a great deal of scholarly theological opinion, Hamill aims her guns at the politicians and religious leaders of the state of Alabama. Politicians are ethically bound by God to break unjust tax structures and provide good government. Priests and preachers must demand justice even from the high and mighty who may not approve. They must also educate the community about injustices in the tax system and encourage them to work for reform. Of the two groups, clergy and politicians, Hamill places the greater burden at the feet of the clergy. If they fail to accept their God-given responsibility out of self-protectiveness or greed, they have abused their call to proclaim God's Word.[9]

Hamill tops the argument off with a variety of statistics, not the least of which is a discussion of Alabama's spiritual demographics. What is unusual about her analysis is not the review of tax and budget numbers but rather her observation that over 90 percent of Alabamians practice Christianity and thus should find her call to reform the tax system compelling. Therefore, she concludes, the movement must begin with churches, synagogues, and other religious organizations demanding "that the old way end." She ends the essay (in the law review of a state university, no less) with a prayer in which she asks personal forgiveness for her blindness toward injustice and that God would touch the hearts of her fellow citizens and the leaders of the state.[10] The prayer of this mainline Protestant law professor was answered in fascinating ways, even though ultimate success remained elusive.

The Governor, the Churches, and the Christian Coalition

Hamill's plea gained instant relevance when Alabama's new governor, Bob Riley, took up her challenge as though she had pierced his heart with the gospel. Though Riley made his reputation as a Reaganite tax-cutter and small-government conservative, he made a massive tax overhaul the centerpiece of his policy. The changes would not merely seek to raise money for balancing budgets; rather, the new tax system would redirect the burden of taxation from the poor to more wealthy citizens and business interests. The state's education system was to be a prime beneficiary of the new funds.[11]

Riley gave Hamill full credit for his decision to pursue tax reform. He explained that he was convinced of the need to take care of the poor and that Alabama's tax code placed the largest burden on that very group. In making the appeal, Riley was never shy about invoking the imperative of following Christ. The Southern Baptist Riley campaigned across the state for the new tax plan, highlighting the immorality of charging an income tax to people making less than five thousand dollars a year. All this was quite a turn for a man who never once voted for a tax increase during his time as a U. S. congressman.[12]

Hamill's Beeson Divinity School supported her and Riley to the hilt. They helped by printing and distributing over ten thousand copies of a shortened version of her argument to churches around the state.[13] The state's churches supported the plan too. Alabama's

Baptist Convention, the United Methodist Church, the Presbyterian Church (USA), and others gave their official approval to Riley's reform.[14] Perhaps surprisingly, perhaps not, the Alabama chapter of the Christian Coalition came out strong against the Riley-Hamill tax proposal. The national Christian Coalition and its African-American female head complicated things by jumping in on Riley's side.[15] The fight over the tax plan ultimately created a schism between the national Christian Coalition and some of its state chapters.[16]

Aftermath

Despite Riley's full-bore campaign to reform the Alabama tax system and Hamill's blossoming celebrity, the constitutional initiative went down to massive defeat at the polls.[17] The state's African-American population simply did not trust the proposed tax increase headed by a rich, white Republican governor even though it redounded largely to their benefit. White Christians in the state did not cohere in a single voting block, which is unsurprising given the mixed message conveyed by the infighting Christian Coalition.[18] Hamill's mustard seed of faith seemed likely to move a mountain but fell short in the end. Alabama ended up solving its budgetary crisis without raising taxes, but it also continues to expect the poor to pay too large a share of the overall tax burden.

Application

There are several lessons to be learned from this episode. The State of Alabama hosted an emotionally charged campaign to change its tax system in which the primary appeal was to voters' religious sentiments. Voters were asked to care for the poor by reforming the tax system to lighten the burden of those less well-off and to provide more funds for education. Hamill appealed primarily to Jewish and Christian scriptures. Riley followed her lead. Both took their message statewide. A seminary and large religious organizations got directly involved in supporting the measure. Pastors preached about it. In short, Alabama was the scene of a tremendous amount of linked religious and political advocacy and action during the time of the campaign.

My research uncovered forty-five news articles, features, interviews, and opinion pieces about the Hamill-Riley tax reform.[19]

It might surprise readers to discover that there were virtually no complaints about forbidden church and state interaction. No legal or academic commentators leaped into the fray to speak of the need for independent secular rationales or for public appeals to be secular appeals. Fears of theocracy simply never played a significant role in the public debate. The ACLU, People for the American Way, and Americans United for the Separation of Church and State steered clear. The governor of the state of Alabama, guided by a professor at the state's largest law school, worked to redistribute several billion dollars from one group of persons to another because of the moral imperative they saw in Jewish and Christian holy writings. The guardians of secularism did not make enough noise to interrupt the song of cicadas in the warm Alabama nights.

Intuition check: does anyone think that this story would have been treated similarly by the press and church-state watchdogs if it had involved an equally religious program aimed at hampering the proclaimed injustice of abortion? We know it would have been treated differently. The charge of theocracy would be loud and frequent. Accusations would fly. Turn the facts around again and the crusade is aimed at establishing greater civil rights for illegal immigrants working for low wages in an underground economy. No worries of theocracy. Turn them around again and see religion aimed at solidifying the traditional understanding of marriage. Theocracy threatens again!

The point is a simple one that Stephen Carter has made before. Carter's perceptive assertion is that religious rhetoric and motivation were once very warmly received in the United States.[20] Calls for progressive positions on civil rights, the Cold War, and Vietnam met with great enthusiasm from the media and government elites. At that time, there were no top academic voices such as those of John Rawls, Bruce Ackerman, Stephen Macedo, Robert Audi, or many others talking about the importance of offering only public reasons that any person could reasonably accept.[21] The only people calling for religion to be separate from politics during that period were fundamentalist Christians like Jerry Falwell.[22]

Carter rightly senses that something has happened and that the rules do not appear to be fairly applied. When religious liberals involve themselves in politics, they are "speaking truth to power" and "filling a prophetic role" in public affairs. Religious conservatives are instead pilloried as potential theocrats and oppressors who want to return us to the Middle Ages, this despite the fact that on the issue they care most about they are certainly speaking prophetically. That issue is abortion. Carter believes the Supreme Court's decision in *Roe v. Wade* and its subsequent mass mobilization of religious conservatives is the watershed event that changed perception of the desirability of the religious voice in the public square.[23] Carter is right. It is an interesting coincidence of history that political philosophers begin making arguments about the need to exclude religious reason in public during the same period when abortion legalization debates began to occupy the consciences of Americans preceding and following *Roe v. Wade*. Religious appeals were fine for the civil rights movement and for anti-Vietnam protesters. Not so fine for pro-lifers.

As Carter describes it, *Roe* was like "a cold shower" for most religious conservatives.[24] The issue of abortion was tailor-made to prick the consciences of evangelicals and wake the sleeping giant fundamentalist community as well.[25] After all, here we had the unborn child, as innocent as a human life can possibly be, legally permitted to be destroyed, with virtually no recourse to the democratic process permitted. Suddenly, religious conservatives, including those who long advocated staying out of politics, leaped into the fray. The change in the nature of religious speakers in politics was obvious. Carter writes:

> And so the public rhetoric of religion, which from the time of the abolitionist movement through the era of the "social gospel" and well into the 1960's and early 1970's had largely been the property of liberalism, was all at once—and quite thunderously, too—the special province of people fighting for a cause that the left considered an affront.[26]

With that sea change in the composition of religious speakers in the public square came the corresponding alteration in how such speakers were viewed and treated. Consider how easily pro-life advocates and demonstrators could have been viewed as latter-day civil rights marchers, and yet to this day they are not seen that way by anyone other than their co-religionists. In point of fact, their right to protest has been restricted and confined in a way that would be decried with great emotion had the same been done to civil rights protesters of the 1960s. Can it be imagined that protesters staging sit-ins at segregated businesses and institutions would have been hit with RICO (Racketeering Influenced Corrupt Organizations) lawsuits, backed by the full force of the federal government, originally designed to deal with organized crime? Several pro-life protesters suffered that fate.[27] When religious conservatives speak truth to power, they just do not seem to earn the esteem of either the society or the "secular state" the way some of their liberal predecessors did.

Carter's main point is that social elites seek to marginalize the religious influence whenever it expresses a worldview with which they disagree. Thus, the left-wing nuclear freeze or poverty rights group speaks in frankly religious terms, and it sounds like music. The right-wing abortion protester or marriage advocate speaks, and it is frightening theocracy all over again.

Some readers are shaking their heads and protesting that the two types of situations are not parallel. I suppose they would contend that the guardians of secularism to whom I refer did not jump in with both feet against Bob Riley and Susan Hamill because, although they canvassed the state appealing directly to the voters' Christian sympathies and belief in Scripture, they were trying to achieve secular values of compassion and charity with which many people can agree. The first answer is to point to the problem I discussed earlier with separating out secular values from religious ones. That problem has never been solved, though many like to pretend that we can simply sift religious from secular and be content with the result. Labeling values-based decisions as acceptable or unacceptable based on an association with religion versus some other system of assigning meaning is bankrupt, particularly if scientific empiricism is expected to serve as a tiebreaker. It simply cannot.

The second answer is to note that Christian campaigns against abortion and even gay marriage, to cite two examples that most often raise the dread specter of theocracy, are quite capable of making their cases on "secular" grounds and often choose to do so. What distinguishes those cases from the Alabama one in which the government proposes to reach directly into one's pocketbook because the lordship of Christ demands it? The Alabama case is, in fact, almost a perfect reversal of the optimum Audi/Rawlsian picture of how public deliberation should work. In their world secular rationales are supposed to be the language of the public square and religionists should find their religious rationales capable of supporting the secular thoughts in their own traditions and communities. In Alabama, the supposedly virtuous Audi/Rawls idea was flatly reversed. The reform campaign was conducted on fully Christian grounds and those uninterested in that were free to debate from their own secular concerns.

The upshot of this story is simple. The use of religious advocacy and reasoning in public affairs is not uniquely harmful and certainly does not present a grave threat to social harmony. If a governor can propose to restructure the tax system, the very heart of the government, because of Christian convictions and can then personally carry that message across the state in religious venues and every other kind of forum without deeply unsettling a pluralistic community, then it seems very reasonable to propose that concerns to the contrary are clearly false. If the answer to that contention is that Alabama is not that pluralistic, then two responses are possible. First, if the lack of pluralism explains the unproblematic nature of the Christian campaign by the governor to change the tax system, then Steven D. Smith is surely right when he proposes that church-state strictures need not necessarily be the same in Massachusetts as in Louisiana.[28] Second, if pluralism were to be more pronounced, then one imagines it is even less likely that Christians would run roughshod in those communities than it was that the same would happen in Alabama.

Pluralism provides its own best defense to monism. Alabama proves what we already know, which is that Christianity is plural within itself and is not today likely to steamroll anyone on anything. No elegant political philosophies or legal rules are needed to police the boundaries of religious and secular argumentation. The focus should be on the wisdom and justice of particular policies, not on the motives for the policies. An endless fascination with perfecting the way we form our reasons for policies, religious or otherwise, leads to absurdity and arbitrary decisions.[29]

Summary

Secularism is not neutral, nor is it something that simply happened thanks to the growing maturity and rationality of human beings. It is an understandable reaction to the various tragedies of church-state alliances in Western history. It is not, however, necessarily more rational nor more harmonious than any number of alternatives. It cannot claim the authority of science. It cannot escape the need to look beyond materialism in order to discover values. Secularism, like realism, is more of a boast or a way to score rhetorical points than it is a concept that performs any actual work.

There are plenty of projects afloat aiming to rehabilitate the concept of secularism by differentiating good secularism from the bad. Those projects are well-meaning but face a tremendous uphill battle. Secularism means "without God," just as liberalism has come to mean "pacifistic, big government" in the common rhetoric instead of "democratic, limited government," which is the historical pedigree for the word. It would be better to simply acknowledge our actual situation, which is that our community life truly depends upon our ability to persuade each other of the right and the wrong and the good and the bad without artificial rules of discourse or boundary-drawing between so-called religious and secular reason. Considering the panoply of rhetorical regulations presented by various political and legal philosophers, Sanford Levinson writes that he finds the game "fundamentally misguided." Instead, no citizen of a democracy should need to "engage in epistemic abstinence." It is "the prerogative of listeners" to reject arguments they find unpersuasive. These are the arguments that are "inaccessible" or "marginal."[1] Neither place cards nor labels are needed to set up guidelines for citizens who are peers.

Here at the end, I recall a question asked by a mentor to whom I explained my project. He wondered how I would respond to the charge that the onset of secularism brought about the end of wars of religion in the West. My answer to him was that secularism is not what brought religious peace to the West. Neither is the waning of religious sensibilities. What brought religious peace to the West is the same thing that brought religious war: pluralism. Religious pluralism created conflict to the point where the various contestants realized none could win convincingly, and the cost was too high to continue. Pluralism is better than secularism because it is not artificial. In a pluralistic environment, we simply enter the public square and say who we are and what we believe. We make arguments that advert to religion or other sources of values, and they are more or less convincing on a case-by-case basis. The result is that our arguments are naturally tempered by reality and we develop the virtue of civility if we pay attention. Pluralism brought about the separation of church and state. Notably, many argued for the separation of church and state on the religious basis that God would not tolerate the kind of hypocritical allegiance brought on by confessional legal regimes. The alternative presented by secularism commits the same sin in a different direction. Secularists ask that individuals with religious reasons pretend to think and act on some other basis.

Removing God from our public deliberations doesn't help us focus on the things we have in common. The truth is that the great majority of us have God in common. God matters. He matters in how we think about human rights and civil rights. He matters in how we think about bioethics and in helping us to know how far we dare to go. He matters in how we treat criminals. He matters in the decisions we make about the economy and in how we go to war. In order to preserve our freedom to talk about him in all that we do, even in politics, we need only respect others by seeking to persuade rather than to coerce. Surely that is preferable to replacing the organic heart of our civilization with a mechanical one.

Selected Bibliography

Alwall, Jonas. Religious Liberty in Sweden: An Overview. *Journal of Church and State* (Winter 2000): 147–72.

Aquinas, Thomas. *St. Thomas Aquinas on Politics and Ethics: A New Translation, Backgrounds, Interpretations*. Translated by Thomas Sigmund and Paul E. Sigmund. 1st ed. New York: Norton, 1988.

Audi, Robert, and Nicholas Wolterstorff. *Religion in the Public Square: The Place of Religious Convictions in Political Debate*. Lanham, MD: Rowman and Littlefield, 1997.

Augustine, Michael W. Tkacz, Douglas Kries, Ernest L. Fortin, and Roland Gunn. *Political Writings*. Indianapolis: Hackett, 1994.

Bader, Veit. Religious Pluralism: Secularism or Priority for Democracy? *Political Theory* 27, no. 5 (October 1999): 597–633.

Bainton, Roland. *Christianity*. Boston: Houghton Mifflin, 1964.

Benson, Iain T. "Notes Towards a (Re)Definition of the Secular." *The University of British Columbia Law Review*, no. 33 (2000): 519–49.

Berg, Thomas. "Church-State Relations and the Social Ethics of Reinhold Niebuhr." *North Carolina Law Review* (April 1995): 1567–1639.

Berger, Peter L. *The Desecularization of the World: Resurgent Religion and World Politics*. Washington, DC; Grand Rapids, MI: Ethics and Public Policy Center; Eerdmans, 1999.

_____. *The Sacred Canopy: Elements of a Sociological Theory of Religion*. New York: Anchor Books, 1990.

Bhargava, Rajeev, ed. *Secularism and Its Critics*. New Delhi: Oxford University Press, 1998.

Bolce, Louis, and Gerald De Maio. "Our Secularist Democratic Party." *The Public Interest* (Fall 2002): 3–20.

Bonomi, Patricia U. *Under the Cope of Heaven: Religion, Society, and Politics in Colonial America*. New York: Oxford University Press, 1986.

Bremer, Francis J. *John Winthrop: America's Forgotten Founding Father*. New York: Oxford University Press, 2003.

Brooke, John. Science and Religion: Lessons from History? *Science* (December 11, 1998): 1985–86.

Bruce, Steve. *Religion and Modernization: Sociologists and Historians Debate the Secularization Thesis*. Oxford; New York: Clarendon Press; Oxford University Press, 1992.

Budziszewski, J. *The Revenge of Conscience: Politics and the Fall of Man*. Dallas: Spence, 1999.

Bullock, Steven C. *Revolutionary Brotherhood: Freemasonry and the Transformation of the American Social Order, 1730–1840*. Chapel Hill: University of North Carolina Press, 1996.

Callahan, Daniel, and Harvey Gallagher Cox. *The Secular City Debate*. New York: Macmillan, 1966.

Campos, Paul F. "Secular Fundamentalism." *Columbia Law Review* (October 1994): 1814–27.

Canavan, Francis. *The Pluralist Game: Pluralism, Liberalism, and the Moral Conscience*. Lanham, MD: Rowman and Littlefield, 1995.

Carpenter, Joel A. "Fundamentalist Institutions and the Rise of Evangelical Protestantism, 1929–1942." *Church History* (March 1980): 62–75.

Carter, Stephen L. *The Culture of Disbelief: How American Law and Politics Trivialize Religious Devotion*. New York: Basic, 1993.

Casanova, José. *Public Religions in the Modern World*. Chicago: University of Chicago Press, 1994.

Chadwick, Owen. *The Secularization of the European Mind in the Nineteenth Century: The Gifford Lectures in the University of Edinburgh for 1973–4*. Cambridge; New York: Cambridge University Press, 1975.

Chambers, Whittaker. *Witness*. Chicago: Regnery Gateway, 1984.

Chesterton, G. K. *Orthodoxy*. San Francisco: Ignatius Press, 1995.

Clapp, Rodney. *Border Crossings: Christian Trespasses on Popular Culture and Public Affairs*. Grand Rapids, MI: Brazos Press, 2000.

Conkle, Daniel O. "Secular Fundamentalism, Religious Fundamentalism, and the Search for Truth in Contemporary America." *Journal of Law and Religion* 12, no. 2 (1995–1996): 337.

_____. "Different Religions, Different Politics: Evaluating the Role of Competing Religious Traditions in American Politics and Law." *Journal of Law and Religion* 10, no. 1 (1993–1994): 1.

Connolly, William E. *Why I Am Not a Secularist*. Minneapolis: University of Minnesota Press, 1999.

Cox, Harvey. *The Secular City*. New York: MacMillan, 1975.

Dewey, John. *The Influence of Darwin on Philosophy, and Other Essays in Contemporary Thought*. Bloomington: Indiana University Press, 1965.

Dreisbach, Daniel L., Mark David Hall, and Jeffry H. Morrison. *The Founders on God and Government*. Lanham, MD: Rowman and Littlefield, 2004.

Durkheim, Emile, Carol Cosman, and Mark Sydney Cladis. *The Elementary Forms of Religious Life*. Oxford; New York: Oxford University Press, 2001.

Eberle, Christopher J. *Religious Convictions in Liberal Politics*. Cambridge: Cambridge University Press, 2002.

Farrow, Douglas. "Three Meanings of Secular." *First Things*, (May 2003): 18–20.

Finke, Roger, and Rodney Stark. *The Churching of America, 1776–1990: Winners and Losers in Our Religious Economy*. New Brunswick, NJ: Rutgers University Press, 1992.

Finnis, John. "On the Practical Meaning of Secularism." *Notre Dame Law Review*, no. 73 (1998): 491–516.

Finocchiaro, Maurice A. "Science, Religion, and the Historiography of the Galileo Affair: On the Undesirability of Oversimplification." *Osiris*, vol. 16 (2001): 114–32.

Fish, Stanley. "Mission Impossible: Settling the Just Bounds between Church and State." *Columbia Law Review* (December 1997): 2255–2333.

_____. "A Reply to J. Judd Owen." *American Political Science Review* (December 1999): 925–30.

Fowler, Robert Booth. *Unconventional Partners: Religion and Liberal Culture in the United States*. Grand Rapids, MI: Eerdmans, 1989.

Selected Bibliography

Garvey, John H. "A Comment on Religious Convictions and Lawmaking." *Michigan Law Review* 84, no. 6 (May 1986): 1288.

Gaustad, Edwin S. *Neither King nor Prelate: Religion and the New Nation, 1776–1826.* Rev. and corr. ed. Grand Rapids, MI: Eerdmans, 1993.

Gedicks, Frederick Mark. "Public Life and Hostility to Religion." *Virginia Law Review* 78, no. 3 (April 1992): 671–96.

_____. *The Rhetoric of Church and State: A Critical Analysis of Religion Clause Jurisprudence.* Durham, NC: Duke University Press, 1995.

George, Robert P. *The Clash of Orthodoxies: Law, Religion, and Morality in Crisis.* Wilmington, DE: ISI Books, 2001.

_____. *Making Men Moral: Civil Liberties and Public Morality.* Oxford; New York: Clarendon Press; Oxford University Press, 1993.

Gill, Anthony James. *Rendering Unto Caesar: The Catholic Church and the State in Latin America.* Chicago, IL: University of Chicago Press, 1998.

Gray, John. "The Myth of Secularism." *The New Statesman* (December 16–30, 2002): 69–71.

Greeley, Andrew M. *Unsecular Man; the Persistence of Religion.* New York: Schocken, 1972.

Greenawalt, Kent. *Religious Convictions and Political Choice.* New York: Oxford University Press, 1988.

Hamburger, Philip. *Separation of Church and State.* Cambridge, MA: Harvard University Press, 2002.

Hart, D. G. *Defending the Faith: J. Gresham Machen and the Crisis of Conservative Protestantism in Modern America.* Grand Rapids, MI: Baker, 1995.

_____. *A Secular Faith: Why Christianity Favors the Separation of Church and State.* Chicago: I. R. Dee, 2006.

Hatch, Nathan O. *The Democratization of American Christianity.* New Haven: Yale University Press, 1989.

Hauerwas, Stanley. *The Peaceable Kingdom: A Primer in Christian Ethics.* Notre Dame, IN: University of Notre Dame Press, 1983.

Henry, Carl F. H. *The Uneasy Conscience of Modern Fundamentalism.* Grand Rapids, MI: Eerdmans, 1947.

Hitchcock, James. "The Enemies of Religious Liberty." *First Things*, no. 140 (February 2004): 26–30.

Hollinger, David A. *Science, Jews, and Secular Culture: Studies in Mid-Twentieth-Century American Intellectual History.* Princeton, NJ: Princeton University Press, 1996.

Hunter, James Davison. *Culture Wars: The Struggle to Define America.* New York: Basic, 1991.

Hurd, Elizabeth Shakman. "The Political Authority of Secularism in International Relations." *European Journal of International Relations* (June 2004): 235–62.

Johnson, Phillip E. *Reason in the Balance: The Case against Naturalism in Science, Law and Education.* Downers Grove, IL: InterVarsity, 1995.

Kagan, Donald, Steven E. Ozment, and Frank M. Turner. *The Western Heritage.* 2nd ed. New York: Macmillan, 1983.

Keddie, Nikki R. "Secularism and Its Discontents." *Daedalus* (Summer 2003): 14–30.

Kelley, Dean M. *Why Conservative Churches Are Growing: A Study in Sociology of Religion.* 1st ed. New York: Harper and Row, 1972.

Selected Bibliography

King, Martin Luther, and James Melvin Washington. *I Have a Dream: Writings and Speeches That Changed the World*. 1st ed. San Francisco: HarperSanFrancisco, 1992.

Kramnick, Isaac, and R. Laurence Moore. *The Godless Constitution: The Case against Religious Correctness*. 1st ed. New York: Norton, 1996.

Kraynak, Robert P. *Christian Faith and Modern Democracy: God and Politics in the Fallen World*. Notre Dame, IN: University of Notre Dame Press, 2001.

Larson, Edward J. *Summer for the Gods: The Scopes Trial and America's Continuing Debate over Science and Religion*. New York: Basic, 1997.

Laycock, Douglas. "Continuity and Change in the Threat to Religious Liberty: The Reformation Era and the Late Twentieth Century." *Minnesota Law Review* (May 1996): 1047–1102.

Lewy, Guenter. *Why America Needs Religion: Secular Modernity and Its Discontents*. Grand Rapids, MI: Eerdmans, 1996.

Lindberg, David C. "Science and the Early Christian Church." *Isis* (December 1983): 509–30.

_____, and Ronald L. Numbers. "Beyond War and Peace: A Reappraisal of the Encounter between Christianity and Science." *Church History* (September 1986): 338–54.

_____. "Medieval Science and Its Religious Context." *Osiris*, vol. 10 (1995): 60–79.

Luther, Martin, and John Calvin. *Luther and Calvin on Secular Authority*. Edited by Harro Hopfl. Cambridge: Cambridge University Press, 1991.

Macedo, Stephen. "Liberal Civic Education and Religious Fundamentalism: The Case of God v. John Rawls?" *Ethics* (April 1995): 468–96.

_____. "Transformative Constitutionalism and the Case of Religion: Defending the Moderate Hegemony of Liberalism." *Political Theory* (February 1998): 56–80.

Machen, J. Gresham. *Christianity and Liberalism*. Grand Rapids, MI: Eerdmans, 1923.

Machiavelli, Niccolo, and Peter E. Bondanella. *The Prince*. Oxford; New York: Oxford University Press, 1984.

MacIntyre, Alasdair C. *After Virtue: A Study in Moral Theory*. 2nd ed. Notre Dame, IN: University of Notre Dame Press, 1984.

_____. *Three Rival Versions of Moral Enquiry: Encyclopaedia, Genealogy, and Tradition*. Notre Dame, IN: University of Notre Dame Press, 1990.

Maritain, Jacques. *Man and the State*. Washington, DC: Catholic University of America Press, 1998.

Marsden, George M. *Fundamentalism and American Culture: The Shaping of Twentieth Century Evangelicalism, 1870–1925*. New York: Oxford University Press, 1980.

_____. *Jonathan Edwards: A Life*. New Haven, CT: Yale University Press, 2003.

_____. *The Outrageous Idea of Christian Scholarship*. New York: Oxford University Press, 1997.

_____. *Reforming Fundamentalism: Fuller Seminary and the New Evangelicalism*. Grand Rapids, MI: Eerdmans, 1987.

_____. *Religion and American Culture*. San Diego: Harcourt Brace Jovanovich, 1990.

_____. *The Soul of the American University: From Protestant Establishment to Established Nonbelief*. New York: Oxford University Press, 1994.

Martin, David. The Secularization Issue: Prospect and Retrospect. *The British Journal of Sociology* (September 1991): 465–74.

_____. *On Secularization: Towards a Revised General Theory*. Aldershot, Hants, England; Burlington, VT: Ashgate, 2005.

Selected Bibliography

May, Henry Farnham. *The Enlightenment in America.* Oxford; New York: Oxford University Press, 1978.

McClay, Wilfred M. "Two Concepts of Secularism." *Wilson Quarterly* (Summer 2000): 54–71.

McConnell, Michael W. "'God Is Dead and We Have Killed Him!': Freedom of Religion in the Post-modern Age." *Brigham Young University Law Review* (1993): 163–88.

_____. "Leary Lecture: Five Reasons to Reject the Claim That Religious Arguments Should Be Excluded from Democratic Deliberation." *Utah Law Review* (1999): 639–57.

McManners, John. *The Oxford History of Christianity.* Oxford; New York: Oxford University Press, 2002.

Mommsen, Wolfgang J. *The Political and Social Theory of Max Weber: Collected Essays.* Chicago: University of Chicago Press, 1989.

Morgan, Edmund Sears. *Puritan Political Ideas, 1558–1794.* Indianapolis, IN: Bobbs-Merrill, 1965.

Murray, John Courtney, S. J. *We Hold These Truths: Catholic Reflections on the American Proposition.* New York: Sheed and Ward, 1960.

Nelson, William Edward, and Robert C. Palmer. *Liberty and Community: Constitution and Rights in the Early American Republic.* New York: Oceana, 1987.

Neuhaus, Richard John. *The Naked Public Square: Religion and Democracy in America.* Grand Rapids, MI: Eerdmans, 1984.

Niebuhr, H. Richard. *Christ and Culture.* New York: Harper, 1956.

Noll, Mark A. *The Civil War as a Theological Crisis.* Chapel Hill, NC: University of North Carolina Press, 2006.

_____. *The Kingdom of God in America.* 1st Wesleyan ed. Middletown, CT: Wesleyan University Press, 1988.

_____. *The Old Religion in a New World: The History of North American Christianity.* Grand Rapids, MI: Eerdmans, 2002.

_____. *The Scandal of the Evangelical Mind.* Grand Rapids, MI: Eerdmans, 1995.

_____, George M. Marsden, and Nathan O. Hatch. *The Search for Christian America.* Colorado Springs: Helmers and Howard, 1989.

Novak, Michael. *On Two Wings: Humble Faith and Common Sense at the American Founding.* 1st ed. San Francisco, CA: Encounter Books, 2002.

Numbers, Ronald L. "Science and Religion." *Osiris,* 2nd series, vol. 1 (1985): 59–80.

Owen, J. Judd. *Religion and the Demise of Liberal Rationalism: The Foundational Crisis of the Separation of Church and State.* Chicago: University of Chicago Press, 2001.

Parsons, Talcott. "1965 Harlan Paul Douglass Lectures: Religion in a Modern Pluralist Society." *Review of Religious Research* (Spring 1966): 125–46.

_____, and Toby Jackson. *The Evolution of Societies.* Englewood Cliff, NJ: Prentice-Hall, 1977.

Perry, Michael J. *Religion in Politics: Constitutional and Moral Perspectives.* Oxford: Oxford University Press, 1997.

Pojman, Louis P., and Robert Westmoreland. *Equality: Selected Readings.* New York: Oxford University Press, 1997.

Ponnuru, Ramesh. "Secularism and Its Discontents." *National Review* (December 27, 2004): 32–35.

Selected Bibliography

Queen, Edward L., Stephen R. Prothero, and Gardiner H. Shattuck. *The Encyclopedia of American Religious History.* New York: Facts on File, 1996.

Rawls, John. *Political Liberalism.* 2nd ed. New York: Columbia University Press, 1996.

Ryan, Halford Ross, and Harry Emerson Fosdick. *Harry Emerson Fosdick: Persuasive Preacher.* New York: Greenwood Press, 1989.

Scott, Franklin Daniel, and American-Scandinavian Foundation. *Sweden, the Nation's History.* Minneapolis: University of Minnesota Press, 1977.

Shafritz, Jay M., and Albert C. Hyde. *Classics of Public Administration.* 1st ed. Oak Park, IL: Moore, 1978.

Smith, Christian. *The Secular Revolution: Power, Interests, and Conflict in the Secularization of American Public Life.* Berkeley, CA: University of California Press, 2003.

Smith, Steven D. "Centennial Symposium: Reconciling the Free Exercise and Establishment Clauses: The Iceberg of Religious Freedom: Sub-Surface Levels of Nonestablishment Discourse." *Creighton Law Review* (June 2005): 799–814.

_____. *Foreordained Failure: The Quest for a Constitutional Principle of Religious Freedom.* New York: Oxford University Press, 1995.

_____. *Getting Over Equality: A Critical Diagnosis of Religious Freedom in America.* New York: New York University Press, 2001.

_____. "Recovering (from) Enlightenment?" *San Diego Law Review* (Summer 2004): 1263–1310.

_____. "The 'Secular,' the 'Religious,' and the 'Moral': What Are We Talking About?" *Wake Forest Law Review* (Summer 2001): 487–509.

_____. "Separation and the Secular: Reconstructing the Disestablishment Decision." *Texas Law Review* 67 (April 1989): 955.

Smolin, David M. "Symposium: Religious Education and the Liberal State: Religion, Education, and the Theoretically Liberal State: Contrasting Evangelical and Secularist Perspectives." *Journal of Catholic Legal Studies*, no. 44 (2005): 99–142.

_____. "Symposium: The Religious Voice in the Public Square: Cracks in the Mirrored Prison: An Evangelical Critique of Secularist Academic and Judicial Myths regarding the Relationship of Religion and American Politics." *Loyola of Los Angeles Law Review*, no. 29 (June 1996): 1487–1512.

Sommerville, C. John. *The Decline of the Secular University.* Oxford; New York: Oxford University Press, 2006.

_____. "Post-Secularism Marginalizes the University: A Rejoinder to Hollinger." *Church History* 71, no. 4 (December 2002): 848–57.

Stark, Rodney. *For the Glory of God: How Monotheism Led to Reformations, Science, Witch-Hunts, and the End of Slavery.* Princeton, NJ: Princeton University Press, 2003.

_____. *The Rise of Christianity: A Sociologist Reconsiders History.* Princeton, NJ: Princeton University Press, 1996.

_____, and Roger Finke. *Acts of Faith: Explaining the Human Side of Religion.* Berkeley, CA: University of California Press, 2000.

Swatos, William H., and James K. Wellman. *The Power of Religious Publics: Staking Claims in American Society.* Westport, CT: Praeger, 1999.

Swatos, William H., and Daniel V. A. Olson. *The Secularization Debate.* Lanham, MD: Rowman and Littlefield; co-published with the Association for the Sociology of Religion, 2000.

Selected Bibliography

Tierney, Brian. *The Crisis of Church and State, 1050–1300: With Selected Documents.* Toronto; Buffalo: University of Toronto Press in association with the Medieval Academy of America, 1988.

Tomasson, Richard F. *Sweden: Prototype of Modern Society.* 1st ed. New York: Random House, 1970.

Turner, Frank M. "The Victorian Conflict between Science and Religion: A Professional Dimension." *Isis* (September 1978): 356–76.

Turner, James. *Without God, Without Creed: The Origins of Unbelief in America.* Baltimore, MD: Johns Hopkins University Press, 1985.

Vidler, Alec. *The Church in an Age of Revolution: 1789 to the Present Day.* London: Penguin, 1990.

Weber, Max, Hans Heinrich Gerth, and C. Wright Mills. *From Max Weber: Essays in Sociology.* New York: Oxford University Press, 1946.

_____. *The Sociology of Religion.* Boston: Beacon Press, 1993.

Witte, John. *Religion and the American Constitutional Experiment: Essential Rights and Liberties.* Boulder, CO: Westview Press, 2000.

Wood, James. "Editorial: The Secular State." *Journal of Church and State* (Spring 1965): 169–78.

Woodward, Kenneth L. "Born Again!" *Newsweek*, October 25, 1976, 68–78.

Notes

Introduction

1. C. John Sommerville, *The Decline of the Secular University* (Oxford: Oxford University Press, 2006), 86.

2. Garry Wills, "The Day the Enlightenment Went Out," *The New York Times*, http://www.nytimes.com/2004/11/04/ opinion/04wills.html?ex=1257397200&en=bbab1b2b70dd433b &ei=5088&partner=rssnyt (accessed Sept. 20, 2006). In the opinion piece, Wills argued that the coalition of conservative religionists who supported George W. Bush were more closely aligned ideologically with Islamic fanatics than with their fellow Americans. Wills is a highly respected public intellectual.

3. "Bush's God," *The American Prospect*, http://www.prospect.org/web/page.ww?section=root&name =ViewPrint&articleId=7858 (accessed Sept. 20, 2006).

4. As I describe the argument for secularism and the privatization of religion, I recall with some amusement a conversation I had with an engineer friend of my father's. He complained to me that all the churches in town represented an incredibly inefficient use of space. What these religious types should do, he explained, is to share a single facility and simply work together to schedule its proper use for their various congregations.

5. Max Weber, "Religious Rejections of the World and Their Directions," in *From Max Weber*, ed. and trans. H. H. Gerth and C. Wright Mills (New York: Oxford University Press, 1946), 323–59.

6. The paradigmatic example is former Cornell University president A. D. White's *The History of Warfare of Science with Theology in Christendom*, which was published in 1896. The book is now in the public domain and can be read free, thanks to Project Gutenberg at http://www.gutenberg.org/etext/505 (accessed Sept. 20, 2006).

7. The best book covering the history of the Scopes trial and its uses in the polemical battle between science and religion is probably Edward J. Larson's *Summer for the Gods: The Scopes Trial and America's Continuing Debate over Science and Religion* (New York: Basic Books, 1997).

8. William H. Swatos Jr. and Kevin J. Christiano, "Secularization Theory: The Course of a Concept," in *The Secularization Debate*, ed. William H. Swatos and Daniel V. Olson (Lanham, MD: Rowman and Littlefield, 2000), 5–7.

Chapter 1: The Early Church and the Empire

1. Brian Tierney, *The Crisis of Church and State 1050–1300* (Toronto: University of Toronto Press, 1988), 1.

2. Matt. 22:21.

3. Some Christians argue for secularism in public affairs as a way of keeping the faith centered on spiritual matters rather than giving in to a temptation to focus too much on the purported diversion of politics. See D. G. Hart, *A Secular Faith: Why Christianity Favors the Separation of Church and State* (Chicago: Ivan R. Dee, 2006).

4. Acts 5:29. For a classical source of the same idea, consider Antigone's determination to give her brother a proper burial despite the fact that it would violate the law of the state.

5. Donald Kagan, Steven Ozment, and Frank M. Turner, *The Western Heritage* (New York: Macmillan, 1983), 213.

6. Roland H. Bainton, *Christianity* (Boston: Houghton Mifflin, 1964), 87.

7. Henry Chadwick, *The Early Church* (New York: Dorset Press, 1986), 127. The deathbed baptism was particularly important for officials who might have things like torture and imprisonment on their conscience despite having performed them in service of the state.

8. Bainton, *Christianity*, 90.

9. Chadwick, *The Early Church*, 125.

10. Ibid., 127.

11. Bainton, *Christianity*, 91.

12. Chadwick, *The Early Church*, 128.
13. Bainton, *Christianity*, 100.
14. Ibid., 118.
15. Chadwick, *The Early Church*, 168.
16. Augustine, "The City of God," in *Augustine: Political Writings*, trans. Michael W. Tkacz and Douglas Kries, ed. Ernest L. Fortin and Douglas Kries (Indianapolis, IN: Hackett, 1994), 30–31.
17. Ibid., 32.
18. Ibid., 35.
19. Ibid., 11.
20. Ibid., 41.
21. Ibid., 44–45.
22. Ibid., 59.
23. Ibid., 44.
24. Martin Luther King Jr., "Letter from Birmingham Jail," in *I Have a Dream: Writings and Speeches That Changed the World*, ed. James Melvin Washington (San Francisco: HarperSanFrancisco, 1992) 84–100.
25. Augustine, "The City of God," 158.
26. Ibid., 149.
27. Ibid., 139.
28. Chadwick, *The Early Church*, 219–20.
29. Ibid., 221.
30. Ibid., 222–23.
31. Ibid., 224–25.

Chapter 2: By What Right? By What Power?

1. Brian Tierney, *The Crisis of Church and State 1050–1300* (Toronto: University of Toronto Press, 1996), 10.
2. Ibid., 17.
3. Ibid., 24–36.
4. Ibid., 54.
5. Ibid., 111.
6. Martin Luther, "On Secular Authority," in *Luther and Calvin on Secular Authority*, ed. and trans. Harro Hopfl (Cambridge: Cambridge University Press, 1991), 32.
7. John Finnis, "On the Practical Meaning of Secularism," *Notre Dame Law Review*, 73: (1998), 491.
8. David Martin, *On Secularization: Towards a Revised General Theory* (Burlington, VT: Ashgate, 2005), 4.
9. Abraham Kuyper, *Lectures on Calvinism* (Grand Rapids, MI: Eerdmans, 1931), 51.
10. Tierney, *The Crisis of Church and State*, 152. Innocent's position anticipated Roger Williams's by several centuries.
11. Ibid., 159.
12. Thomas Aquinas, "Summa Theologiae," *St. Thomas Aquinas on Politics and Ethics*, trans. and ed. Paul E. Sigmund (New York: Norton, 1988), 61.
13. Ibid., 62.
14. Ibid., 96.
15. Ibid., 97.
16. Roland H. Bainton, *Christianity* (Boston: Houghton Mifflin, 1964), 202–3.
17. Understanding citizens in the restrictive sense of the times, e.g., no slaves, no women.
18. Marsilius of Padua, "Defensor Pacis," *Medieval Sourcebook*, http://www.fordham.edu/halsall/source/marsiglio4.html (accessed Oct. 16, 2006).
19. Marsilius of Padua, "Conclusions from Defensor Pacis," *Medieval Sourcebook*, http://www.fordham.edu/halsall/source/marsiglio1.html (accessed Oct. 16, 2006).

Chapter 3: New Winds Blowing

1. John T. McNeill, *God and Duty: The Political Thought of John Calvin* (New York: Bobbs-Merrill, 1956), 41.

2. Ibid., 46.
3. Ibid., 81.
4. Ibid., 54.
5. Martin Luther, "On Secular Authority," in *Luther and Calvin on Secular Authority*, ed. and trans. Harro Hopfl (Cambridge: Cambridge University Press, 1991), 8.
6. Ibid., 9.
7. 1 Tim. 1:9.
8. Luther, "On Secular Authority," 7.
9. Ibid., 10.
10. Ibid., 11.
11. Ibid., 12.
12. Ibid., 14.
13. Ibid., 15.
14. Ibid., 18.
15. Ibid., 20.
16. Ibid., 23–24.
17. Ibid., 25.
18. Ibid., 27.
19. Ibid., 28.
20. Ibid., 30.
21. Ibid., 32.
22. Wolfhart Pannenberg, "The Christian Division of Church and State," Becket Fund; http://www.becketfund.org/other/Prague2000/PannenbergPaper.html (accessed Apr. 27, 2007).
23. Niccolo Machiavelli, *The Prince* (New York: Oxford University Press, 1984), 11.
24. Ibid., 9.
25. Ibid., 58–60.
26. Ibid., 39–41.

Chapter 4: Reformation's Wake
1. Thomas Hobbes, *Leviathan, or The Matter, Forme, and Power of a Common-Wealth Ecclesiastical and Civill* (London: University Press, 1651), 83–89.
2. John Locke, "A Letter Concerning Toleration," The Constitution Society, http://www.constitution.org/jl/tolerati.htm (accessed April 27, 2007).
3. Ibid.
4. Ibid.
5. Jean-Jacques, Rousseau, "The Social Contract: Book One," The Constitution Society, http://www.constitution.org/jjr/socon_01.htm (accessed Apr. 27, 2007).
6. Jean-Jacques, Rousseau, "The Social Contract: Book Four," The Constitution Society, http://www.constitution.org/jjr/socon_04.htm (accessed Apr. 27, 2007).
7. Ibid.
8. Ibid.
9. Ibid.
10. Ibid.

Chapter 5: American Story
1. Edmund S. Morgan, *Puritan Political Ideas* (Indianapolis, IN: Bobbs-Merrill, 1965), *xv–xvii*.
2. Ibid., *xx–xxviii*.
3. Francis Bremer, *John Winthrop: America's Forgotten Founding Father* (New York: Oxford University Press, 2003), 251–52.
4. Ibid., 298.
5. Roger Williams, "The Bloudy Tenet of Persecution," in *Puritan Political Ideas*, ed. Edmund S. Morgan (Indianapolis, IN: Bobbs-Merrill, 1965), 208.
6. Ibid., 212.
7. Roger Williams, "Williams to Daniel Abbot, Town Clerk of Providence (January 15, 1681)," in *Puritan Political Ideas*, 224.

8. George M. Marsden, *Religion and American Culture* (New York: Harcourt Brace Jovanovich, 1990), 24–26. In the section at hand, Marsden references Harry S. Stout, *The New England Soul: Preaching and Religious Culture in Colonial New England* (New York: Oxford University Press, 1986). Also see George M. Marsden, *Jonathan Edwards: A Life* (New Haven, CT: Yale University Press, 2003), 238.
9. Marsden, *Jonathan Edwards*, 350–56; 369–71.
10. Mark Noll, *The Old Religion in the New World: The History of North American Christianity* (Grand Rapids, MI: Eerdmans, 2002), 96.
11. H. Richard Niebuhr, *The Kingdom of God in America* (Middletown, CT: Wesleyan University Press, 1988), 100.
12. Noll, *The Old Religion in the New World*, 54.
13. Patricia U. Bonomi, *Under the Cope of Heaven: Religion, Society, and Politics in Colonial America* (New York: Oxford University Press, 1986), 161.
14. The treatment of this theme *nonpareil* can be found in Nathan O. Hatch, *The Democratization of American Christianity* (New Haven, CT: Yale University Press, 1989).
15. José Casanova, *Public Religions in the Modern World* (Chicago: University of Chicago Press, 1994), 27–29.

Chapter 6: France
1. Alec Vidler, *The Church in an Age of Revolution: 1789 to the Present Day* (London: Penguin, 1990), 11.
2. Ibid., 12.
3. John McManners, *The Oxford History of Christianity* (Oxford: Oxford University Press, 2002), 290.
4. Vidler, *The Church in an Age of Revolution*, 13.
5. Ibid., 13.
6. Donald Kagan, Steven Ozment, and Frank M. Turner, *The Western Heritage* (New York: Macmillan, 1983), 658.
7. Ibid., 666–67.
8. John Hall Stewart, *A Documentary Survey of the French Revolution* (New York: Macmillan, 1951), 526–27. Quoted in Kagan, et al., *The Western Heritage*, 668.
9. Ibid.
10. Kagan, et al., *The Western Heritage*, 679.
11. Ibid., 681.

Chapter 7: Analyzing the Evolution
1. Alasdair MacIntyre, *After Virtue: A Study in Moral Theory* (Notre Dame, IN: University of Notre Dame Press, 1984), 185.
2. The Christian church in various manifestations has struggled with the decision to include everyone in a comprehensive church-state model or to opt for voluntary associations of true believers. The first choice is referred to as a comprehensive model. The second characterizes the regenerate church (believers only).
3. Robert P. Kraynak has written in support of what I'm calling the European proposition. See Robert P. Kraynak, *Christian Faith and Modern Democracy: God and Politics in a Fallen World* (Notre Dame, IN: University of Notre Dame Press, 2001).
4. Thomas Paine, *The Age of Reason* (New York: Putnam, 1895).

Chapter 8: The American Model
1. Of course, Paine did not make his deistic critique of Judeo-Christian religion clear until well after the American Revolution, which he helped foster with his wildly successful pamphlet *Common Sense*. *Common Sense* is far more friendly to the Bible than his later *The Age of Reason*.
2. For a good summation of this general case, see Isaac Kramnick and R. Laurence Moore, *The Godless Constitution: The Case against Religious Correctness* (New York: Norton, 1996).
3. A good presentation of this position, without veering off into sheer advocacy, can be found in Daniel L. Dreisbach, Mark D. Hall, and Jeffry H. Morrison, eds., *The Founders on God and Government* (Lanham, MD: Rowman and Littlefield, 2004). Another highly

readable example comes from Michael Novak, *On Two Wings: Humble Faith and Common Sense at the American Founding* (San Francisco: Encounter Books, 2002). The case is made in the way of a lawyer speaking zealously (and perhaps not very objectively) for his client by David Barton, *Original Intent: The Courts, the Constitution, and Religion* (Aledo, TX: Wallbuilder Press, 1996).

4. Henry F. May, *The Enlightenment in America* (Oxford: Oxford University Press, 1976), *xvi*.

5. Ibid., *xv*.

6. Mark Noll, *The Old Religion in the New World: The History of North American Christianity* (Grand Rapids, MI: Eerdmans, 2002), 35–36.

7. H. Richard Niebuhr, *The Kingdom of God in America* (Middletown, CT: Wesleyan University Press, 1988), 124.

8. John Witte Jr., *Religion and the American Constitutional Experiment: Essential Rights and Liberties* (Boulder, CO: Westview Press, 2000), 37.

9. Patricia U. Bonomi, *Under the Cope of Heaven: Religion, Society, and Politics in Colonial America* (New York: Oxford University Press, 1986), 6–11, 220.

10. Edwin Gaustad, *Neither King Nor Prelate: Religion and the New Nation 1776–1826* (Grand Rapids, MI: Eerdmans, 1993), 2.

11. Bonomi, *Under the Cope of Heaven*, 88–89.

12. Ibid., 15–16, 75.

13. Ibid., 220.

14. Niebuhr, *The Kingdom of God in America*, 100.

15. Bonomi, *Under the Cope of Heaven*, 161.

16. Philip Hamburger, *The Separation of Church and State* (Cambridge: Harvard University Press, 2002), 111–20.

17. Ibid., 19.

18. John Locke, "A Letter Concerning Toleration," The Constitution Society, http://www.constitution.org/jl/tolerati.htm (accessed April 27, 2007).

19. E.g., see Vincent Phillip Munoz, "Religion and the Common Good: George Washington on Church and State," in *The Founders on God and Government*, ed. Daniel L. Dreisbach, Mark D. Hall, and Jeffry H. Morrison (Lanham MD: Rowman and Littlefield, 2004), 7.

20. In the mold of David Barton and his Wallbuilders organization (see p. 77).

21. Mark A. Noll, Nathan O. Hatch, and George M. Marsden, *The Search for Christian America* (Colorado Springs, CO: Helmers and Howard, 1989).

22. Ibid., 148.

23. Gaustad, *Neither King Nor Prelate*, 130.

24. Robert C. Palmer, "Liberties as Constitutional Provisions," in William E. Nelson and Robert C. Palmer, *Liberty and Community: Constitution and Rights in the Early American Republic* (New York: Oceana, 1987), 139.

25. Ibid., 55.

26. Ibid., 86–87.

27. Ibid., 55.

28. See Article I, Section 8, of the United States Constitution for a list of the expressly delegated powers of the new government made available as the basis for legislative action.

29. Palmer, "Liberties as Constitutional Provisions," 104.

30. Ibid., 113.

31. Ibid., 104–5.

32. Ibid., 56.

33. Ibid., 87.

34. Ibid., 57.

35. *Everson v. Board of Education*, 330 U.S. 1, 15–16 (1947).

36. Steven D. Smith, *Foreordained Failure: The Quest for a Constitutional Principle of Religious Freedom* (New York: Oxford University Press, 1995), 6.

37. Ibid., 13.

38. Ibid., 16.

39. Ibid., 17.

40. Ibid., 19.

41. Ibid., 21.

42. Ibid., 20–21.
43. Ibid., 21.
44. Ibid., 26–27.
45. Kramnick and Moore, *The Godless Constitution*, 10. They are building their case, incorrectly I think, on Article VI of the United States Constitution, which declares, "No religious test shall ever be required as a qualification to any office or public trust under the United States."
46. Hamburger, *The Separation of Church and State*, 436–37.
47. Daniel O. Conkle, "Toward a General Theory of the Establishment Clause," *Northwestern University Law Review*, no. 82: (1988), 1138. Quoted in Smith, *Foreordained Failure*, 52–53.

Chapter 9: American Christianity
1. Steven C. Bullock, *Revolutionary Brotherhood: Freemasonry and the Transformation of the American Social Order, 1730–1840* (Chapel Hill, NC: University of North Carolina Press, 1996), 281.
2. Roger Finke and Rodney Stark, *The Churching of America, 1776–1990: Winners and Losers in Our Religious Economy* (New Brunswick, NJ: Rutgers University Press, 1992), 56.
3. Edwin Gaustad, *Neither King Nor Prelate: Religion and the New Nation 1776–1826* (Grand Rapids, MI: Eerdmans, 1993), 129.
4. Mark A. Noll, *The Scandal of the Evangelical Mind* (Grand Rapids, MI: Eerdmans, 1994).
5. Ibid., 102, 112–13.
6. Donald Kagan, Steven Ozment, Frank M. Turner, *The Western Heritage* (New York: Macmillan, 1983), 144.
7. Ibid.
8. Ibid., 145.
9. Mark Noll, *The Old Religion in the New World: The History of North American Christianity* (Grand Rapids, MI: Eerdmans, 2002), 108–11. Also see Mark A. Noll, *The Civil War as a Theological Crisis* (Chapel Hill, NC: University of North Carolina Press, 2006).
10. J. Gresham Machen, *Christianity and Liberalism* (Grand Rapids, MI: Eerdmans, 1923), 7.
11. The famous sermon through which Fosdick made his signature point is reproduced in Halford R. Ryan, *Harry Emerson Fosdick: Persuasive Preacher* (Westport, CT: Greenwood Press, 1989), 79–90.
12. D. G. Hart, *Defending the Faith: J. Gresham Machen and the Crisis of Conservative Protestantism in Modern America* (Grand Rapids, MI: Baker, 1995), 163–64.
13. George M. Marsden, *Fundamentalism and American Culture: The Shaping of Twentieth-Century Evangelicalism 1870–1925* (Oxford: Oxford University Press, 1980), 28–32. The difference is particularly well illustrated through Marsden's portrayal of the different attitudes over time of the father-son Blanchards who ran Wheaton College for the first several decades of that institution's existence.
14. Joel A. Carpenter, "Fundamentalist Institutions and the Rise of Evangelical Protestantism, 1929–1942," *Church History* (Mar. 1980): 72.
15. Though it may seem hard to believe now, Jimmy Carter once had the strong support of Pat Robertson. One of the best contemporaneous sources for the seemingly sudden rise of evangelicalism and fundamentalism in America is Kenneth L. Woodward, John Barnes, and Laurie Lisle, "Born Again," *Newsweek*, October 25, 1976, 68–78. Another milestone in the public recognition of conservative Christianity as a force in the late twentieth century was Charles W. Colson, *Born Again* (Grand Rapids, MI: Spire, 1976).
16. Carl F. H. Henry, *The Uneasy Conscience of Modern Fundamentalism* (Grand Rapids, MI: Eerdmans, 1947).
17. Ibid., 20.
18. Ibid., 22–23.
19. Ibid., 26–27.
20. Ibid., 30.
21. Ibid., 37.
22. Ibid., 44.
23. Marsden, *Fundamentalism and American Culture*, 207.

24. George M. Marsden, *Reforming Fundamentalism: Fuller Seminary and the New Evangelicalism* (Grand Rapids, MI: Eerdmans, 1987), 61.

25. Henry, *The Uneasy Conscience*, 45.

26. Ibid., 72.

27. Ibid., 73.

28. Marsden, *Reforming Fundamentalism*, 63. Over time, of course, evangelicals and Catholics would see their commonalities overwhelm their differences and this last part of Henry's message (the anti-"Romanism") would be dropped. It is one of the ironies of American history that Protestant Christians opened the door to much greater secularization than they envisioned because of their obsession with preventing the Catholic Church from making gains while hostile secularism was tearing at the faith's roots in the culture. This point is addressed further in the chapter on secularism and cultural harmony.

29. H. Richard Niebuhr, *The Kingdom of God in America* (Middletown, CT: Wesleyan University Press, 1988), 193.

30. Ibid., 196–97.

31. The granddaddy of all such studies was Dean M. Kelley, *Why Conservative Churches Are Growing: A Study in Sociology of Religion* (New York: Harper and Row, 1972).

Chapter 10: Secularism

1. Rodney Stark and Roger Finke, *Acts of Faith: Explaining the Human Side of Religion* (Berkeley, CA: University of California Press, 2000), 15.

2. Ibid., 1.

3. David Martin, *On Secularization: Towards a Revised General Theory* (Burlington, VT: Ashgate, 2005), 18.

4. Emile Durkheim, *The Elementary Forms of the Religious Life* (Oxford: Oxford University Press, 2001).

5. Max Weber, *The Sociology of Religion* (Boston: Beacon Press, 1991), 151.

6. Max Weber, "Religious Rejections of the World and Their Directions," in *From Max Weber*, ed. and trans. H. H. Gerth and C. Wright Mills (New York: Oxford University Press, 1946), 323–59.

7. Peter L. Berger, *The Sacred Canopy: Elements of a Sociological Theory of Religion* (New York: Anchor, 1990), 107.

8. Ibid.

9. Ibid.

10. Ibid.

11. Ibid., 108.

12. See, e.g., Talcott Parsons, "1965 Harlan Paul Douglass Lectures: Religion in a Modern Pluralistic Society," *Review of Religious Research* (Spring 1966): 125.

13. Talcott Parsons, *The Evolution of Societies* (Englewood Cliffs, NJ: Prentice Hall, 1977).

14. William H. Swatos Jr. and Kevin J. Christiano, "Secularization Theory: The Course of a Concept," in *The Secularization Debate*, ed. William H. Swatos and Daniel V. Olson (Lanham, MD: Rowman and Littlefield, 2000), 11.

15. Martin, *On Secularization*, 20. One can observe an example of that to which Martin refers in Thomas Luckmann, "On Religion in Modern Society: Individual Consciousness, World View, Institution," *Journal for the Scientific Study of Religion* (Spring 1963): 160.

16. Harvey Cox, *The Secular City: Secularization and Urbanization in Theological Perspective* (New York: MacMillan, 1975). I hasten to add that we never had the opportunity to hear Bonhoeffer offer his own explication of "religionless Christianity" because of his execution by the Nazis prior to the end of the war. What is available can be found in Dietrich Bonhoeffer, *Letters and Papers from Prison: The Enlarged Edition* (New York: Touchstone, 1997), 280–82.

17. Berger, *The Sacred Canopy*, 45.

18. Ibid., 156.

19. Berger, "A Bleak Outlook Seen for Religion," *New York Times*, February 25, 1968, 3.

20. Anthony Gill, *Rendering unto Caesar: The Catholic Church and the State in Latin America* (Chicago: University of Chicago Press, 1998), 50–65.

21. Peter Berger, "The Desecularization of the World: A Global Overview," in *The Desecularization of the World: Resurgent Religion and World Politics*, ed. Peter Berger (Grand Rapids, MI: Ethics and Public Policy Center and Eerdmans, 1999), 10–11.

22. David Martin, "Towards Eliminating the Concept of Secularization," in *Penguin Survey of the Social Sciences*, ed. J. Gould (Harmondsworth: Penguin, 1965).

23. Andrew M. Greeley, *Unsecular Man: The Persistence of Religion* (New York: Schocken, 1972).

24. Rodney Stark, "Secularization, R.I.P.," in *The Secularization Debate*, 43.

25. Berger, "The Desecularization of the World," 2–4.

26. Ibid., 6.

27. José Casanova, *Public Religions in the Modern World* (Chicago: University of Chicago Press, 1994), 3.

28. Stark, "Secularization, R.I.P.," 41.

29. Stark and Finke, *Acts of Faith*, 18.

30. Stark, "Secularization, R.I.P.," 47.

31. Ibid., 52.

32. Stark and Finke, *Acts of Faith*, 228–29.

33. Ibid., 238.

34. Martin, *On Secularization*, 3–4.

35. Berger, "The Desecularization of the World," 12.

36. Ibid., 12–14.

37. Casanova, *Public Religions*, 55.

38. Robert Audi and Nicholas Wolterstorff, *Religion in the Public Square: The Place of Religious Convictions in Political Debate* (Lanham, MD: Rowman and Littlefield, 1997), 25–28.

39. Elizabeth Shakman-Hurd, "The Political Authority of Secularism in International Relations," *European Journal of International Relations* (June 2004): 236–37.

40. Ibid., 237.

41. Casanova, *Public Religions*, 20.

42. Shakman-Hurd, "*The Political Authority of Secularism*," 239–40.

43. Ibid, 240.

44. Martin, 187.

45. Shakman-Hurd, "The Political Authority of Secularism," 240.

46. Ibid., 255.

47. Ibid., 246.

48. Ibid., 252.

49. Berger, *The Sacred Canopy*, 156.

50. George M. Marsden, *The Outrageous Idea of Christian Scholarship* (New York: Oxford University Press, 1997), 81.

51. Martin, *On Secularization*, 8.

52. Ibid., 76.

53. *Antifoundationalism* is a near synonym to *postmodernism*. It likewise disavows the existence of a disinterested view from nowhere in human discourse.

54. Stanley Fish, "A Reply to J. Judd Owen," *American Political Science Review* 93 (Dec. 1999): 925.

55. Francis Canavan merits special attention for *The Pluralist Game: Pluralism, Liberalism, and the Moral Conscience* (Lanham, MD: Rowman and Littlefield, 1995).

56. Stanley Fish, "Mission Impossible: Settling the Just Bounds between Church and State," *Columbia Law Review* 97 (Dec. 1997): 2258, quoting John Locke, "A Letter Concerning Toleration," The Constitution Society, http://www.constitution.org/jl/tolerati.htm (accessed April 27, 2007).

57. Fish, "A Reply to Judd Owen," 2261.

58. Ibid.

59. Ibid., 2262, quoting Locke.

60. Ibid.

61. Ibid., 2263.

62. Ibid., 2266.

63. Ibid.

64. Ibid., 2269.
65. Michael W. McConnell, "'God Is Dead and We Have Killed Him!': Freedom of Religion in the Post-modern Age," *Brigham Young University Law Review* (1993): 164–65.
66. Stanley Fish, "A Reply to J. Judd Owen," 925–26.
67. Ibid.
68. Ibid., 926.
69. Ibid.
70. Ibid., 929.
71. Ibid.
72. Ibid.
73. Ibid.
74. Ibid.
75. Gen. 3:18.
76. Matt. 7:1.
77. Steven D. Smith, *Getting Over Equality: A Critical Diagnosis of Religious Freedom in America* (New York: New York University Press, 2001), 169. Smith refers to this position as ultra-Protestant because he means to take Luther's notions of imputed righteousness and justification by faith and extend them from conduct to belief.
78. Canavan, *The Pluralist Game*, 73.
79. One might make a nod to Robert Audi's work at this point, as well. His arguments are dealt with in more detail in the next chapter.
80. John Rawls, *Political Liberalism* (New York: Columbia University Press, 1993), *xxiv*.
81. Ibid., 134–35.
82. Ibid., (1996 ed.), l.
83. Ibid., 225.
84. Ibid., 243, n. 2.
85. Paul F. Campos, "Secular Fundamentalism," *Columbia Law Review* (Oct. 1994): 1820, n. 16.
86. Ibid., 1820–21.
87. Alasdair MacIntyre, *After Virtue* (Notre Dame, IN: Notre Dame University Press), 1984.
88. Smith, *Getting Over Equality*, 45.
89. Robert P. George, *The Clash of the Orthodoxies: Law, Religion, and Morality in Crisis* (Wilmington, DE: ISI Books, 2001), 325–26.

Chapter 11: Purpose-driven Secularism

1. George M. Marsden, *The Outrageous Idea of Christian Scholarship* (New York: Oxford University Press, 1997), 83.
2. Richard John Neuhaus, *The Naked Public Square: Religion and Democracy in America* (Grand Rapids, MI: Eerdmans, 1984), 28.
3. Christian Smith, "Introduction: Rethinking the Secularization of American Public Life," in *The Secular Revolution: Power, Interests, and Conflict in the Secularization of American Public Life*, ed. Christian Smith (Berkeley, CA: University of California Press, 2003), 19–20.
4. Stanley Fish, "A Reply to J. Judd Owen," *American Political Science Review* 93 (Dec. 1999): 925–26.
5. Smith, "Preface," in *The Secular Revolution*, vii.
6. Smith, *The Secular Revolution*, 1.
7. Ibid., 3.
8. Ibid., 5.
9. Ibid., 10.
10. Bryan Wilson, *Contemporary Transformations of Religion* (Oxford: Oxford University Press, 1976), 6–7.
11. *Church of the Holy Trinity v. United States*, 143 U.S. 457, 471 (1892).
12. Smith, *The Secular Revolution*, 29.
13. Ibid., 34–35.
14. Ibid., 35.
15. Ibid., 37.

16. Ibid. Though this discussion may sound like a harsh indictment of some kind of conspiracy, it may be balanced by the realization that secularization was also a liberating move for some who might have been held back by Protestant tribalism. David Hollinger, a strong advocate of secularism, has pointed out that secularization was an avenue to opportunity for Jews. See David Hollinger, *Science, Jews, and Secular Culture* (Princeton, NJ: Princeton University Press, 1996), 25.
17. Smith, *The Secular Revolution*, 63.
18. Ibid., 65–66.
19. Ibid., 67–69.
20. Ibid., 70–71.
21. Ellen Lagemann, *Private Power for the Public Good* (Middletown, CT: Wesleyan University Press, 1983), 35.
22. George M. Marsden, *The Soul of the American University: From Protestant Establishment to Established Nonbelief* (New York: Oxford University Press, 1994), 282.
23. Smith, *The Secular Revolution*, 114.
24. Ibid., 117–47. These themes may be found as numbered on pages 117, 121, 126, 129, 132, 134, 139, 141, 144, and 147.
25. Marsden, *The Outrageous Idea of Christian Scholarship*, 28.
26. Smith, *The Secular Revolution*, 153.
27. James Davison Hunter has written about this demographic group and its preferences (as well as their counterparts) in *Culture Wars: The Struggle to Define America* (New York: Basic, 1991). The best depiction of the two sides comes in his presentation of the orthodox vision and the progressivist vision which can be found on pages 108–16.
28. Louis Bolce and Gerald De Maio, "Our Secularist Democratic Party," *The Public Interest* (Fall 2002): 6.
29. Ibid., 14.
30. Ibid., 9–10.
31. Ibid., 15–16.
32. Alan Cooperman, "Democrats Win Bigger Share of Religious Vote: Parties Disagree on Why Gap Has Narrowed," *Washington Post*, http://www.msnbc.msn.com/id/15662295/ (accessed May 1, 2007). The story is a perfect example. It discusses how Democrats managed to significantly narrow the "God gap" in 2006. The story features no discussion of the voting habits of secularists.
33. Bolce and De Maio, "Our Secularist Democratic Party," 18–20.

Chapter 12: Theocratic Danger

1. It is, of course, the record of the twentieth century that requires a scholar like John Rawls to set up a system theoretically avoiding the problems of "comprehensive doctrines" rather than merely those of religious doctrines.
2. Douglas Laycock, "Continuity and Change in the Threat to Religious Liberty: The Reformation Era and the Late Twentieth Century," *Minnesota Law Review* 80 (May 1996): 1094–95.
3. Robert Audi and Nicholas Wolterstorff, *Religion in the Public Square: The Place of Religious Convictions in Political Debate* (Lanham, MD: Rowman and Littlefield, 1997), 8.
4. Michael W. McConnell, "'God Is Dead and We Have Killed Him!': Freedom of Religion in the Post-modern Age," *Brigham Young University Law Review* (1993): 177.
5. Ibid., 177–78.
6. Thomas Berg, "Church-State Relations and the Social Ethics of Reinhold Neibuhr," *North Carolina Law Review* 73 (Apr. 1995): 1614.
7. McConnell, "God Is Dead and We Have Killed HIm," 179.
8. Ibid., 181.
9. Berg, "Church-State Relations," 1634.
10. Ibid.
11. Ibid.
12. Francis Canavan, *The Pluralist Game: Pluralism, Liberalism, and the Moral Conscience* (Lanham, MD: Rowman and Littlefield, 1995), 6.
13. Ibid., 38.
14. Ibid., 38–39.
15. Ibid., 57–58.

16. William H. Swatos Jr., "The Public and the Public: Is Nothing Private Anymore?" in *The Power of Religious Publics: Staking Claims in American Society*, ed. William H. Swatos Jr. and James K. Wellman (Westport, CT: Praeger, 1999), 192–95.

Chapter 13: The Department of God

1. José Casanova, *Public Religions in the Modern World* (Chicago: University of Chicago Press, 1994), 43.
2. Islam, for example, presents a different case. David Martin has pointed out that Islam was born as both a faith community and a political community at the same time, and it has often expanded via simple conquest. The result is that the Muslim's self-understanding naturally involves political rule as well as spiritual discipline. Inferentially, one might conclude that the bargain Casanova and Swatos are speaking of may not be one many Muslims feel they can easily accept, which may be part of the problem on the international scene at present. David Martin, *On Secularization: Towards a Revised General Theory* (Burlington, VT: Ashgate, 2005), 105.
3. Rodney Stark and Roger Finke, *Acts of Faith: Explaining the Human Side of Religion* (Berkeley, CA: University of California Press, 2000), 228–29.
4. Ibid., 36.
5. Matt. 6:24.
6. Casanova, *Public Religions*, 27.
7. Richard F. Tomasson, *Sweden: Prototype of Modern Society* (Random House: New York, 1970), 77–78.
8. Franklin D. Scott, *Sweden: The Nation's History* (Minneapolis: University of Minnesota Press, 1977), 377.
9. Tomasson, *Sweden*, 79.
10. Scott, *Sweden*, 433.
11. Gunnar Edqvist, "Freedom of Religion and New Relations between Church and State in Sweden," *Studia Theologica* 54 (2000): 35–37, provides a sense of the process.
12. Ibid., 40.
13. Arne Rasmusson, "Church and State in Sweden: A New Relationship," *Christian Century*, May 3, 2000, 494.
14. "Shorn of Tax Support, Sweden Church Slips," *Christian Century*, Apr. 6, 2004, 16.
15. Rasmusson, "Church and State in Sweden," 495.
16. Ibid.
17. Tomas Dixon, "Locked Out: Are Evangelical Lutherans a 'Doomed Species'?" *Christianity Today*, Jan. 8, 2001, 30.
18. Ibid., 31.
19. Edqvist, "Freedom of Religion," 40.
20. Tomas Dixon, "'Hate Speech' Law Could Chill Sermons," *Christianity Today*, Aug. 5, 2002, 22.

Chapter 14: The Legend of Warfare

1. The current controversy over embryonic stem cell research is an excellent example. Those who opposed embryonic stem cell research are often accused of putting religion (or ideology) before science. The reality, of course, is that ideology is up against ideology because the question is over whether something *should* be done, not whether it *can* be done.
2. John William Draper, *The Conflict between Religion and Science*, 7th ed. (London: Henry S. King, 1876), 51–52. Quoted in David C. Lindberg, "Science and the Early Christian Church," *Isis*, vol. 74 (Dec. 1983): 509.
3. Ibid.
4. Owen Chadwick, *The Secularization of the European Mind in the Nineteenth Century* (Cambridge: Cambridge University Press, 1975), 162.
5. Ibid.
6. David C. Lindberg and Ronald L. Numbers, "Beyond War and Peace: A Reappraisal of the Encounter between Christianity and Science," *Church History*, vol. 55 (Sept. 1986): 340.
7. Lindberg, "Science and the Early Christian Church," 510.
8. Lindberg and Numbers, "Beyond War and Peace," 342–50.
9. Ibid., 353.

10. John Brooke, "Science and Religion: Lessons from History?" *Science*, New Series, vol. 282 (Dec. 11, 1998): 1986.
11. Chadwick, *The Secularization of the European Mind*, 163.
12. See chap. 3.
13. Maurice A. Finocchiaro, "Science, Religion, and the Historiography of the Galileo Affair: On the Undesirability of Oversimplification," *Osiris*, 2nd Series, vol. 16 (2001): 114–15.
14. Ibid., 116.
15. Ibid., 132.
16. Lindberg, "Science and the Early Christian Church," 510.
17. Chadwick, *The Secularization of the European Mind*, 163.
18. Ibid., 179.
19. In particular see Richard Dawkins, *The God Delusion* (Boston: Houghton Mifflin, 2006) and Sam Harris, *The End of Faith: Religion, Terror, and the Future of Reason* (New York: Norton, 2005).
20. Chadwick, *The Secularization of the European Mind*, 179–80.
21. Ibid., 175.
22. Lindberg, "Science and the Early Christian Church," 517–18. The extended quote from Augustine comes from Augustine, Letter 120, ed. A. Goldbacher, in Corpus scriptorium ecclesiasticorum latinorum, vol. xxxiv (Vienna: F. Tempsky, 1895), 708–9.
23. Ibid., 519–22.
24. Mark A. Noll, *The Scandal of the Evangelical Mind* (Grand Rapids, MI: Eerdmans, 1994), 203.
25. Lindberg, "Science and the Early Christian Church," 522.
26. Ibid., 529.
27. David C. Lindberg, "Medieval Science and Its Religious Context," *Osiris*, 2nd Series, vol. 10, Constructing Knowledge in the History of Science (1995): 61.
28. Ibid., 67.
29. Ibid., 74.
30. Ibid.
31. Ibid., 74–75.
32. Ibid., 75–76. To see the way Bacon has been used, see Andrew Dickson White's claim that Bacon was persecuted and jailed, in *A History of the Warfare between Science and Theology in Christendom* (New York: Dover, 1960), 38.
33. Lindberg, "Medieval Science," 78.
34. Frank M. Turner, "The Victorian Conflict between Science and Religion: A Professional Dimension," *Isis*, vol. 69 (Sept. 1978): 357–58.
35. Ibid., 360.
36. Ibid., 363.
37. Ibid., 364.
38. Ibid., 364–65.
39. Ibid., 370–71.
40. Ibid., 366.
41. Ibid., 368–71.
42. Ibid., 375–76.
43. Edward J. Larson, *Summer for the Gods: The Scopes Trial and America's Continuing Debate over Science and Religion* (Cambridge, MA: Harvard University Press, 1997), 4–5.
44. Ibid., 3–6.
45. Ibid.
46. See 1998 Gallup poll numbers discussed by John Carpenter, "Creationists Get a Leg Up in Kansas," *Chicago Sun-Times*, August 29, 1999, sec. Sunday News 20. More recently see "Poll: Majority Reject Evolution," http://www.cbsnews.com/stories/2005/10/22/opinion/polls/main965223.shtml (accessed July 17, 2007).
47. During most of the twentieth century, opposition to the implications of evolutionary theory took the form of "creation-science," which sought to reconcile the fossil record and old-earth estimates with the Genesis account. Early on, creationists tried to ban the teaching of evolution from tax-supported public schools and universities as an establishment of atheism and a dangerous philosophy. Some, such as William Jennings Bryan, pointed to the effect of evolution on the German nation's aggressive stance in World War I and Darwinism's

sometimes direct, sometimes indirect support of eugenics movements designed to weed out the weak. Accordingly, evolutionary thought had to be opposed as a great threat to Christian civilization and the dignity of the person. Eventually, the nation settled into an uneasy compromise. Anti-evolutionists were not able to put in place a systematic ban on the teaching of evolution, but were able to have references to evolution toned down or removed entirely from the textbooks used in many school districts. Later challenges from creationists came in the form of equal treatment laws, such as the one struck down by the Supreme Court in *Edwards v. Aguillard*, 482 U.S. 578 (1987).

48. But at least one prominent church-state scholar believes creationist perspectives can be constitutionally taught in public school science classrooms. See Derek Davis, "Kansas versus Darwin: Examining the History and Future of the Creationism-Evolution Controversy in American Public Schools," *The Kansas Journal of Law and Public Policy* (Winter 1999).

49. Noll, *The Scandal of the Evangelical Mind*, 186.

50. Ibid., 186–87.

Chapter 15: The Knowledge Situation

1. Steven D. Smith, "Centennial Symposium: Reconciling the Free Exercise and Establishment Clauses: The Iceberg of Religious Freedom: Sub-Surface Levels of Nonestablishment Discourse," *Creighton University Law Review* (June 2005): 810.

2. Rodney Stark and Roger Finke, *Acts of Faith: Explaining the Human Side of Religion* (Berkeley: University of California Press, 2000), 8.

3. For an excellent example of this kind of aggressive Darwinism that might give any sane person pause, consider Daniel Dennett, *Darwin's Dangerous Idea: Evolution and the Meanings of Life* (New York: Simon and Schuster, 1995), 61–84. In the section indicated, Dennett makes an analogy between Darwinism and universal acid that eats through everything until nothing is left. According to Dennett's account, Darwinism is corrosive to things such as morals.

4. Wolfgang Justin Mommsen, *The Political and Social Theory of Max Weber* (Chicago: University of Chicago Press, 1992), 163.

5. Whittaker Chambers, *Witness* (Washington: Regnery, 1987).

6. Outstanding examples of books that helped shape Western perception of the Soviet Union include Aleksandr Solzhenitsyn, *A Day in the Life of Ivan Denisovich* (New York: Bantam, 1973) and Arthur Koestler, *Darkness at Noon* (New York: Bantam, 1984).

7. For an excellent example see H. George Frederickson, "Organization Theory and New Public Administration," in *Classics of Public Administration*, ed. Jay M. Shafritz and Albert C. Hyde (Oak Park, IL: Moore, 1978), 391–405. Also see the argument and narrative of the previous chapter.

8. For a book-length treatment of the difficulties involved in presenting management as a science, see Henry Mintzberg, *Managers Not MBAs: A Hard Look at the Soft Practice of Managing and Management Development* (San Francisco: Berrett-Koehler, 2005).

9. Ray Kurzweil, *The Singularity Is Near: When Humans Transcend Biology* (New York: Viking Penguin, 2005).

10. G. K. Chesterton, *Orthodoxy* (San Francisco: Ignatius Press, 1995), 59.

11. Wesley J. Smith, "Kass, in the Firing Line," *National Review Online*, http://www.nationalreview.com/smithw/smith200312050930.asp (accessed April 25, 2007).

12. I think the inflatable appearance of certain body parts is very much what Aldous Huxley was driving at when his characters in *Brave New World* referred to attractive men and women as being "pneumatic" in their looks. Aldous Huxley, *Brave New World* (New York: Harper Perennial Modern Classics, 1998), 44, 49, 56, 60, 80, 93, 96.

13. Francis A. Schaeffer, *The Complete Works of Francis A. Schaeffer: A Christian Worldview*, vol. 1, *He Is There and He Is Not Silent* (Wheaton, IL: Crossway, 1982), 280.

14. Rodney Stark, *For the Glory of God: How Monotheism Led to Reformations, Science, Witch-Hunts, and the End of Slavery* (Princeton: Princeton University Press, 2003), 160–62.

15. Stark and Finke, *Acts of Faith*, 33.

16. John Gray, "The Myth of Secularism," *The New Statesman* (Dec. 16, 2002): 71.

17. John Dewey, *The Influence of Darwin on Philosophy: And Other Essays in Contemporary Thought* (Bloomington, IN: Indiana University Press, 1965), 19.

18. Ibid., 21. I do not doubt some might protest that I am attributing to Dewey a view that he puts in the mouth of a fictitious discussion participant named Grimes. However, I think that if one reads what Grimes has to say, one will find Grimes's views are quite consonant with Dewey's expressed in the previous chapter. He wants philosophy to climb down from the world of abstraction and to deal with the problems of "a just social order." For whatever reason, Dewey does not recognize that he has not climbed down from anywhere in considering just such a question. To bolster my point, I advert to the *Humanist Manifesto.* Dewey cowrote and signed the document, which calls for the same kind of industrial order. The manifesto remains available at the American Humanist Web site.
19. Richard Dawkins, "What Is Natural," Greenpeace, http://richarddawkins.net/article, 40, What-Is-Natural, Greenpeace (accessed April 26, 2007).
20. Louis Pojman, "Are All Humans Equal? A Critique of Contemporary Egalitarianism," in *Equality: A Reader*, ed. Robert Westmoreland and Louis Pojman (Oxford: Oxford University Press, 1996), 24.
21. Ibid., 3–23. In this section Pojman categorizes the various defenses of equality theory and describes difficulties in more detail than is needed here.
22. Ibid., 24.
23. Larry Arnhart has tried to justify various moral points of view from Darwinism, but the effort is not particularly convincing. Larry Arnhart, *Darwinian Conservatism* (Charlottesville, VA: Imprint Academic, 2005). See Carson Holloway for a detailed refutation of Arnhart and others who argue that a Darwinian view can sustain a conservative morality. Carson Holloway, *The Right Darwin: Evolution, Religion, and the Future of Democracy* (Dallas: Spence, 2006).
24. Stephen D. Smith, "Recovering (from) Enlightenment?" *San Diego Law Review* (Summer 2004): 1289.
25. Ibid.
26. Louis Pojman, "Are All Humans Equal?" 26–27.
27. C. John Sommerville, "Post-secularism Marginalizes the University: A Rejoinder to Hollinger," *Church History* (December 2002): 855–56.
28. Christopher J. Eberle, *Religious Convictions in Liberal Politics* (Cambridge: Cambridge University Press, 2002), 332–33.
29. Ramesh Ponnuru, "Secularism and Its Discontents," *National Review* (Dec. 27, 2004): 34.
30. Frederick Mark Gedicks, "Public Life and Hostility to Religion," *Virginia Law Review* (Apr. 1992): 694–95.
31. Stephen D. Smith, "The 'Secular,' the 'Religious,' and the 'Moral: What Are We Talking About?" *Wake Forest Law Review* (Summer 2001): 487–88.
32. Iain T. Benson, "Notes towards a (Re)Definition of the 'Secular,'" *The University of British Columbia Law Review*, vol. 33 (2000): 520–21.
33. Robert P. George, *The Clash of the Orthodoxies* (Wilmington, DE: Intercollegiate Studies Institute, 2001), 7–8.

Chapter 16: Secularists Sit One Out

1. "Unjustly Taxed: The Bible and Politics in Alabama," *The Christian Century*, http://findarticles.com/p/articles/mi_m1058/is_19_121/ai_n6355212 (accessed May 16, 2007).
2. Ibid.
3. Susan Pace Hamill, "An Argument for Tax Reform Based on Judeo-Christian Ethics," *Alabama Law Review*, vol. 54 (Fall 2002).
4. Ibid., 1.
5. Ibid., 9–46.
6. Ibid., 58.
7. Ibid., 59.
8. Ibid., 61–66.
9. Ibid., 74–75.
10. Ibid., 80–81.
11. Jeffrey Gettleman, "A Tax Increase? $1.2 Billion? Alabamians, It Seems, Say No," *New York Times*, Sept. 6, 2003.
12. Mike Wilson, "What Is 'Bama to Render to Caesar?" *St. Petersburg Times*, Sept. 9, 2003.

13. Shailagh Murray, "Divinity School Article Debates Morality of Alabama Tax Code," *Wall Street Journal*, http://www.law.ua.edu/lawreview/WSJ_hamill.html (accessed May 16, 2007).
14. Cynthia Tucker, "Our Opinion: Tax Code Keeps Alabama Down," *The Atlanta Journal-Constitution*, Editorial, 10P (August 24, 2003).
15. Collin Hansen, "'Jesus Tax' Plan Dies: Alabama's Fiscal Debate Exposes a Divide between Christians," *Christianity Today*, http://www.christianitytoday.com/ct/2003/011/7.25.html (accessed May 16, 2007).
16. This goes to my personal knowledge of the situation as a former lobbyist in Georgia connected with religion and public affairs. My source was a conversation with the current head of the Georgia Christian Coalition, Jim Beck, who confirmed that Georgia and Alabama both broke from the national organization. He heads up the new state chapter that is designed to coordinate with the national group.
17. Tom Baxter, "Alabama Voters Turn Back Record $1.2 Billion Tax Plan," *Atlanta Journal-Constitution,* September 10, 2003.
18. Larry Copeland, "Alabama Governor's Tax Increase Plan Is a Switch with High Stakes," *USA Today*, September 5, 2003.
19. There were many more, but I weeded out obvious duplicates based on shared wire copy. The full list is easily accessible via Lexis-Nexis or other news databases.
20. Stephen Carter, *The Culture of Disbelief: How American Law and Politics Trivializes Religious Devotion* (New York: Basic Books, 1993), 57.
21. Robert Audi has already been discussed at length. For good examples of Ackerman and Macedo, see Bruce Ackerman, "Political Liberalisms," *The Journal of Philosophy* (July 1994): 364–86 and Stephen Macedo, "Transformative Constitutionalism and the Case of Religion: Defending the Moderate Hegemony of Liberalism," *Political Theory* (February 1998): 56–89.
22. Falwell, of course, eventually saw things differently and long ago repented of his blindness toward the just calls for civil rights legislation.
23. Carter, *The Culture of Disbelief*, 57.
24. Ibid., 58.
25. Using the labels "evangelical" and "fundamentalist" is a tricky business. Both are orthodox in their faith. The biggest difference may well be that evangelicals emphasized engaging the world, while many fundamentalists isolated themselves. Tolerance for disagreement within the Christian community may be another hallmark that distinguishes evangelicals from fundamentalists.
26. Carter, *The Culture of Disbelief*, 58.
27. The history of the legal battle over the use of RICO suits and their treble damages against pro-life protesters is documented in *Scheidler v. National Organization for Women*, 537 U.S. 393 (2003). The Scheidler decision finally disallowed the use of the RICO suits in this fashion.
28. Steven D. Smith, *Getting Over Equality: A Critical Diagnosis of Religious Freedom in America* (New York: New York University Press, 2001), 66.
29. Nicholas Wolterstorff, "The Role of Religion in Political Issues," in Robert Audi and Nicholas Wolterstorff, *Religion in the Public Square: The Place of Religious Convictions in Political Debate* (Lanham, MD: Rowman and Littlefield, 1997), 95–96.

Summary
1. Sanford Levinson, "Book Review: Religious Language and the Public Square," *Harvard Law Review* (June 1992): 2077.

Index

Index

Carter, Stephen, 188–90

Carthage, church council in, 31

Casanova, José, 102, 135–36, 139, 212n2

Cathers, 31

Catholics/Catholicism, 30, 31, 52, 62, 101, 208n28

Catholic Church, 33, 39, 54, 66, 135; clergy of, 34; and the creation of secularism, 35; critique of, 46; political power of, 59–60; vulnerability of, 47–48

Catholic Solidarity Union, 102–3

Chadwick, Henry, 27

Chadwick, Owen, 154, 155

Chambers, Whittaker, 170

Charlemagne, 33

Chesterton, G. K., 172

Christendom model, 55–56

Christian church, the: authority of, 37; makeup of, 65–66; medieval church, 65–66; political power of, 33

Christian Coalition, 131, 184; schism within, 187, 216n16

Christian states, 50

Christianity, 26–27, 44, 73, 77, 82, 108, 139, 140, 141, 156–57, 168, 181, 191; appeal of, 89–90; bias against, 52; decline of, 88–89, 94; and the founding of the United States, 76–77; growth of, 88, 94; and modernism, 91; myth that Christianity is hostile to science, 22, 149–53; public, 94–95; "religionless Christianity," 100, 208n16; rise of in the West, 26; Rousseau's view of, 50–51; and the slavery issue, 90–91; under Constantine, 27–28; under Theodosius, 28

Christianity and Liberalism (Machen), 91

Christians, 13, 17, 54, 66, 113–14, 202n3; Catholic/Donatist strife among, 30–31; conservative, 91, 94, 189; different classes of, 34–35; participation of in government, 41–42; and political authority, 26; self-interest of, 139–40

church membership, 73–74

church/state model of community, 64, 205n2

church/state power relationships, 33–34; Luther's view of 40–44

church/state separation, 19–20, 75–76, 80, 148, 194

citizens/citizenship, 51, 65

city of God, the, 29–30; members of, 30

Civil Constitution of the Clergy (1790), 60–61

Common Sense (Paine), 205n1

communion, 74

Comte, 98

Conkle, Daniel, 85

Constantine, 27, 63, 65

Copernicus, 151, 152

counter-secularization, 102

Cox, Harvey, 100

creation science, 164, 213–14n47, 214n48

Crisis of Church and State, The (Tierney), 33

Crusades, 35, 36

Dana, Dwight, 152

Darrow, Clarence, 91, 162–63, 165

Darwin, Charles, 89, 90, 152, 170

Darwinism, 176, 213–14n47, 215n23; in America, 162–65